WIVES AND OTHER WOMEN

WIVES AND OTHER WOMEN

NORMA KLEIN

St. Martin's/Marek
New York

For information, write: St. Martin's/Marek
175 Fifth Avenue, New York, N.Y. 10010
Manufactured in the United States of America

Library of Congress Cataloging in Publication Data

Klein, Norma, 1938-
  Wives and other women.

  "A St. Martin's/Marek book"

  I. Title.
PS3561.L35W5   813'.54   81-21544
ISBN 0-312-88626-8   AACR2

Design by Manuela Paul

10 9 8 7 6 5 4 3 2 1

First Edition

For Berl

WIVES AND OTHER WOMEN

Summer 1970

"**A**re they yours?"

He looked startled. "Yes."

Nira was struggling to get the baby into a comfortable position. "No, I just meant—my brother sometimes looks after our kids if we go away on a trip, he's a bachelor, so I thought . . ." She was flustered, in part because she'd been spying on him, watching his porch from theirs, ever since he'd moved into the cottage next to their country house at the beginning of August. She and the children had been there since July; Adlai would be doing his city-husband, long-weekend bit until the two weeks at the end, before Labor Day.

"That's nice, that you have someone in the family who can do that. My wife and I never—"

"Where is she?" Suddenly the baby snapped onto the bottle and began sucking lustily. Nira leaned back, stretching, in the beach chair. She was in cutoff shorts and a T-shirt, braless, no makeup, barefoot—typical husband-free attire, balanced precariously between respectability and slovenliness.

"What?"

"Your wife—I didn't see her."

He hesitated. "She's in the city."

"In August?"

"Well—"

"Is she working?"

"We're divorced." He said it flatly and somewhat curtly.

Nira bit her lip, then plunged on. "So who was that woman with your kids?"

He laughed. "Which woman?"

"The one with the braid."

"She's the baby-sitter." He smiled at her. "You see a lot from your porch, don't you?"

Nira blushed. "Well, I just—"

"I can see your porch too. . . . Your husband arrives at seven-thirty, Thursday evenings, right?"

She felt relieved, but tried to justify herself anyway. "It's that I'm stuck here, I *feel* stuck, with the baby and all . . . I have nothing to do! Plus I have this weird obsession with other people's lives. They always seem so much more interesting than mine."

"Till you come close."

"What do you mean?"

"Up close, most people's lives are about the same, don't you think? The same confusions, anxieties, whatever."

Nira thought this over. "I don't know . . . No, I guess I *don't* think so. Lots of people are really *doing* things, people *I* know, women. They have interesting jobs, they're back in law school, or they're editors. They do stuff with computers. Nobody my age is fiddling around with babies anymore . . . I'm thirty-six," she blurted before he could ask, if he was going to.

"That doesn't seem that old to have a baby."

"Oh, it's not just that. It's that I had her for all the wrong reasons, and now look at her!" The baby was almost asleep, but still sucking, the milk dribbling out of her mouth on one side.

"She's beautiful."

"Yes, that's what I mean." Nira sighed, frowning. "She's gorgeous."

He looked puzzled. "I don't think I understand."

She knew she was getting breathless, talking too fast as she always did when she was nervous. "What I mean is, anyone else, any average, normal person, mother, would be *crazy* about a baby like this. They'd just be gaga! . . . And I don't even like her. Not just love, I don't even *like* her." Nira took a deep breath, afraid that, crazily, she was going to cry.

"You act very . . . loving with her," he said softly.

She stared at him. "I do?"

"Sure . . . The way you handle her, touch her."

"That's hypocrisy, though. I'm just pretending."

"I'm sure she can't tell," he said.

"Really? I thought they said babies could."

He was staring at the baby. With her eyes shut, her black eyelashes made a long, artistically perfect fringe on each heat-flushed cheek. "It makes me feel nostalgic," he said. "It's been so long since mine were that age."

"So, why don't you have some more?"

"I'm divorced."

"Oh, right . . . I'm sorry. You said that. Anyway, even if you weren't, two is plenty. Were those both yours that I saw on the porch? Both girls?"

He nodded.

"What're their names?"

"Jane and Stacey."

Nira mulled this over. "You're not Jewish?"

"No, why?"

"I never heard of a Jewish Jane."

"There aren't that many non-Jewish ones either," he said, smiling. "My wife liked the name. It was after her favorite aunt."

"So, what went wrong?" Nira said. She shifted the baby to the other arm.

"Pardon me?"

"I mean, with your marriage? Like, was it some particular thing? Sex or something?"

He looked uncomfortable. Terrific. Let's try some more small talk to put him at his ease. "It's hard to talk about."

"I'm sorry. I tend to ask overly personal questions." She stopped. "Listen, could I ask you a favor?"

"Sure." He looked slightly wary. Gee, I wonder why.

"The thing is, I don't have any photos of her, the baby . . . and I saw you taking some of your girls the other day, and I just wondered. I have a camera. It's loaded and everything. Would you mind?"

"I'd be glad to." He seemed relieved that the favor was so prosaic. What had he expected? Will you ravish me on the dunes instantly in exchange for letting you use our Manhattan phone book? "Do you want to hold her?"

"Let me get the camera first." Nira set the baby down in the carriage and scampered into the house, the grass tickling her feet. The camera was in the kitchen, on the ledge next to three days' worth of unwashed dishes. "It's an old camera," she said, returning. He had stood up and was looking down at the baby.

"She has wonderful coloring," he said. He looked up. "Like you."

"Me?" She looked around, startled, as though there were someone else he might have been referring to.

"The black hair and very fair skin." He cleared his throat. "By the way, do you know my name? It's Jerome Gardener, Jerry. I know yours."

"What's mine?" Nira said, out of curiosity.

"Nora Goldschmitt, isn't it?"

She shook her head.

He looked surprised. "They once delivered your Sunday *Times* to me and it said—"

"It's Nira, not Nora."

"That's an interesting name. I've never heard of it."

"My parents made it up." She smiled, feeling suddenly relaxed with him, not knowing why. "They were very left-wing, and it was the thirties, the New Deal. There was a headline the day I was born about the National Industrial Recovery Act: 'NIRA PASSES.' So my father named me Nira."

"What's *her* name?" He pointed to the baby, seeming relaxed himself now. When he'd come over, an hour earlier, to borrow the phone book, he'd looked stiff and ill at ease.

"It's weird," Nira said, "but on my husband's side of the family—he's English—they call all girls by the names of flowers. It's kind of a sickly thing, but Ad's mother would have died if I'd broken with it. So we have a Heather, a Posey and—behold!—a Jasmine. . . . If I go on, God forbid, we may end up with a Ragweed."

"She looks like a flower, velvety." He looked down at the baby again, pensively. "I think it would be good if you were holding her. Will she wake up if you lift her out of the carriage?"

Nira gave him the camera and sat back down on the beach chair, once again lifting the sleeping baby into her arms. The baby was getting wet, but not enough to soak through. Trying to see herself through his eyes, Nira wondered if she looked maternal and full-breasted, or just phony and ill at ease. She looked up at him. "Should I, like, not talk? Look off in the distance? Do something special?"

"Just be natural." He had the camera around his neck and was circling around her, focusing, about two feet away.

"Who was the *other* woman?" Nira asked. "Not the baby-sitter. The blond one."

"Paige?"

Nira grinned. "*She* arrives Wednesdays at eight and leaves Fridays. That's a funny schedule."

He clicked the shutter. "She's a free-lance writer."

"Oh." Intellectual women scared Nira. She remembered the dashing way the woman looked in her broad-brimmed straw hat and denim skirt, looking out at the ocean, like a scene from a magazine. "What does she write?"

"She's a science writer. . . . That's my field. I'm a molecular biologist."

Nira swallowed. "She must be smart."

"She is." He clicked again.

"Hey, there's only twelve on the roll," Nira warned him. "Don't go so fast."

"Don't worry. I know what I'm doing."

Nira looked up at him. Despite his two weeks at the beach and the fact that he was fair-haired, he wasn't very tan. He was thin, like her, skinny almost, which gave him a boyish look. A long beakish nose, blue eyes. I know what I'm doing. The methodical type. Men are always methodical, they always know what they're doing. No, they don't. They pretend. Maybe. "Is your wife a writer too?"

He shook his head and clicked the shutter again. I'm *not* looking maternal, Nira thought. I'm holding her like a sack of wheat. She'll look at these photos when she's twenty and hate me. "So, how come she's in the city? I thought you said she was working there."

"Did I say that?" He looked puzzled.

"I thought you said she was in the city."

"She is . . . But she's not working."

"What's she doing, then?"

His mouth tightened. "Sitting around getting stoned with her boyfriend."

"Oh."

"He's nineteen."

Nira didn't know what to say. "Well, I guess she must be having a good time," she said carefully.

"Is that your idea of a good time? Sex and drugs with a high school dropout?"

His voice was so cutting Nira was taken aback. "Well, I don't know, actually. I guess I never . . . what kind of drugs? Heroin?"

"He's white."

"What do you mean?"

"It's not hard drugs, just pot."

Nira wiggled her foot which was starting to go to sleep. "I'm bad about drugs," she admitted. "I've tried, but . . . it's that I don't smoke or something. Maybe I'm just not the type."

"Why sound apologetic?"

"Did I? I'm sorry."

"No, I just don't understand why you're apologizing for not having a drug habit." His voice had eased, now that they were one distance removed from discussing his wife.

"Was that what broke up your marriage? That she was on drugs?"

There was a pause. He clicked the shutter one more time. "That's the end of the roll."

Nira stared at him, concerned. He had a funny expression. "Am I asking too many questions?"

"We'll talk about it some other time," he suggested.

"When we know each other better."

She felt humiliated, put in her place, though he'd done it politely. "Okay, well . . . Listen, thanks for taking the photos! That was really nice. I'll cook you a meal some night, if you want, in exchange. I'm a rotten cook but—"

"I'd like that." His expression softened. "I'm not too great myself."

"How about the baby-sitter?"

He laughed. "That's not one of her functions . . . I'm beginning to wonder if there's anything she *is* good at. She can't make a bed, she doesn't know what to do with the kids."

"So, why do you need one, anyway?"

"I'm trying to get some work done. . . . It's hard with the girls around."

"They can come over here, if you want . . . I think Heather's about the age of . . . which is your oldest one?"

"Jane . . . she's eleven."

"Heather's twelve, Po's ten. . . . They know a lot of kids around here. We've been coming here ten years."

The baby was dripping now, having consumed a bottle and a half. Nira put her back in the carriage, face down, her chubby arms flat on the crumpled sheet.

"I think these will be nice photos," he said, almost formally. He set the camera down on the picnic table. "The light was good."

"Not too dark?" They'd been in the shade.

"I don't think so. . . . If you like, I'll bring it to the place in the city I use. They do a good job, usually." He opened the camera, took out the film and pocketed it.

"Thanks . . . when would you like to come for dinner?"

"What day would be convenient?"

"Thursday?"

"I thought your husband arrived Thursday." He looked at her, hesitated. "I'd like to meet him."

"He's away in London this week," she explained. "His family's still there. Usually I go with him, but with the baby—"

To her relief *he* looked awkward now, reversing the tone of the rest of the conversation. "It'll be nice for the girls. I think they're a little lonely."

"Sure." She stood on one foot, scratching her leg with her big toe.

To her surprise he took her hand and shook it, making her lose her balance. "I'll see you Thursday, then. Around six?"

After he left, Nira tried to nap, before the girls came back from the beach. Now that Heather was almost a teenager, they went everywhere by themselves. They were good swimmers, knew everyone for miles around, often drifted from house to house on sleepovers, always welcome. She had stopped worrying.

She didn't sleep. Instead, she spent the afternoon thinking about Jerry Gardener's wife, alone in the hot city with her teenage boyfriend. Nira had almost picked up a teenage boy a month earlier. It had been her first day out after the baby's birth, a beautiful May day, warm, radiant. She walked slowly, stiffly, wearing an old, faded pair of jeans, a flowered T-shirt, sneakers. Maybe it was that outfit, grabbed haphazardly from the closet, that had made the boy start talking to her.

He was beautiful. Black curly hair, big eyes, a brash, ingenuous manner. He was looking after his sister's kid, he said, a two-year-old who was playing in the sandbox.

"He's cute," Nira said, mainly aware of a mild claustrophobia at being in the playground again.

"Yeah, he is. Kids just really turn me on, you know?" he said. "Little kids, I mean. I don't know what it is about them." He talked easily, as though talking were easier than not talking, about kids, his sister, his ambition to be a rock singer. "I wish I had my guitar. I could play you something. I'm good. I'm not great, but I'm good. . . . Where do you live? You live around here?"

Was he a mugger in disguise? He didn't seem the type, but how could you tell? He seemed to guess her thoughts. "I never saw you before," he said. "I come here a lot."

"My other kids are practically teenagers," Nira said, wanting to scare him off. She showed him some recent photos.

His face lit up. "Hey, gee, they're terrific. They look just like you," he said, seeming delighted at this fact. "You have three? I guess you really like kids, huh? Just like me."

"Sometimes I do, and sometimes I don't," she admitted. She looked around the playground. "I've just spent too many years of my life in this playground. I'm getting sick of it."

He looked more sympathetic than was justified. "You know, I have a great idea," he said. "I live right around here and I have this guitar at home? I could go back and get it and play you some of my songs. Would you like that? I wrote some of them myself. They're not great . . . but they're good."

"Well, I don't know, I—"

"You just keep an eye on Danny. He'll be fine. I'll be back in five minutes." Before she could answer, he raced out of the playground, returning in even less time than he'd said he would. He knew a lot of songs, folk songs of her era, pop songs. Nira couldn't tell the difference between the ones he'd written himself and the others. "The lyrics *are* kind of corny," he admitted. "But you have to do that, you know? That's what the public wants."

"Right," Nira said, smiling, delighted with him, at being serenaded on this beautiful spring day. He was so beautiful! Like a Picasso drawing, his body falling into effortlessly graceful, angular poses in his faded jeans and checked shirt.

At the end of the afternoon, as he was about to leave, her brother appeared, having arrived at their apartment and not found her in. Joel was a year older than her, back in medical school after a series of jobs in other professions that hadn't worked out. Now that they were adults, their childhood competitiveness had eased into a joshing camaraderie. He was the only man with whom Nira felt totally at ease, to whom she confided everything, as she did with her women friends. Sometimes there were months when they didn't speak. Other times he'd call several times a week.

"Who's that? Your husband?" the boy asked, looking up, scowling as Joel came closer. Portly and perspiring in his business suit, Joel carried a leather briefcase bulging with papers.

"My brother."

He looked uncertain, as though not sure she was telling the truth.

She introduced them. "Joel, this is Orson. He writes his own songs."

"Hi there, Orson," Joel said easily.

"She really your sister?" Orson asked, good-naturedly.

"Yeah, don't we look alike?" Joel grinned, bringing his round, bearded face next to Nira's.

Orson wrinkled his nose. "Kind of, I guess." He ambled off, his guitar over his shoulder, his nephew trotting ahead of him toward the ice-cream truck.

"Who's he?" Joel looked amused.

"Just cradle-robbing." Nira stretched in the sun which had appeared through a veil of leaves overhead. "God, wasn't he beautiful,

Joel? He's been serenading me all afternoon! What should I have done with him? Maybe I should have taken him home and hung him on the wall—just to stare at."

"Cindy would call him a come-puppy," Joel said, lighting up a cigarillo.

"What's that?" Nira asked, bumming one off him.

"He probably has an erection all day long."

Nira sighed wistfully. "I'm an idiot. What a cure for postpartum depression! It would be enough to make anyone have a baby a year." She frowned. "What about VD, though?"

"What about it? You get a few shots of penicillin."

"True . . . Fay used to pick guys up in hotel lobbies and she never got a darn thing."

"Still?" Joel had had an affair with Fay, her best friend, years earlier.

Staring at the ceiling of the beach house bedroom, Nira wondered if Jerry Gardener's wife's lover was anything like her long-haired, guitar-playing sweetie. She had not seen him again. Not wanting even to be tempted, she had avoided that playground for the few weeks before they'd left for the beach. Hell, why shouldn't his wife have a pot-smoking teenage lover? Why shouldn't all wives? They ought to hand them out at the door, as you left the hospital. *He* had his blond in the straw hat. Look, you know nothing about it, right? Maybe she's been screwing everyone in sight. Maybe he has. Anyway, they're divorced so it's different than if . . .

She waited for Thursday, halfway between anticipation and uneasiness. Something would go wrong. How wrong or what it would be she didn't know.

It was an unqualified disaster. Nira felt a premonition as he arrived with his daughters, promptly at six, the three of them all looking incredibly neat and preppy in khaki slacks and button-down white shirts. His older daughter had wispy hair, so fair it was almost white. There was a lost, imperious look in her long, dreamy eyes, an expression of subdued protest: I didn't want to come. Daddy made me. She held a copy of *Anne of Green Gables* in one hand. The younger one looked fragile and delicate, the kind who might have asthma or special food allergies. She looked startlingly like her father. Her hand was clutched tightly in his, as though for support.

"This is our baby," Posey announced gaily. She was dressed in her Robin-Hood green leotard, her cardboard, aluminum-foil-covered sword dangling rakishly at her side. Her favorite game of the summer was one she had invented with her best friend, Abra: Knights and Princesses. They, of course, were the knights. The "princesses" varied from an old rag doll to Jasmine, the baby, who was often "rescued" from her carriage and then carried wildly around the lawn, tucked precariously under one of Posey's arms. Oddly, the baby adored this. Far from being terrified at Posey's appearance, she let out strange yelping sounds of delight whenever she came near. Usually Posey spoke of the baby with an oddly arched irony, a peculiar imitation of adult speech. "Look at her tiny hands and feet," she said now, to the guests. "Aren't they darling?"

His older daughter regarded the baby impassively, then sat down under a tree to read her book. The younger one, peering into the carriage, said softly, "She's cute."

"She's going to be a knockout when she grows up," Posey informed her. "But right now, with three double chins, the kid has some problems. . . . Do you duel?"

"I–I don't know." The little girl looked at Posey uneasily.

"Listen, it's easy, I'll show you." Posey raced into the house and returned with the smaller of the two swords. "En garde!" she shouted, aiming at Jerry Gardener's daughter's pale, blue-veined throat.

"Po, I mean it, cut that out," Nira snapped. She had wanted to be the graciously effortless earth mother with her swarm of delightful children, a fantasy as doomed to failure as those about teenage lovers.

"I'll teach her how," Posey said defiantly. "She *needs* to learn." She handed the other girl the sword. "Come on, move it around. Attack me."

"Posey, if you don't stop this second, I'm breaking that sword," Nira said, glaring at her. Her cheeks were hot from the fire which she had started before their arrival.

Posey marched over and handed Nira the sword. "Okay, break it," she said coolly.

Nira, furious, tried to and failed. Exasperated, she threw the sword as far as she could over the lawn. It landed, with a plunk, five feet from the house. Posey cocked her head to one side. "Nice try, Mom."

The steaks got overdone. Heather stood by Nira's side with instructions. "Don't make it all gross and bloody, like last time."

"Can I help in some way?" Jerry Gardener asked. His younger daughter had retreated into his lap, from whence she looked out at Nira's daughters, especially Posey, with some trepidation.

"The salad's on the counter in the kitchen," Nira said, almost ashamed to look at him. "Could you bring it out?"

Once the food was ready, the meat overcooked, the salad taste-less, the baby let out a blood-curdling howl.

"Heather, could you and Po take care of her?" Nira suggested, smiling obsequiously at them as they gnawed on their bones. They looked up like two wolverine cubs, their cheeks smeared with fat.

Sighing, Posey lifted the baby out of her carriage, then staggered backward. "God, she stinks! What a stinking baby! Come here," she said to Stacey. "You want to smell something that'll make you want to throw up?"

"No," Stacey said, leaning against her father.

"We do all the shit work around here," Posey continued bale-fully. "In *every* sense of the word." But she lugged the baby into the house where the cries, for the moment, were muted.

Heather approached his older daughter, who had eaten almost nothing, sweeping the gray-brown meat to one side with a graciously decisive gesture. "I have a full deck," she said, pulling a pack of cards out of her pocket. "Want to play?"

"I think I'd like to finish this chapter," Jane said.

"I read that in fourth grade," Heather informed her with barely veiled contempt.

Jane looked at her. "So did I . . . I'm *re*reading it."

Jerry had brought his camera. Nira noticed it lying on the grass, under the tree.

"I think it's getting a little dark," he said, following her glance.

Nira drank some more red wine. She had hoped it would make her buoyant. Instead, it seemed to be bringing on a migraine. Her eyelid was twitching; she touched it lightly. She had washed her hair, she had put on a dress, she had shaved her legs. If I were staggeringly, overwhelmingly beautiful, none of this would matter, she thought. He wouldn't notice any of it, not the girls, not the overcooked steak, not the stinking baby, not that she couldn't break or throw foil-covered swords. How do you know? He looks like the type who would notice anyway.

She had begun to hate him. He seemed like the kind of man who didn't sweat, who, if he lost his temper, did it with icy control, saying careful, irrefutable, damaging things. No wonder your wife has a teenage lover, she told him silently, gulping her wine. She wanted someone playful, silly. She didn't want to be looked at with that blue-eyed, detached stare.

"I'm sorry the meat was overcooked," she found herself saying. Grovel, grovel. Do your groveling act. You're good at that. "The girls don't like it rare."

"It was fine." He hesitated. "My wife is a vegetarian . . . so the girls aren't used to eating much meat."

"She cooks fish," his younger daughter said, her eyes half-shut, then fell asleep, her head on his shoulder. Gently he lifted her up and set her down on the grass.

"She hasn't been sleeping that well," Jerry explained. "She has bad dreams and then she can't fall back to sleep."

"I know," Nira said.

He looked puzzled.

"No, I mean, I do too . . . I have insomnia. I always have. I meant, I know what it's like."

"What kind do you have?"

She couldn't tell if he was asking in a clinically detached or sympathetic way. "The kind where you obsess about everything that's gone wrong the day before and everything that can go wrong the next day." Like today.

"I tend more to wake up at some ungodly hour, like three or four, and lie there, thinking of all the mistakes I've made in my life."

"Yeah, I have that kind too." What mistakes had he made? Horrible ones? Or just easily correctable errors?"

"Daddy, I want to go home," his older daughter said.

Jerry glanced at her, then at the younger one, asleep under the tree, as limp and pale as a starfish. It was nighttime now, dark. Nira had been about to bring out candles and coffee. "Maybe I *had* better," he said.

"Sure," she smiled tremulously, acutely disappointed. "You could come over later for coffee, if you feel like it."

"I'm a little reluctant to leave them alone," he said. "Maybe some other time?"

Nira stared at him. Damn. They're not babies. So she has bad dreams? How about me? She watched as he carefully scooped the younger one up in his arms. She snuggled against him, burying her face in his chest. "Carry me home, Daddy," she murmured.

"I am, darling," Jerry said. He smiled at Nira. "It's lucky she still weighs seventy pounds."

"That *is* lucky," Nira said. And she's lucky to have a daddy who carries her off to bed with that effortless, tender warmth. You had one once, kid. Shut up.

She watched the three of them walk off, his older daughter slightly ahead, he with the sleeping child in his arms. Slowly, Nira cleared what was left of the dishes, did some perfunctory cleaning up in the kitchen, and checked on the girls. They were watching TV in the master bedroom. Posey, a pillow under her head, her sword by her side, was resting her feet on the baby, as though she were a pillow.

"Watch her, Po," Nira said, but languidly, too tired and sad to care. "Don't let her roll off the bed."

"She won't," Posey said.

"You should be in bed," Nira felt obliged to say.

"It's vacation," Heather said automatically, not even moving her eyes from the screen. "We'll sleep late."

"I'm going for a walk," Nira told them. "Put Jas in before you turn in, okay?"

"Who was that man, Mom?" Heather wanted to know.

"Our neighbor, I told you," Nira said, changing into sneakers.

"He's sexy," Heather said. "But his daughter is a real drag. . . . She's reading *Anne of Green Gables* and she's eleven?"

"There are a lot of retards up here. . . . What is he, divorced or something?" Posey yawned.

Nira nodded.

"Yeah, you can tell," Heather said.

"How?"

"That hangdog look." Heather glanced over at her mother. "That's what Angie's mother said. You know, like they haven't had a square meal in months."

"Why can't he cook?" Posey said.

"They never do," Heather said. "Angie's mother kicked out Angie's father, and Angie went over there for lunch, and you know all he had in the house? Peanut butter!"

"I'm not going to get married," Posey said.

"I am," Heather said. "But I'm marrying someone who can cook."

"Kids, will you remember about the baby?" Nira said, putting on her sweater.

Posey's voice got that ironical tone. "Of course we'll remember about the baby. How could we forget about the baby?"

Heather gave the baby a light pat on the stomach with her foot. "Look, this is a *good* baby . . . Mom, really she is. Angie's baby cries all the *time!* All day, all night! And she's ugly. Really ugly. . . . *Our* baby is beautiful."

"Let's enter her in a contest," Posey said with sudden enthusiasm. "Maybe she'd win some prizes. Can we, Mom?"

"Po, listen, I'm tired. . . . Just—let's talk it over in the morning."

"I bet we could win millions!" Posey said. She looked over at Nira. "What're you so tired about?"

"She misses Daddy," Heather said. "She's lonely."

"I miss him," Posey said. "When's he coming back, Mom?"

"Thursday," Nira said. She started down the hall. She heard Heather saying, "You don't miss him the same *way,* dodo. . . . They're married."

"Yeah, I guess" was Posey's languid reply.

What if I had had boys? Nira wondered. Chunky, redoubtable boys who collected frogs and played baseball? She had always expected she would have boys, had seen herself out on the baseball field with them, slugging home runs. "Wow, your mom's really terrific." Of the many bad reasons for having a third child, one had definitely been to make one final try for a boy. Now it seemed clear. God, be she male or female, had selected her as the target of smart-assed, sharp-eyed little girls. So? There are worse fates.

Nira trudged along the beach. It was dark and windy. Her sneakered feet sank into the sand. I'm a failure at everything! she thought, almost in wonder. I can't do complicated things, I can't do simple things. So, what did you want to happen tonight? What *didn't* happen that you expected or wanted? Out with it. Tell the good doctor everything. Look, I don't know. It wasn't that clear cut. Okay, he's attractive. He has a baleful, sensitive look. I wanted him to gaze at me with quiet lust. I wanted us to have a long intimate talk about life, love, marriage . . . And then? I don't know "and then." Just that. I wanted to see if a man, a real man, not a teenage cutie with a guitar, could like me, want me, desire me, the way Adlai is probably at this very second liking, lusting after, and admiring some English feminist whom he knew from Oxford. I'm losing my husband, okay? And that's painful, no matter how ambivalent I feel about him or marriage. It hurts!

She saw it as a cartoon. A big room with a sign over it: Lost Husbands. Some were sitting around in business suits, reading *The New York Times,* others were practicing their squash games. Nira was led up to the room by a harried-looking man with a bunch of keys at his waist. "Any of these seem to be yours, miss?" Nira looked around. "No, I don't think so." Wait, was that Adlai? No, just looked like him. That same bald head, wry expression, sensitive hands. But no, that one was studying a score for *La Traviata;* Adlai, who hated opera, was tone-deaf.

Her best friend, Fay, claimed marriage was a power struggle. "When you marry, it's set up one way. Then, somewhere along the line, the power shifts. That's what happened with you. You had the power, maybe without knowing it or realizing it, and now you're

losing it . . . and that makes you mad and scared, and Adlai's de-
lighted." Shit! If I had it, why didn't I at least appreciate it, savor it
while I did? Did I really have it? When?

Maybe it was true. When they'd met, that summer in England
in 1952, when Nira had been nineteen and Adlai twenty-three, she
had, for some odd, inexplicable reason, blossomed. From a gawky,
toothy, five-foot-eight weed into an energetic, sparkling, wholesome
American girl. That was how he had seen her anyway, and you be-
come, Nira felt, what you were seen as. Everything she did, Adlai
exclaimed about. An English girl would never do that. An English
girl would be too reserved, too stiff, too conscious of manners. English
girls didn't talk loudly and openly about anything and everything,
didn't run to meet him with such eagerness that once she slipped and
gashed her knee open. In America she was, if not a dime a dozen,
certainly not all that remarkable. Or maybe she had just never found
anyone before who regarded her as such.

It was partly, too, the way Adlai had regarded himself, a sort of
English version of Woody Allen—bad at sports, already balding in his
early twenties, inhibited by a slight stutter, which he'd overcome but
which had left him tense and awkward at even casual, everyday con-
versation. Once they were married and moved to America, it had
been more of the same, at least in the early years. Adlai had felt,
despite its having been his decision to settle in New York perma-
nently, ill at ease, uncertain how to act. What was the "American"
thing to do? All their friends were Nira's friends—which made sense
since she had lived in New York all her life and still had a vast, not
always connected, network of friends she'd gone to high school with,
friends from the Parsons School of Design, friends she'd met at the
sportswear firm where she had worked as a designer till Heather was
born. It was as though Adlai stood quietly while Nira wove a net
around him, of warmth and family life and children, and he eased
into it, gradually making it his own, but still seeing her as the star,
the creator of all these wonderful things.

And, ah yes, it was the sixties, those magical pre-Women's
Movement days, when just having babies, doing it well, enjoying it,
was justification enough in one's own eyes, in the eyes of the world, in
the eyes of one's husband. And Nira had been one of the "lucky"
ones. Her father had come to her, even before she'd gotten pregnant
with Heather, and said, "Nira, I never want you to sink into a world
of diapers and dishes. You must never become a household drone, a
complainer, a nag. You must go on with your art. I will give you all

the money you need for child care; I will rent you a studio. I will give you everything you need—and more."

Of course it had been, in its own eccentric way, a trap. So Nira saw it now, fifteen years later. It had not only been Adlai around whom a net had been cast, but her as well. Still, at the time it had not seemed that way. She had only felt guilty, hideously guilty. Gorgeous babies, full-time help, her own studio in the country, a husband who was almost obsequiously devoted, who clung to her at parties, who told her every night that she was beautiful. If she babbled on at parties incoherently—about politics, art, anything—Adlai would tell her later, "You express yourself so well, Ni! Your ideas are so fascinating, so original." And her friends, whose husbands wouldn't let them get a word out edgewise, envied her. "Where did you find him?" "Maybe *I* should go to England." "Does he have a twin brother?" She had beamed. Oh God, riding for a fall, all right. Galloping was more like it.

When had the worm turned? It had started turning in the mid- to late-sixties when all her friends, who had staggered and limped through the early child-filled years without help, those poor "unlucky" ones, were emerging, some timorously, some aggressively, but emerging. Getting jobs, going back to school, entering The World. Complaining, bitching about it, but entering. "What else can I do? The kids are in school all day. They have after-school stuff, gymnastics, art. I *have* to do something, Nira. I'm going crazy. It's different for you. You have your art. That's different. I don't *have* anything like that. I'm not talented. I need to get out or I'll go bananas." Out they went, to a woman, the shy ones, the bold ones. Now if Nira wanted to have lunch with a friend, it meant a forty-minute bus ride to midtown Manhattan to meet—yes, even Yvonne, with her voice that hardly raised above a whisper—for a quick, I've-got-to-get-back-to-the-office-for-a-meeting-at-two lunch. No more lazy playground lunches, gossiping about trivia. Who, except her, had time for trivia anymore? "Listen, the kids are flourishing," they all confided. "I should have gotten out years ago! We all should have."

And Adlai was going through his own transformation. He was good at what he did. He was promoted. He was an authority. He forgot, himself, that he'd once had a stutter. At sales meetings, he made eloquent pitches for books that he privately confessed he would never have foisted on his worst enemy. No matter that Nira never read the books he published or even the lists he brought home. Someone read them. Someone thought they were good. Instead of trying

vainly to sweep his thinning hair over his bald head, he let himself go
proudly, openly bald. And looked a hundred times better. Like a
Russian expatriate poet, with his dark, humorous eyes. He had a wry
wit. God, where had that come from? Women laughed at his jokes,
rushed over to him at parties. He no longer clung to Nira's side. He
mingled. At parties she often didn't see him from the time they ar-
rived to the time they left. Suddenly he was jogging! Unathletic
Adlai was getting in shape, was gazing at himself approvingly in the
mirror, selecting his wardrobe with care, watching what he ate.

Nira panicked. Everyone knew the ending to *this* story. You
didn't even have to be able to put two and two together. But she was
convinced she might have dug out of it or past it, might have found
her own peculiar version of self-renewal, if her father—who had prom-
ised, had *sworn,* he would be there forever—hadn't died. Nira felt like
the acrobat on the high wire who has been performing effortlessly for
years and, one day, looking down, sees that for some reason they have
removed the net. But I *need* the net! I can't do my tricks otherwise.
Sorry, kid. It wasn't *just* the net. It was everything. It was the image
her father had had of her, which was subtly, crucially different from
Adlai's early, clinging admiration. Her father, damn him, had "be-
lieved" in her. "Nira, you're an artist. You don't want to waste your
life telling women to wear yellow gloves this season or frills on their
hemlines. You can do more than that. You can be an Important
Artist."

Even Adlai, bless him, had seen the insanity of the important-
artist routine, but had let it continue. Had let the whole thing con-
tinue. The little intimate dinners at which her father would pour out
all his troubles, complain about her mother, stuff hundred-dollar bills
in her pocket. "If it makes you both happy, why not?" was his atti-
tude. Daddy, you said you wouldn't die. *That* wasn't fair. You prom-
ised. You said you'd always be there.

A year of emptiness, pain, a "breakdown," a four-month stint at
an expensive mental hospital . . . and then the same world. You came
back to the same world, Nira realized. Madness is just a break. Not
fun, not helpful, but in any case a break. You come back to the same
world where friends are working and doing well, where you have kids
that are growing up, into their own things, a husband who is success-
ful, who travels, whom other women admire. None of that has
changed or gone away. You still have no profession. Only a studio in
the Berkshires full of artwork no one wants to buy, a father you can't
scream at beyond the grave.

So you get pregnant. The great non-answer to everything. Another baby. The illusion: you can start over. You can bring back the past. You have a function, something you're good at. Maybe a boy this time. Only you know, from Day One, it won't work, and so does everyone else. Adlai wasn't the type to suggest an abortion. He knew what she was doing and why. He pitied her. He wanted, hoped the baby might "tide her over," whatever the hell that meant.

The awful part was that now, when she realized she needed him so much, when she had nothing else, she wasn't even sure she loved him! Had she ever? Had she married his vision of her? Was it just fear that no one else would ever appear and want her, not just for the odd date or half-assed affair, but permanently? Nira would have liked, now that she knew she could lose her husband, that it wasn't just a paranoid fantasy but a reality, to lure him back, to be peppy and fun and energetic. But she didn't feel that way. She felt shattered and anxious and held together with Elmer's glue. Her attempts to pretend sudden enthusiasm about his work rang as false to her as they probably did to him. Suddenly *she* was the clinger. She was the one who hovered in corners at parties, who questioned him nervously, "Who did you have lunch with today?" who choked on hideous thoughts about who he was jogging with. Rage and obsequiousness were not a fun combination. You *know* who he's jogging with! He's jogging with someone who really, *genuinely,* thinks he's terrific, who really, genuinely, finds his ideas interesting, who's young, who's in good shape, who's doting, who has a good job. Why shouldn't he? Wouldn't you?

Nira had no firm thoughts about adultery. She wished she did. She wished she could be like Helena, who had never forgiven her husband for "betraying" her. An abstraction: betrayal. Maybe Jews just weren't good at abstractions like that, that fierce, unyielding Protestant morality. "If he even went around the block for a sand-wich, I knew I could never trust him again." All she seemed to be good at was jealous panic. And it had not even reached "that point" yet! There were not, as yet, lipsticked handkerchiefs, interrupted phone calls. And there might never be. Adlai was discreet, kind. If he was fooling around, she knew it wasn't to hurt her—look Mom, I can fuck with other women. He was doing it for the same reason she had had babies—because he had discovered, probably to his surprise, that he was good at it, that it was fun, that it made him feel good. For the same reason that Jerry Gardener's wife had found her teenage sweetie. And Jerry Gardener had found his free-lance writer in the straw hat.

Nira didn't believe in psychiatry or drugs. The baby era, for all

its flaws and delights, was over. Jasmine would have to raise herself.
You have to get a job, kid. You have to get your act together. It's up
to *you*, Nira. Not Daddy, not Adlai. . . . You're the only one who cares,
and you're the only one who can do it. Yeah, okay, I will. I'm going
to. Come Labor Day I will be a new woman.

The night Adlai returned from England, Nira let the girls stay
up late. He arrived at ten. Posey, creature of many unpredictable
moods, had changed from her everyday grungy leotard into a floor-
length violet dress sprinkled with flowers. Nira, after giving up design
as a career, had continued making clothes for herself, as she had done
since she was a teenager, and then for the girls. Until they had van-
ished into the anonymity of jeans and T-shirts, she had stitched beau-
tiful smocked dresses of Liberty lawn, Marimekko jumpers, dozens of
"mother-and-daughter" dresses. Heather, once she passed the age of
six, would not be seen dead in any of these creations. "I don't want to
look different," she announced firmly. "I want to look the same." But
Posey, whose love of fantasy ran deep, liked occasionally to transform
herself into a princess-gamin, perfumed, limpid, a "nymphet in train-
ing," as Adlai called her when she was in those moods.

On this particular evening, Posey took her first bath of the sum-
mer, trimmed her insanely long, filthy fingernails into round half-
moons, arranged her black, shiny hair in a "new" way, with plastic
barrettes holding it back from her face.

"Do I look pretty, Mom? How do I look?"

"You look great, Po . . . I can't believe it." It reminded Nira of
those overweight, middle-aged women who go to fat farms to "sur-
prise" their husbands. "I think Daddy likes you the regular way too,"
she felt, for some reason, obliged to add.

"Oh, I know that." Posey looked intense. "Of course he likes me
any way. I'm his child. He *has* to love me."

"He does not *have* to love you," Heather, precise, informed her.
"No one has to love anyone. Lots of parents hate their children. Lots
of parents beat their children to death!" She was dressed simply in a
clean shirt and slacks, her hair in a pony tail.

"Even if they're nice?" Posey looked suddenly alarmed.

"Hon," Nira intervened, feeling anxious, "those are crazy
people."

"You were crazy once." Heather didn't say it accusingly, but just
to relay a piece of information that might somehow have slipped
Nira's mind.

"I wasn't crazy so much," Nira said. "I was depressed." In fact, so effortlessly had the girls seemed to adjust while she had been in the hospital, so smoothly had they welcomed her back, that Nira had wondered what, if any, effect the whole incident had had on them. On her, apart from anything else, it had proven her own dispensability, even at the one role she had felt confident she was doing well. When they were older, she had promised herself, she would explain it to them, tell them what it had been like. Now it seemed easier to go along with the way it had appeared on the surface: she had been sick, had gone away to get well, and was now fine again.

"Yeah, but you *acted* crazy," Heather said. "Remember how you yelled at me that time about practicing the piano."

"I act crazy *lots* of times," Posey said suddenly. "I *like* to do crazy things." Her expression became furtive. "Only I don't always tell anyone."

Heather said, "Mom, will Daddy think the baby looks different? Will he notice?"

"Notice what?"

"Her tooth!"

"Of course he'll notice," Posey said scornfully. "He's not blind. . . . Let's wake her up when he comes, okay, Mom? She'll be mad if we don't."

"Absolutely not," Nira said. "That doesn't make sense."

She herself was somewhere between Heather and Posey in elegance—showered, fragrant, in a gypsy skirt she had made ten years earlier and an off-the-shoulder Mexican blouse, but still barefoot. Perfect elegance now, after fifteen years of marriage, would seem obsequious, she felt.

When Adlai appeared, at ten-forty, Posey made an ecstatic leap into his arms, clinging to him like a monkey, covering his bald head with thousands of nibbling kisses. Heather, more shyly, hugged him quietly from the side. Nira waited her turn and, once Posey had slipped to the ground, kissed him on the lips. "Hi, sweetie."

The baby, either due to extrasensory perception or her own wiles, woke up at just that instant and let out her own welcoming howl. Nira changed her and brought her in.

"What's different about her?" Posey questioned him. "Guess!"

Adlai, head to one side, surveyed the plump baby that Nira held in her arms. "She's fatter?"

"No! You only have three guesses."

"More hair?"

"Her tooth!" Posey pried up the baby's upper lip. "See! She can bite now. *Don't* put your finger in her mouth."

"Definitely not."

The girls stayed up till almost midnight, listening to his stories about England, their English grandmother. Finally at twelve-thirty, Nira was alone with him. They sat on the porch, sipping wine.

"You look tired," she said. It seemed almost ominously quiet with the girls' chatter silenced.

"I am . . . I've been running around a lot. I met some interesting people. I'll tell you about it tomorrow, okay?" He reached out and touched her hand.

"Sure."

They were both looking over at Jerry Gardener's porch. A light was on in one of the rooms. "Have the Richardsons taken it again this year?"

Nira shook her head. "It's a scientist. . . . He has two kids about the age of ours, but they seem kind of shy."

"I suppose we could have him over for a drink. . . . Is his wife nice?"

"I haven't met her. . . . I—I think they're divorced."

At that moment, as though it were a play they were watching or a movie, a woman appeared at one of the windows and looked out, not in their direction. It was not the blond, but a woman with brown hair and bangs.

"Who's she?" Adlai asked with a smile, setting down his glass of wine.

"A girlfriend, I guess." Nira watched, her stomach tight, as Jerry Gardener appeared, shadowy, behind the woman and put one hand on her shoulder. She turned, as though to embrace him. Then they both vanished.

"Looks like it," Adlai said.

The image, shadowy and diffused as it had been, followed them into the bedroom. She was there, while her husband made love to her in that bedroom, now a blond in a straw hat, now a dark-haired woman seen in shadow, a lover's arm on her shoulder. Who was in Adlai's mind as he moved inside her, murmuring incoherently, kissing her neck, her hair? Does it matter? She wondered if the condescension she felt in his familiar, husbandly caresses was in her mind, just an invention.

At two, unable to sleep, she sat on the porch again, a sweater around her shoulders. It was cooler now, and windy. The light in Jerry Gardener's house was off. Guess what's going on over there. So what do you want—to be in Ripley's Believe It or Not? Here we have a couple, married almost fifteen years, who are still having ecstatic sex. Ecstasy has a six-month time limit. Romantic love has a two-year time limit. He still wants to make love to you. Perhaps not as often or as enthusiastically as you'd like, but occasionally. Fortnightly, as the English would say. Quit complaining. Think of Sallie's husband who took the sexy au pair girl home after the theater and returned four hours later "because he got caught in traffic." What do you want, kid? Shall I tell you? Do you really want to know? I want two totally incompatible, unrealizable things.

I want a desert-island-type idyll with an impassioned lover who, for any idiotic reason on earth, is besotted with me, loves sex, wants to do it four times a day, in every position, oral sex, the works. Okay, so that you can buy at the corner supermarket for seventy-five cents. No, I don't want a historical romance. I want a contemporary setting. I want him to be nice, even smart, at least not dumb. So find your guitar player.

Fantasy Two was a twenty-year affair, a second marriage, sex once a month with someone who was married, but dully, who would think she was great, who would be urbane and courteous and write her long, descriptive, avuncular letters entwined with occasional bemused romantic yearnings.

You want Charles Boyer crossed with Gérard Philipe. Not crossed with. Both. Both?

Like everyone she had had offers. Most recently it had been the psychologist who used to live in their apartment building prior to his divorce. He had taken her out to a lavish lunch at an elegant restaurant in hopes, he confessed, that the sleepy, languorous nudes on the wall would "put her in the right mood." He was seeking—optimistic man—"someone with whom to fulfill his sexual fantasies." Beneath Nira's quiet exterior he saw wild burblings, a desire to kick up her heels in some hypothetical flower-strewn meadow. For that he needed a PhD in psychology? A little high, well-fed, Nira allowed her own feelings of confusion to come drifting incoherently forth. He looked delighted. "And what are you doing about these feelings?" Nira looked at him myopically, fuzzily. "Musing," she said. Musing! He sat back in his chair and heaved a heavy sigh. For a twenty-dollar lunch he'd ended up with a muser. Better luck next time.

Taking a lover is like having a third child, kid, a non-answer. You need a job, you need a focus for your life. Don't I need pleasure? Don't I need to have fun? Why should you be different from the rest of the world? Who's having fun? Anyone you know?

Behind that shuttered screen, something was going on that, Nira felt certain, if not fun, was a damn good substitute.

They invited Jerry Gardener over for a drink. He was about to go back to the city. His children were no longer with him. He came alone, sans blond, sans brunette. Nira was mostly silent as Adlai questioned him about his work.

"I'd been hoping to get more done this summer," Jerry said. "But with my daughters. . . ."

Adlai smiled sympathetically. "It's impossible. I've tried it. . . . What is it you're working on?"

"Well, I've had an idea for a history of modern biology. Something for non-scientists, that could also be read by people in the field."

"Popularized but not condescending?"

"Exactly."

Adlai leaned forward eagerly. Nira could see the wheels churning in his head. "How far have you gotten?"

"Basically I just have an outline. . . . I have a friend who works for a university press, and he said if I could do a sample chapter or two, he might bring it in."

"Why just a university press?"

"Well, I don't know. . . . They do that kind of thing well, and this isn't really a commercial idea."

"It could be," Adlai said. "It sounds like it definitely could be."

"Could it?"

"Look, I don't want to interfere with anything you've set up with your friend, but . . . would you be willing to let me see it once you have the chapters done? We'd definitely be interested."

Jerry sipped his gin and tonic. "The university press thing isn't anything definite. My real problem is time. You see, I'm doing research now, and there's no way you can do that halfway. It's too competitive. If you can't get grants, you're out. . . . There's no such thing as running a small lab. And you get sucked into more and more administrative duties."

Adlai smiled. "I know all about that."

"I've thought, but only in the vaguest way, of giving it up altogether—research, I mean—maybe going into teaching. But it would be terribly difficult finding a job at an equivalent salary. Now that I'm divorced, I just can't afford to—"

"A friend of mine," Adlai said, "claims no one can afford to get divorced any more."

What friend was that? Nira wondered. It sounded like a great conversation. Gee, I'd love to marry you, sweetie, but how about Nira and the kids? We'd be broke. We'd starve. Don't worry, darling, once I'm made vice-president of Lord and Taylor's. . . . Shit.

Jerry Gardener smiled painfully. "I couldn't afford it either, but . . ."

"Of course," Adlai said. "Sometimes it just becomes impossible."

There was a pause.

"Would either of you like another drink?" Nira said, just to indicate to both of them that she was there.

They looked up in surprise—as though she were a waitress that had suddenly appeared after an overly long absence—then shook their heads.

"You have a lovely family," Jerry Gardener said, his eyes leaving Nira. "Beautiful girls."

Adlai's expression softened. "Yes, I . . . I feel I'm very lucky." He cleared his throat. "Have you been divorced a long time?"

"Just a year . . . but things have been"—he gestured—"not good for longer than that."

"It's always especially hard for the children," Adlai said.

"Yes, terrible . . . worse than people say. I had no choice, though. My wife simply—"

"They live with her? How often do you see them?"

Nira was beginning to feel sick. Why is he so interested in all of this?

"Not often enough," Jerry said. "It's not a fair arrangement. But I'm trying—"

"We have a friend who's just been devastated at losing his children," Adlai said. He glanced over at Nira. "Skipp."

"Women are devastated too," Nira said suddenly, exploding.

They both stared at her.

"I mean, you're talking as though it were just bad for men!"

"The law favors mothers, at least in terms of custody," Jerry Gardener said.

"And in many cases the father is actually the better parent," Adlai said. "The more responsible one."

"Absolutely," Jerry said.

"But what is the mother supposed to have?" Nira cried, her voice trembling. "She had the children, she raised them, and then they're taken away from her? She doesn't have a job, she has no money. What of her?"

Both of them looked uncomfortable. Hysterical woman versus detached men. You know who wins that one.

"It's not a matter of all mothers, sweetie," Adlai said softly.

He'll take the children if we get divorced, Nira thought in horror. But you're not *getting* divorced! Shut up and sit down.

At that moment, as though on cue, Heather and Posey in bathing suits appeared, pushing the baby in her carriage.

"Girls, you remember Mr. Gardener," Nira said quickly.

"Hi," Posey flung out. She pointed in at the carriage. "Boy, is she in a lousy mood today."

"I think she's cutting a new tooth," Heather said. To Jerry, she added, "She has two already, and she's just five months old."

"She bites," Posey said. "I mean, really *bites.*"

"Mom, I think she's going to need braces," Heather said. "Her teeth are crooked." Heather was going to be fitted for braces in the fall.

"Those teeth don't count," Posey said. "Baby teeth fall out."

"Yeah, but if her baby ones are crooked, her regular ones will be worse."

They took the baby inside. Jerry got up to leave. "She's an extraordinarily beautiful baby," he said to both of them.

Nira felt he was looking at them with envy: the self-possessed, successful husband; the beautiful kids; the mildly fragmented, obsequious, but still physically appealing wife. She stared at him, willing him to see through it. She could sense he was disconcerted by the intensity of her stare.

"Keep in touch about the book," Adlai said. "Even if all you have is an outline. Are you in the phone book?"

"I live in a funny neighborhood. It's temporary, I hope. Near Ninth Avenue in the Forties."

"Let's have lunch and talk about it."

Back in the city Nira made a bargain with herself: You can call him by November first or when you get a job. You can call him as soon as you get a job, but if you don't have one by November first, you can call him anyway. He was going to be, in her fantasy, her reward for getting a job or her consolation for not getting one.

The day after they got back, she called Fay.

Fay had graduated Parsons the same year as Nira, but had

stayed in fashion all those years, designing sportswear for various Seventh Avenue houses, finally apprenticing herself to a name designer. At thirty-seven, she had just married her boss and, for the first time since she was sixteen, she told Nira, she was taking a break. "I'm doing nothing," she said. "I'm going to do all those crazy things ordinary people do. I might even have a baby."

Her lover had five children, mostly grown. Statistically, Fay said, the chances of their having gotten married were minus one hundred. Reality should have dictated that he would be the thousandth *meshugunah* married man to whose mournful stories she would listen, who would be momentarily captivated by her vivacity, with whom marvelous sex and manic guilt would alternate with an almost Mozartean inevitability. But, behold, he had invented another script; he had appeared at her door one week after their first night together and said, "I love you. I am going to marry you. I am leaving my wife and five children." And had done it. And had married her.

"I don't believe it," Fay told Nira after the wedding. "Just because it happened doesn't mean I have to believe it, right? I mean, he's a nice guy, Nira! He's a *mensch*. I wouldn't even have room for him in my Complete Guide to Schmucks. He wouldn't even deserve a footnote."

"What about the one-night stands?" Nira wanted to know. "Can you give them up?"

To Nira, Fay had always been a role model, the only woman of their generation whom Nira knew personally who had said *phooey* to all the Prince Charming nonsense, who had had great sex (and not so great) with an unlikely crew of characters. There had been the conductor of the Tokyo Symphony Orchestra ("I want more than the winds"), the worm farmer who looked like William Buckley and was a male model on the side, with whom she spent ecstatic four days in her father's old-age home in Florida, the piano player in the bar in Cincinnati who thought she was a dead ringer for his twin sister, the guilt-ridden cardiologist whose wife beeped him while he was in motels and whom Fay used to meet after his psychiatric appointment at eight in the morning ("Doing it in a car in twenty-degree weather is no fun," Fay had informed her. "No sir."). In her next life Nira wanted to be reborn as Fay. Right now she needed her, if she was really going to go through with her job plan.

"I can try," Fay said, in response to the one-night stand question. "What can anyone do but try? Look Ni, I know to you it sounded like piles of fun, but there was, like, an hour of fun for every thousand hours of angst and idiocy. Not that I regret it, not that I'd have missed it for the world . . . But it's the way you feel about babies. I did it. It's over."

"About the job thing," Nira began.

"How desperate are you?" Fay wanted to know.

"Totally," Nira admitted. "Rock bottom."

"But you worked for two years. You didn't keep up with any of those contacts?"

"I got fired twice . . . And, no, I don't have any idea what happened to Ira Simpson of Glorious Garments, and if I saw him coming, I'd run and hide."

"I thought you were kind of a hotshot back then," Fay said. "I'm not rubbing salt; I'm just gathering information. Didn't they interview you in *Women's Wear?*"

"Fay, that was 1955! Okay? Those pages are yellow. Nobody remembers. I'm not that *person* anymore."

In fact, the night before calling Fay, Nira had looked at some old photos of herself from that era. Look at that girl! That cocky, impish grin, fantastic legs, that breezy "I can conquer the world" expression. Nira felt the same pangs of envy as if she were looking at photos of some older sister who had always, no matter what you did, been prettier and smarter. Somewhere within you, she encouraged herself, that person lurks, freeze-dried.

"Okay, well, look, never forget that you said you were totally desperate," Fay said. "The good part is this: they will probably hire you."

"Who's they?"

" 'They' are partners, Murray and Sol. Mystique Sports Wear. They're poker pals of Oscar's. Murray is the money; Sol has, you should pardon the expression, the 'ideas.' They're linked together for all time due to some classic male-bonding idiocy in some war. . . . What was that war in the fifties?"

"Korea?" Nira offered.

"Some such thing. Sol saved Murray, not from a fate worse than death but from the real McCoy; so Murray, who has his finger in nine million pies and is pretty sharp money-wise, is backing him in this sportswear deal."

"What's the bad part?"

"The bad part is they've fired four designers in six months. Murray, who probably *could* get the thing off the ground, is too busy to bother and feels he has to leave it up to Sol, who is one of those wonderful masculine combinations we all know and love so well of raving arrogance and total incompetence. I mean, he'd dress women in Saran Wrap and safety pins if he could get away with it. The wages are unspeakable and possibly even illegal. You'll be lucky if you have enough for subway fare and half a tuna fish sandwich for lunch. They'll work you around the clock . . . except for Friday. It's a four-day week, which allows them the option of calling it a part-time job and paying you shit."

"Will I be designing, though?"

"So to speak . . . Look, hon, probably you'll just be *schlepping* stuff from stores and copying anything they decide can make it. Lousy fabrics. It's cheapo stuff. They don't want to take any chances. They've fired anyone who ever tried to do anything even *vaguely* innovative. It's aiming for the lowest level. Low, lower, lowest."

"But, Fay, listen, are they really going to hire me? I haven't worked in ten years!"

"Ni, you don't understand. They are desperate. Their reputation has spread. No one with any options would go near them. You have no options so you're made for each other."

"Should I bring my portfolio?"

"Bring it but, believe me, they'll hire you without it. Be sure to bring the *Women's Wear* interview. Sol loves publicity. He's the type who would have his dying dog interviewed if he had the chance."

"Is he the one who'll interview me?"

"I just don't know. . . . Look, Oscar'll call them. He'll set it up."

The interview was for Thursday at two, a week after Nira called Fay, two weeks after Labor Day. It was Sol she spoke to on the phone, but he said he'd be out of the office Thursday. "My partner'll fill you in on everything you need to know. Murray Farber. He's a great guy. If Murray likes you, it's fine with me."

Mystique Sports Wear was on Seventh Avenue—Fashion Avenue. Murray Farber was five ten or eleven, tan, with a mane of frizzled grayish hair and a nervous habit of drumming on the desk top while he talked.

"You made *Women's Wear?*" he asked Nira after looking through her portfolio. "Pretty impressive for a kid. What were you—twenty-three?"

"Twenty-two."

He closed the portfolio. "Okay, terrific . . . But here you'll have to forget all of that."

"All of what?" Nira asked nervously.

"Originality, creativity. . . . Leave that at home, honey, okay? Be creative with your husband, be creative with your baby. I don't know what your friend Fay told you, but we're not operating on that level. It's not that I don't have the cash, but that's not what I want to do with it right now. Do you get what I mean? We're still groping a little bit. Once we've hit it, we may try something fancier."

"I understand," Nira said.

He was squinting at her. "I like your stuff, Don't misunderstand me. It's good. You've got a good eye. It's simple . . . But you were designing for upper middle-class ladies—it's a different world. We're aiming at what you'd call shop girls . . . who want to look like they're having careers, not just selling stockings at Macy's."

Nira nodded. "Uh, when do I start?"

He grinned. "You're eager, huh? What happened? Your husband's business go under? I know, the same thing happened with my brother-in-law. He was doing fine and in one week—whammo. He's out of a job, four kids. . . . His wife had to go back to work. In one week—straight from the golf course to junior dresses at Lord and Taylor's. She wasn't like you. She didn't have training. She'd never worked."

"I'm not here because of that," Nira said. "My husband hasn't been fired. I just felt, well, once you have children—"

"Listen, I know! You want to give them the best. You want them to have all the extras. Better than what you had. I know all of it. I have three. Once you add it up—piano lessons, horseback riding, what have you? Your husband doesn't even *have* to lose his job. It's still hard . . . Who looks after the baby? Your mother?"

"I have a housekeeper," Nira said.

He looked mournful. "It's a pity . . . You're missing out. Your baby's going to grow up without you. I'm not blaming you. You have no choice, but it's hard."

"I have two others," Nira said. "And I did stay at home with them, so I know what it's like."

"You have *three* kids?"

"Yeah, three girls."

"All girls? Three? Three *babies?*"

"Not babies, girls. . . . One ten, one twelve."

"You've been busy!" he exclaimed, as though she'd been keeping things from him. "I thought from what you said you'd been just sitting around at home, watching the soaps, buffing your nails. I didn't know you had three kids . . . Three girls?"

"Right."

"I like girls," he said. "*I* have a girl . . . But you've got your hands full with girls these days. It isn't like it used to be. You've got to watch them. In the old days, it was the boys you had to watch. Nowadays it's the girls. My wife says her hair is white—at forty-three—because of our daughter. She's not a wild kid either. But they keep you on your toes." He stood up. "Okay, what more can I say? Welcome!"

"Thanks," Nira said, trying to smile. Her hands were wet. She bent to pick up the portfolio.

"So, what does your husband say about all this?" Murray Farber asked as they walked out.

"All what?"

"It's hard for him, I guess. It always is . . . No one likes to see their wife out in the marketplace like that. It's no place for a woman, believe me. You stay in this business long enough and you become just like a man. That's a fact."

"Will I grow a penis?" Nira asked.

He looked startled, then laughed. "I think you're safe, honey. . . . But it's not like sitting at home with babies. It's not all fun and games. You show a profit or you're out."

"It sounds just like marriage." She grinned.

He smiled back. "You got a sense of humor, huh?"

"Sometimes."

In the phone booth downstairs, Nira sat trembling. She was soaked through with perspiration. *I don't think I groveled. Did I?* The interview had gone so fast that she could hardly remember anything. *You have a job.* She stared at the phone. *It doesn't mean you have to call him this second. I want to.* It was like the job interview. If she didn't do it right away she might never do it at all. If she thought about it for longer than one minute, she would never do it.

"Hello?" He answered after the third ring.

"Is this Jerry Gardener?"

"Yes?"

"Hi, uh, this is Nira Goldschmitt . . . I don't know if you remember. Our house was near yours this summer and—"

"Of course." He sounded pleased. "I've been meaning to call you."

"You have?"

"Those photos came out really nicely. I think you'll like them."

The photos! Why hadn't she thought of that? It would have been a perfect excuse. "Could I come over and see them?"

There was a moment's pause. "Over here?"

"I thought I might . . . I work near where you live."

"Oh . . . well. Why don't we meet for lunch some day, then?"

Nira swallowed. "I think it would be easier if I just come over. I don't have that much of a lunch hour. I don't know if I *have* a lunch hour. I just started work."

"When did you start?"

"Well, actually, I start next week . . . But I could come over tomorrow, Friday. I don't work Friday."

He didn't answer for a moment.

"Is Friday a not-good day?" she said.

"No, Friday's fine. . . . What time?"

"Two? Is that okay? I mean, it could be any time, but—"

"Two is fine."

She was glad she had made it for the following day. Even if she was up all night with insomnia, even if she obsessed non-stop from now until two on Friday about all that could go wrong, she would be out of her misery in thirty-six hours. Whatever that meant.

Nira had once dated a scientist in college. His apartment had been so neat, it had made her upper middle-class English mother-in-law's house look like a hovel. It was not so much that it had been elegant, but there were clean, totally uncluttered surfaces everywhere. On his desk, a ceramic jar with three perfectly sharpened pencils. About four magazines, perfectly arranged, on a glass coffee table. He had explained, unnecessarily, that he threw out the old issue the moment the new one arrived.

She dressed in an outfit she had made two years earlier and still loved. Bright yellow not only suited her, but it always cheered her up with its symbolic connections to sunlight, butter, kitchens. It fit nicely, had a lowered waist, and the black piping along the neck accented her black hair. Her intention, particularly now that the weather was doing its Indian Summer routine, was to appear crisp and unruffled, composed, a working woman, a woman of the world. She wanted to eradicate from Jerry Gardener's mind the braless, barefoot mother of three who blurted out over-eager questions or hovered obsequiously in the background while her husband held forth on the complexities of the modern world.

His apartment was a walk-up. Four flights. A run-down building, which surprised Nira though she remembered his saying something about not being able to afford being divorced. People said so many things though.

Nira knocked tentatively at the door. After a moment he opened it. "Hi," he said, looking—oh thank God!—delighted to see her. "You found it all right?"

The address was odd—43½—and had an entrance below street-level. "Yeah, it was no trouble."

A brief look around the apartment surprised her. It was a mess. A lot like Joel's apartment when he'd first graduated college: piles of books scattered around, a wilted fig tree in one corner, studenty-looking furniture. He saw her glance. "It's not exactly. . . . Frankly, it's all I could afford. My wife has our rent-controlled apartment."

"Actually, I'm sort of relieved," Nira admitted, breathless both from the climb and the fact of being within a few feet of him, with no child or husband chaperon lurking nearby. "I thought all scientists were horribly neat and organized."

Jerry laughed. "Maybe at the lab, but not always there either. . . . Anyway, that's why I was a little reluctant to have you come here."

They moved over to the table near the window.

"The photos are in that envelope," he said, pointing. "Why don't you look at them while I get the sandwiches out?"

"Oh." Nira frowned. "Listen, I ate already."

He looked puzzled. "I thought we were meeting for lunch."

"We were?"

"I thought on the phone you said . . ."

Nira swallowed. Her dress was clinging to her. "I'm sorry . . . it's just . . . I usually eat with the baby on Friday and she gets hungry by eleven-thirty."

"How about some iced tea, then?"

"Sure."

While he went into the kitchen, Nira took the photos out of the folder and glanced through them. They were unbelievably beautiful. What stunned her was not just the color, the sharpness and clarity of it, but that what he had captured on film was so totally unlike her own memory of that afternoon. Her expression in the photos, whether looking down or gazing directly into the camera or off into the distance, was dreamy, soft, pensive. Her hysteria, confusion, ambivalence about the baby had, somehow, been airbrushed out. Strange. The camera cannot lie? Evidently, anything can lie.

"These are really lovely," she said as he set a glass of iced tea before her.

"I'm glad you like them." He was gazing at her intently. God, he was wonderful—those blue eyes, the quietness of his voice. That's why you're here. It is? Panic and lust edged back and forth as Nira gulped at the iced tea, then remembered to add sugar from a bowl right in front of her.

She forced herself to look at him. "I guess I'm sort of here for ulterior motives."

He smiled. "Which ones?"

She cleared her throat. "Well, I just was wondering if maybe you'd like to have an affair with me. . . . The thing is, I know you probably have millions of girlfriends, and I'm not sure I'm your type, or even if I'm the type in general, or that I'd be good at it or anything, but I . . . well, I thought I would ask you."

"I feel very flattered."

"You do? Why?"

"There must be a great many men who find you extremely appealing."

"I don't know." Nira frowned. "A couple, maybe, but—"

He hesitated. "Also, I guess I thought you were happily married."

She smiled nervously. "Did I seem that way?"

"You seem very involved with your family—in a good way. I envied your husband."

"I didn't seem trapped and anxious?"

"Well, maybe a little." He was gazing at her with a melting, intense expression. "Were you thinking of this afternoon?"

"This afternoon?"

"There's no reason why we couldn't—"

"You mean, right now?"

"Sure."

Nira gulped some more tea. Her heart was thumping like mad. "I guess I was expecting you to say no."

"Is that why you asked me?"

"No . . . I mean, I wanted you to say yes, but . . . you just want to do it?"

He smiled. "Well, we could see how it goes."

"Don't you want to know the bad things about me, just so you'll be prepared? Or do you think you know them already? Or don't you think it matters?"

"What bad things?"

"Well, just my personality in general . . . like, maybe you've noticed all this, but I'm one of these people who—I'm terribly moody. I mean, I either feel ecstatically happy or suicidally depressed. I kind of go from one extreme to the other. And, well, I'm scattered in some ways, but underneath I'm extremely ambitious and competitive. I want to do well! I really do. I haven't yet, but I want to terribly. I may have seemed obsequious and I am, but I'm also—I get into rages and depressions. I'm not a soothing person, if that's what you're looking for . . . And the thing is, I just don't even know about this whole thing!"

"Which whole thing?"

"The whole thing of having an affair . . . I'm not sure I'm the type."

"Who is?"

"Well, some people are. Like my friend, Fay. . . . The thing is, some women are carefree and blithe. I *can* be carefree, sometimes, but not all the time." Nira stopped. "Do you want to think it over? I could come back next week."

Jerry stood up and took Nira's hand. "Let's go inside and talk about it. I'll tell you the bad things about me."

Nira stood up. "Is that a way of saying you want to do it now?"

He nodded. They were almost touching, just inches away from each other. "I want you very much." He bent down and kissed her. Their lips touched and opened. Her tongue darted into his mouth, his into hers. She was drowning! "Let's go inside, Nira, please."

Lust was stronger than panic, which for Nira was a welcome relief. They were naked before she had time to think of anything except that kissing him was wonderful, and that she wanted him more than she could remember wanting anything. He caressed her slowly, but by the time his hand was between her legs, sliding moistly inside her, she was so excited, she was afraid she might come before he entered her. She clung to him, drenched in sweat, forgetting everything, only wanting this moment, of his entering her, even the initial awkwardness and pain of accommodating to his unfamiliar, angular body, to go on forever. Despite wanting to prolong it, she came too quickly. He thrust into her again and again, murmuring her name. She heard herself cry out, "I love you." Afterward he lay on top of her, still inside her, their breathing melting together.

"Am I too heavy?" he said very softly.

"No," Nira said.

She didn't want him to withdraw, the heaviness of his body felt so comforting and good. He rolled over, pulling her into his arms. Nira turned to fit her body against his more comfortably. There she saw, on the wall of his bedroom among a lot of other photos, many of his children, a photo of herself. It was one of the ones from the group he had taken. He had put a photo of her on his wall! She felt dazed, paralyzed with happiness.

"What if I hadn't called?" she said, caressing his shoulder, speaking into his skin. "Would you have called me?"

Jerry hesitated. "I don't know . . . I thought of it so many times, but then . . . the thing with your husband. I felt too uncomfortable; his eagerness about the manuscript I was working on." He hesitated. "And my own marriage was wrecked, partly, by my wife's taking a lover."

"You didn't also?"

He looked down at her. He sighed. "Yeah, I did also."

"Who did it first?"

"It was simultaneous . . . I mean, neither of us knew that. It wasn't revenge on either side: 'If you're doing it, I will.' We both just . . . needed something."

"How long were you married?"

"Ten years."

"That's not long. . . . Usually it takes fifteen or twenty."

"We rushed it." He was looking at her intently. "Oh, it was a lot of things, Nira. It wasn't like what you have with your husband."

"Who was your . . . Who did you do it with?"

"I was out in La Jolla for the summer, doing research out there. She was doing postdoctoral work in the lab I was in."

A female version of him formed in Nira's mind—blond, crisp, blue-eyed. "Was it the doting thing, primarily?"

"What doting thing?"

"You know, wanting someone who looked up to you, who thought you were terrific."

"Sure, a bit."

"What happened with her, I mean after the summer?"

"I came back. Claire—"

"Your wife?"

"My wife—was looking limpid and radiant. Her mother had taken the girls for a month. She kept smiling mysteriously and making enigmatic remarks about how womanly she felt. Finally I asked her point-blank if she'd had an affair while I was away. She said yes."

Nira looked at him. His profile was sharp. "Were you angry? I guess you couldn't have been too much if you'd been doing the same thing."

"Well, maybe I didn't have a right to be, but I was furious. I remember following her around, yelling, 'Who is he, who is he?' I even hit her." He frowned. "We didn't have that kind of marriage. It had never been violent. Claire's more the type—everything takes place underground. And I grew up in a family where no one showed their feelings much. It wasn't the done thing."

"And did she confess?" Nira asked wryly. "Who he was, I mean?"

"Finally . . . Look, I know it all sounds unbelievably sexist, but it wasn't just injured male pride. It was that the guy she picked was so— I told you, this teenage kid, stoned all day."

"He didn't judge her," Nira said, staring at the ceiling.

"Yes." Jerry looked at her. "You're right, I think that was part of it."

"Did you ever tell her about your . . . thing?"

He nodded. "I had the obviously naive idea that if we sat down and talked about why it had happened, we could understand what was going wrong, maybe even do something about it. . . . But the second I told her, she went berserk, started throwing things, ordered me out of the apartment. I couldn't believe it, the depth of her rage. It was like nuclear war."

"Well, marriage is like that," Nira said, her stomach clenching.

"Yours doesn't seem to be." He gazed at her with a thoughtful expression. "I remember one night this summer. I was trying to work one evening, sitting at my desk, starting around six or seven. Every time I got up to take a break, you and your husband were sitting together outside, just the two of you under that tree, talking. For hours! Claire and I never had that. That quiet kind of back and forth."

"It isn't really the way it seems," Nira said. "It's—" She stopped.

"What were you going to say?"

"It just seems so strange, all of this—my being here, your saying yes . . . I feel like someone who just suddenly decided to run for president and won. I never thought you'd say yes! I can't believe it somehow."

He brushed her hair back from the side of her face. "What if I hadn't? Who would you have asked second?"

"There was no second," Nira admitted wryly. "You were the only one."

"I'm surprised."

"Well, no, it's that I've been at home with the kids for ten years. Our social life is just other married couples . . . And I guess I didn't want to just do it in the abstract. That seemed too classically mad housewifeish."

"You don't seem like a mad housewife."

"Didn't you see the movie?"

"Yes, but—"

Nira decided to skip telling him about her breakdown on a "first date." Instead she said, "I've felt a bit of what she felt in the movie—the social-climbing, ambitious husband thing."

"Is your husband like that?"

She was reluctant to plunge into criticizing him, it seemed so classic and easy. "He's English, shy in a certain way. . . . Maybe making it here has been harder for him than it would have been in England. I think he wanted me as the gracious hostess, weaving back and forth, chatting cheerfully with the right people."

He looked amused. "And you couldn't . . . or wouldn't?"

Nira laughed. "Oh, a bit of both. I'm not a disaster. I mean, I don't hide in the bathroom or get drunk or forget people's names. It's just . . . it all seems kind of dumb and meaningless. It's not what I like best is what it comes down to, I guess. I'd rather have a few friends over for dinner, even if they aren't people who could ever be helpful in one's career or anything else." She was afraid she was babbling, out of nervousness and also pleasure at his seeming interested in her life. "Listen, what should we do? I've never done this before. Should we meet once a week? Is Friday a good day?"

He hesitated. For a terrified second, Nira was afraid he was going to say this was it, this one time, that he was about to remarry or move to Africa to work with impoverished and needy natives. "Usually I work weekdays, pretty long hours, till seven, eight at night. . . . Would Saturday be possible?"

"Sure," Nira said. "Adlai takes the girls on outings then, to the movies and things like that."

When she was in the bathroom washing herself, she glanced in the mirror. God, I look beautiful, she thought, and she felt stabbed, after delight, by anxiety. I look different than when I came. Will Adlai notice?

"Why do you look so worried?" Jerry asked as she emerged. He had dressed again and was sitting on the edge of the bed.

"Partly it's that I feel so happy," Nira said. "I'm afraid I'll have to pay in some way. Like, maybe I'll get run over on the way home."

Jerry stood up. He was gazing at her and also, somehow, through her. "Life is usually more devious than that in the way it wrecks things for people, don't you think?"

His assumption that things had to be ultimately wrecked pierced

through Nira's happiness, not destroying it but clouding it. She felt
he was probably right. "Can I take the photos?" she asked.

"Of course."

Nira smiled at him, the tenderness of their sexual exchange still
brightening inside her. "I'm so glad," she confessed, "that you put the
one of me on your wall."

Summer 1980

"**I** thought you were a woman." Puzzled, Penny looked down for the letter which had accompanied his manuscript.

"I'm sorry." He smiled sheepishly. "I did that deliberately. I guess I thought writing a novel with a female heroine might have seemed presumptuous."

She thought for a moment, pushing her glasses back. "It didn't occur to me. . . . I mean, you carried it off beautifully. We were really more surprised at your submitting a novel here. We want to do it, but we've never done anything like this before. . . . What made you think of a university press?"

He was sitting in the chair opposite her desk, legs crossed. The air conditioner in Penny's office was, as always, on the blink, but he looked unruffled in a seersucker suit. "I didn't think of it totally as a novel," he said. "More a cross between a history-of-science text and a novel."

"Is that your field—history? You did the historical background extremely well, I thought."

"I'm really a scientist, or was. . . . I switched to teaching several years ago."

"Here? At Princeton?"

"Yes . . . Only I'm half in the history department and half in biology. There wasn't a tenured position open in either one at the time I was looking."

Penny tried to piece it together. It was late in the afternoon and the August heat was making concentration difficult. "So, you thought of us because you didn't think it was a novel?"

"Partly . . . But, well, also, you've done another book by me, and it's always been an agreeable association."

She was intrigued. "We have? Which one? I've only worked here four years, but I know the back list pretty well. Not under Gold-schmitt? Or is that just a pseudonym?"

"It's my wife's name, actually . . . My name's Gardener, Jerry Gardener."

"Oh, of course. *The Molecular Revolution in Twentieth Century Biology.*" She smiled at him. She had not actually read it, but she knew it was still in print and doing reasonably well. "This is seeming more and more like a mystery."

"I simply used my wife's name because I wanted to use an actual name so you could get in touch with me," he explained, sounding apologetic. "Also, it was her idea, in a way."

That interested Penny, that his wife had been involved in the book's inception. She wondered if she were a scientist also. "The idea of taking a hypothetical woman scientist and writing about her as though she were real?"

"No, she suggested that the main character be a woman. You see, I'd wanted to write a book like this, something between the history of science and a novel. I wanted to get inside the mind of a scientist living in that era, and I thought framing it as a novel would give me more freedom. . . . But my wife suggested that if I made it a woman scientist, it would have, well, a feminist aspect as well."

"Sort of a Shakespeare's sister thing?" That appealed to Penny, as it had when she had read the manuscript a few weeks earlier.

He leaned forward. He had fair hair, graying on the sides. Late forties, she concluded, or thereabouts. An academic—a variant on their usual contributor, but better looking. Probably jogs. "You don't think it's too stiff? I was afraid the science might overwhelm the rest of it."

"It does, a bit. . . . For us that's all right, since our readers are pretty knowledgeable. You aren't in that position of having to explain everything from scratch.

"I know a fair amount about the eighteenth century, but not a great deal about astronomy. You made it lucid."

"I tried." He sounded genuinely pleased rather than falsely humble.

"Is it based on any particular historical figure?"

"Well, there was a brother and sister who worked together in the late eighteenth century, William and Caroline Herschel. He was a court musician actually, but he built telescopes on the side and she worked with him."

"Just the two of them?"

"Once he discovered a new planet, George the Third gave him a pension so he was able to devote himself exclusively to astronomy. . . . The telescopes were gigantic." He took a pencil and sketched one for her. "Forty feet long, five feet across. You could walk through them."

"But was it the construction of them?" Penny asked. "Or what they saw through them?"

"It was what they discovered about the universe—double stars, the Milky Way. Not all their conclusions were accurate, but it was a crucial beginning."

Penny looked down at her notes. "I do have some suggestions for revision," she said. "Will you be willing to consider that?"

"I expected it."

He was making it easier for her, which was a relief. It was one of the first books her boss had trusted to her from scratch. Probably for no better reason than that the main character was a woman, but who cared. She had wanted that responsibility since she had taken the job.

"The science part, the historical background is very clear," she said. "I just think you might be a little looser. You've gone far enough so that really delving into Antonia's personality a bit more would"— she gestured—"make her more real. At the moment she's almost more of a symbol."

"I have a sabbatical until January," he said. "There's no reason I can't work on it pretty steadily till then."

Standing up, Penny handed him the manuscript. "I've written down some suggestions in the margins. . . . Why don't you read it over and call me once you're done? You don't have to follow it all literally. Feel free to disagree if you think I'm trying to force it into a direction you hadn't intended."

"I know it needs work." He put it into his briefcase.

"Has your wife read it?"

He shook his head. "She never reads my books."

"Oh . . . I thought you said it was her idea."

"Well, we talk about what I'm going to do, but she's in a completely different field. She designs clothes. Science doesn't really interest her."

"Does she never read them?" Penny was curious. "Even when they're published?"

"She doesn't read," he said dismissively.

He was standing, obviously ready to depart. Penny took her sweater from the back of the chair. "I'm going too now," she said. A glance at her watch showed it was past five.

Downstairs, they stood on the tree-lined street together. The press was in a small brick building, three stories high.

"Can I give you a lift?" he asked.

Penny hesitated. "To the train station, if you have time."

"Where are you going?"

"Into the city, actually."

"I can drive you, if you like. I'm going back tonight."

"Don't you live out here?"

"No, I commute. . . . How about you?" He leaned over and opened the car door for her.

Penny got into one of the bucket seats. "I live out here," she explained, grateful for the chance to relax in the comfort of a tilted chair. "But I go in occasionally." She glanced at him. "I used to review movies for a small magazine a friend started. It folded about a year ago, but they still send me announcements of screenings. I figured: why tell them to stop?"

"Was it a hobby, the reviewing? Or were you doing it professionally?"

"In between." She smiled. "I had fantasies of becoming Pauline Kael, you know, writing terse, brilliant analyses of the modern world in the guise of movie reviews. I love movies! I guess it's a kind of escape. I must have seen two or three a week since I was twelve. . . . Also, well, my husband's a movie actor."

"One I'd know of?"

She sighed. "Not yet . . . he's done a lot of TV and a few grade-B features. It's . . . well, hard."

"Can he get work in the East? I have a friend who said most of the jobs were out in Hollywood."

"They are . . . That's why he lives there."

Jerry Gardener glanced at her. "And you live here?"

Penny hesitated. Explaining her marriage to a new person always made her uncomfortable. "I don't know, I just can't . . . A week in L.A. seems like a year in—well, maybe hell is too strong, but . . . All this is excuses, I guess. I'm really afraid I'd be swallowed up if I moved out there."

"They don't have university presses?"

"It isn't that." She looked ahead. "When I'm with him, Cal, my husband, I go under somehow. It's not his fault. Well, no, it's a bit his fault. It's *both* our faults. He says he's not going to be overbearing, and I say I'm going to stand up to him . . . But either I don't . . . or I do and it drains me of the energy to do anything else."

"My wife's first marriage was a little like that. She married very young."

Penny grimaced. "I did too. . . . Insanely young."

He laughed. "How insane? Or rather, how young?"

"Sixteen . . . It was crazy. We started going together in high school, and the night of our senior prom, we just drove to Pennsylvania and did it. Our families had been friends for years. His mother and mine played bridge together; his father and mine played golf at the same club. We're both the youngest of two children. His oldest sister used to be friends with mine. It was one of those—he used to bite me in the sandbox. I used to throw sand at his face." She smiled. "I can't believe it, but we've been married almost twenty years." The air conditioning in the car was beginning to soothe her, almost like a stiff drink.

"You don't look old enough to have even been married ten."

"I don't *feel* old enough. . . . Does it sound crazy, our living so far apart?"

"Well, anything that works."

"Yes, that's what I always say, but I feel like it sounds defensive. The point is, we're together. Neither of us wants anyone else."

"That's all that matters then."

They were silent for a few minutes.

"Do you have children?" he asked. "That's the only thing that would make a setup like that tricky, I would think."

"No, we don't . . . Do you?"

"Four . . . four girls." He looked strange, as though upset.

"Goodness! Are you independently wealthy or just terribly brave?"

"Definitely not the former. . . . A bit of the latter, but also . . . Well, our generation did it more unthinkingly than yours. Two are my wife's; two are mine. We were each married before."

"You didn't want any together?"

"Don't you think two on each side sounds difficult enough?"

"I guess," Penny looked reflective. "My best friend, Meredith, says that if you love someone you want to blend with them and create a child. I don't know. We've thought of it a lot . . . But I just feel in the end it would be mine. Cal would be off making movies or whatever, and I just don't know. How old are yours?"

"My older daughter is just finishing college and the younger one's in her last year of high school. . . . My wife's older daughter finished college last year, but she's living at home with us till she can find a place of her own. And Jasmine, the youngest, is just ten."

Penny knew a few couples with one child, even fewer with two. Four seemed almost unthinkable. "Do you sit at night at a long oak table and preside, like in a Victorian novel?"

"I might . . . if we ever ate together. But they all seem to have different schedules now. I've stopped even trying to figure it out, I just eat out or in with Nira, if she's home."

"Is that your wife? Nira?"

"Yes."

"Why wouldn't she be home?"

"Her career is very demanding right now. She and a friend have started their own firm, designing children's clothes mainly, and they need to get financial backing. Right now they're in Paris, pursuing a contact. It takes a lot of work and, well . . . something has to give."

Penny had been trying to pick up on the tone in which he said all this, rather than just the information. It was hard—he spoke smoothly, not revealing anything of how he felt. "You don't mind, then?" she said.

"Mind?"

"Whatever—her not being there, no hot meal on the table, her being so involved, the whole thing?"

He hesitated a long time. "Well . . . I don't think I have the right to mind, basically."

"Why not?"

"I've always been very involved in my work. . . . It's her turn now."

"That sounds suspiciously liberated."

"Why suspiciously?"

"I think men always mind," Penny said. "No matter what they say."

He hesitated again. "Okay, you're right. . . . It's not so much that I mind for myself. But I wish when our kids were younger, she'd been around more. My mother worked when I was a child and I always hated that, her not being there."

Penny smiled. "Well, mine didn't and I think the one thing I wouldn't ever inflict on a child is a mother who *is* there. . . . But you don't mind for yourself?"

He glanced at her. "You're rather intrepid about wanting the truth, aren't you? Okay, honesty! I mind, which I shouldn't . . . just for this reason. When we met, about ten years ago, I was racing around in circles, doing research, getting grants, no free time for anything. Now my life is different, more the way I wanted it to be, more relaxed, more free time. Part of me would like someone to share that with."

"That's understandable," Penny said.

"It's not being in synchrony," he went on. "Before, Nira sat around patiently, delighted when I had a spare moment. Then gradually she got fed up and found her own life . . . well, for all the reasons women do, but also needing a life of her own. . . . And now she has it."

"And you're sitting around, delighted when *she* has a spare moment?"

"A bit of that . . . more than I ever envisioned possible."

"It's like that adage," Penny said. "There are two tragedies in life—not getting what you want and getting it."

"Exactly."

"My husband is the same way," she said. "When I'm out in L.A., he waxes on so beamingly about how wonderfully my career is going, and it's such an act!"

"What would he rather have you do?"

"Sit around dotingly, the way I used to, when I was a kid." Penny laughed. "You can't be doting after thirty! Not that I was ever a smash at it. But the thing is, at sixteen I really thought he was terrific. And I still do, basically . . . But it was also I thought *I* was nothing, a nonentity . . . And I *don't* think that anymore. I'm not—I mean, Cal is brilliant; he has a real talent, even if he screws up a lot of things out of self-destructiveness or what have you. I'm more of a plodder. But I'm not a nonentity."

They were nearing the city. The traffic had become heavier. Jerry pulled over into another lane. "From nonentity to plodder? It doesn't sound like your self-image has shot up all *that* high."

"Oh, it has . . . I'm being self-deprecating, trying to charm you or something. I'm a good editor."

"I'm sure you are."

"How can you be sure? You haven't seen my notes yet."

"I can tell."

Penny watched him as he drove. "You don't mind then?"

"What?"

"My being young . . . not having been at the press that long. I was afraid you might insist on someone more experienced."

"Not at all. You seem like you know what you're doing."

She felt pleased. "I'm glad I came across that way. . . . No, I do, really. Know what I'm doing, I mean."

"You sound uncertain."

"Listen, this is all so unprofessional, burbling on like this. It's just been such a dog of a week, the heat. Cal is opening in *Richard the Third* in Camden, and he's even more manic than usual. I guess today it all got to me. . . . Your being a man when I'd expected a woman. I'm frazzled."

"I'm glad you're my editor," he said. "Your age doesn't bother me. I think I was brighter at thirty-five than I am now. Brain cells disintegrate."

Penny laughed. "That's reassuring. . . . Listen, you can let me off at Eighty-sixth and First, if that's okay."

"Fine . . . Whom do you stay with in the city?"

"A friend, a psychiatrist, actually. The next corner will be fine." Before she got out, she wrote Meredith's number on a piece of paper. "If you have any questions about the suggestions I've made, you can call me at the office . . . or here. I'll be one place or another."

"Never at home?" He looked surprised.

"No, of course . . . I'll give you that number too." She wrote the Princeton number on the other side.

"Enjoy the movie," he said. "Which one is it?"

"I'll try. The director is a woman, which always makes me nervous. I always want women to do well . . . and they don't always."

"Men don't always either."

"They don't have to." With the last word tucked comfortably under her belt, Penny strode off.

Meredith was home, lying on the couch, reading *The New York Times,* when Penny let herself in after the movie. "How was it?" Meredith asked, glancing up. At thirty-five, she was as small and femininely rosy as she'd been when they were college roommates. But her long, thick hair was coiled back in a bun; an attempt, she claimed, to look dowdy and older. It didn't work.

"Rotten." Penny locked the door behind her. "It was some idiocy about a housewife floundering in the suburbs who gets a job at a striptease joint at night without telling her husband."

"Well, that's life," Meredith said, grinning. She had a can of beer beside her on the floor.

"Is it?" Penny stared at her, kicked off her shoes, and collapsed on the adjoining couch. "Since when?"

"Since they invented housewives and suburbs and striptease joints."

"Who invented them, Doctor?"

"Sir Harold Bergson in 1715. . . . Unfortunately he never went beyond that. He rested on his laurels for the remaining two years of his life. . . . Listen, Pen, do you want to get up and jog with me tomorrow?"

Penny cringed. "Do I have to?"

"No . . . But it would do you a world of good."

"I don't like things that do me a world of good."

"You don't get any more exercise than I do. . . . You'll be all flab and fatty tissue before you turn forty."

"Good, I'm looking forward to it." Penny sighed. "Shit."

"What?"

"I forgot to call Cal."

"What were you supposed to call him about?"

Penny opened a pack of cigarettes and lit one. "He's opening in *Richard the Third* in a few weeks. They started rehearsals Monday."

Meredith tossed *The Times* on the floor. She began pulling hairpins out of her hair and dropping them into an ashtray. "You know what I don't get about you and Cal?"

"What?" Penny said, knowing she was too tired to rebut anything.

"Sex."

"Sex? What sex? He's three thousand miles away."

"That's what I mean . . . Don't you go crazy?"

Penny laughed. "Crazier than who, or whom?"

"Pen, seriously . . . When were you last laid?"

"When were *you?*"

"First of all, I *am* crazy . . . Have you ever met an uncrazy psychiatrist? Second, I'm not married. One of the supposed advantages of marriage is a regular sex life."

"You were married, jerk. . . . Is your memory that short?"

Meredith had married a fellow med student her first year of medical school. She was divorced by her third. "Sex, strangely enough, was not our problem. We just never saw each other."

"Bull."

"No, I mean it. All I really want to know is what do you do about those sudden unspeakable cravings in the middle of the night? You have no impulse to do foolish and regrettable things with passing strangers?"

"I don't meet passing strangers. Or they pass by so fast I don't see them. Celibacy is like dieting, Mer. After a while you get used to it. You wake up occasionally and think, 'Sex, that's right. There was once this thing called sex.' Then you roll over and go back to sleep."

"And meanwhile Cal is still—"

"Of course! Look, he's surrounded by gorgeous young things . . . I mean, gorgeous! Not just your attractive, put-together New York types. Real starlets, the whole bit."

"And you really don't mind?"

Penny sat up. "I'll tell you what I mind. I mind hearing about it. I mind blow by blow accounts of how and when and with whom . . . Because he does it just to get a rise out of me, and I'm damned if he will."

"So, he'll keep doing it till he does."

"Maybe." She crushed out the cigarette. It was her sixth. Her new rule was six on regular days, ten on murderous ones.

Penny fixed the bed in Meredith's living room and lay in the dark, sleepily reviewing the day. She wished either that her life were conventional enough so that she didn't have to explain it to everyone, defend it, justify it; or that she just didn't care. Meredith's theory was that everyone's life, once you got past the first layer, was strange and nonsensical, but that most people had learned to erect some public screen to ward off embarrassing questions. She thought of Jerry Gardener and his four daughters, his successful wife, his feminist book. Did *he* want to have one great love affair before he died? Or had he come to terms with everything and was channeling all that superfluous energy into work, as Penny had always wanted to do? He seemed self-possessed and in control. But then so, people always told her, did she.

I'll call Cal in the morning, she decided. He wouldn't have been in tonight anyway.

In the end she didn't reach him till Sunday, when she was back at Princeton. Penny lived in a large wooden house surrounded by six acres of wooded land. It had been bequeathed to her by her parents.

Everyone assumed the size of the house—six bedrooms—would bother her living there alone, but it didn't. She slept in the room she'd had as a child and ignored most of the others. The quiet, the peacefulness of being in the middle of nowhere, which drove Cal crazy, was soothing to her. She liked coming home, after a day of talking to people for eight straight hours, and hearing no human voices except the ones she chose to hear if she answered the telephone or turned on the radio or TV.

"So, are you coming out?" he demanded. He had answered on the fifth ring.

"When? For the opening?"

"Sure . . . Don't you want to see me make a fool of myself?"

"Cal, come on. You won't. You'll be great."

"When did I last do Shakespeare?"

"It'll come back. . . . Is your voice okay?"

"Fair . . . Listen, Pen, will you answer me? Are you going to come or not?"

"Do you want me to?"

"Yeah."

"Then, I'll try to."

"Try to!"

"Cal, I have a job. We're overloaded."

"And you're so indispensable that the whole place will collapse if you're gone one week?"

"I've just signed up a new book. The author may need help with revisions. I—"

"And that's more important than my opening as the lead in *Richard?*"

"It's not a *matter* of what's more important! Look, I said I'd try to come. It's complicated but I'll try, if you really want me there."

"Oh, shit, forget it . . . Don't come."

"Cal, Jesus, don't pull this. . . . You're always saying you act worse if I'm in the audience. I don't want to be some scapegoat. If you get lousy reviews, you'll say it's because I was there."

"Why are you assuming I'm going to get lousy reviews?"

"I'm not . . . I'm assuming you'll get brilliant reviews."

"Listen, I'll tell you something. I'm going to get lousy reviews."

"Why?"

"Because I can't do Shakespeare anymore! I can't speak the goddamn *lines,* that's why. I sound like I was chewing on a loaf of Wonder Bread."

"You *know* you'll be terrific."

"Pen, listen, will you do me a huge favor?"

"What?"

"Don't come."

"Okay, I won't."

"You're right . . . If you're sitting there, with that damn critical expression, waiting for me to wreck the whole play, of course I'll do terribly."

"You don't even see me! I don't have that expression. I may be anxious because I know you are, but—"

He let out an exasperated sigh. "Why the fuck are we having this conversation for the millionth time?"

"I don't know."

"So, tell me about all the fascinating books you've signed up? Anything dirty?"

"Yeah, a really filthy inside story of a woman scientist who lived in the eighteenth century. It's about—"

"You really want to know if Karen came out, right? That's why you're hesitating about coming out here."

"Nope . . . I don't want to know."

"She broke her leg and she's in L.A. resting. . . . She said she'd try and make it for the opening . . . Pen?"

"Yeah."

"I really would sort of like you to be here." His voice had changed.

"Are you being straight?"

"Yeah . . . I think maybe I *can* pull it off." He laughed mirthlessly. "If it goes well, I'll wish you'd have been there."

"I *know* it'll go well. I *know* it."

"Then come."

"Okay, I'll come."

She hung up and for half an hour sat staring at the wall. The play opened in five weeks. Which gave him about a dozen times to change and rechange his mind. To panic about losing his voice. To meet someone new on the set. To call his ex-lover Karen in L.A. The strange thing was that she actually liked watching Cal perform. Even when he did badly, when he overacted, when he was off into some weird personal interpretation of the part, there was some spark of the goofy, intense teenage kid who had shown up at her parents' house every night, wanting her to help him with his math homework, which he never understood, no matter how many times she explained it. "I bet you think I'm dumb, Pen, don't you?" "I don't think you're really concentrating." "I can't concentrate when I'm with you. It's hormonal or something. My mind starts to do strange things."

By now they had spent almost as many years living apart as living together. It had been 1973 when he had moved to L.A., supposedly just for the summer. She had thought she would just spend the summer in the house. There was a lake nearby, a stable where she could ride on weekends. She had been doing free-lance copy-editing, and going into the city once a week seemed convenient. It had never occurred to her that there would be any jobs out there nor that she would want, as a permanent arrangement, to live in the same house in which she'd grown up.

Meredith had thought it was crazy. Like Cal, she was a city person, had never lived anywhere but New York, claimed she suffered from withdrawal symptoms if she was deprived of city air, shopping bag ladies, muggers. "All these trees!" she would exclaim when she came out to visit. "And it's so quiet."

"The local crime rate is rising," Penny tried to reassure her.

"Still, it's not the same. . . . You can hear crickets. You have fireflies."

"I know," Penny said blissfully. "But you know what I love the most?"

"What?"

"Getting up at six Sunday morning and taking Ginger—she's the horse I ride—across those fields for an hour or two. It's so incredibly peaceful, the smells, the air."

"What does Cal say? I can't imagine him on a horse somehow."

In the abstract Cal liked the idea. He had inveighed against New York for years, claimed it was a prison, claimed the noise level was doing something unspeakable to his hearing, claimed even that he wanted to give up acting completely and run a general store in some small hamlet in New England. But all of those fantasies vanished after even one weekend at her parents. Penny remembered with amusement the first time she'd taken him riding. He'd been in his first movie Western by then and had looked terrific. A stunt man did most of the chase sequences. Faced with an actual horse, Cal had eyed it suspiciously. "Why is it so big?"

"They come that way, Cal. Come on, she's really gentle."

"She's going to throw me."

"Never."

"Why does she keep showing me her teeth that way?"

"The bridle may be too tight. Don't pull on the reins. Just hold them lightly, unless she's going too fast and you want her to stop."

Their ride through the meadow had been fine, but for some reason Cal's horse, on the way home, eased into a gallop.

"Shit," he yelled as Penny galloped up beside him. "She's gone crazy. What should I do?"

"Lean forward," Penny called. "Just flow with it." When the ride was over, he accused her of wanting deliberately to make a fool of him. "I thought you'd want to practice now that you were such a success as a cowboy," she had replied, smiling slyly. In truth, she had enjoyed his discomfiture. It was nice having an area, however irrelevant, where she excelled more than he did.

In L.A. all of that was reversed. He had acquired his friends, other actors mainly, some screenwriters. All of them, to a man (or woman), regarded Penny as strange. She didn't enjoy drugs, even socially; her idea of makeup was an occasional swipe of lipstick; she liked to go to bed at ten. And the distrust was mutual. The men were variations on Cal, but lacking his goofy charm. The women struck her as unbelievably affected and strung out. There seemed to be no Merediths, no potential friends to talk to at lonely moments. Sometimes she accompanied Cal to the set where he had a smallish part in a made-for-TV movie about a frontier family. During the shooting, Penny tried to sit quietly on the sidelines reading, sometimes going off for walks and photographing wild flowers with her ancient, twin-lens Minolta. If she stayed on the set, Cal claimed her expression behind her sunglasses was cool and judgmental. If she wasn't there, he felt she wasn't interested.

But what had turned her off most of all was another actor's wife, five or six years younger than herself, who was on the set also. A pretty, bouncy girl with fluffy blond hair, she kept trying to give Penny tips. "You don't have to *be* interested," she whispered after overhearing one of their blowups. "Just *look* interested. . . . Look at me." She put on an expression of wide-eyed awe that, Penny thought, wouldn't fool a two-year-old. "Don't you feel phony and awkward though?" she asked. "And isn't it a bore?" "Listen, if I'm not here, he'll find someone else," the girl announced. "That happened once. It's *not* going to happen again." "And it doesn't seem demeaning?" Penny had asked rhetorically. "Hanging around to prevent that from happening? You don't want a life of your own in some way?" "As what?" the girl demanded. "I'm not talented at anything. I'm not like him. He's a genius. You might not be able to tell in this 'cause he doesn't have that many lines, but Blake is going to be *big* one day." "Sure," Penny said. Where had she heard that one before?

And, ironically, given that her presence was supposed to fend off idle script girls and adoring starlets, Cal didn't even seem interested in sex while the movie was being shot. At night they might lie naked and entwined, but mainly so that she could rehearse his lines with him. Once, about one second after they finished making love, he sat up, inspired. "Pen, I just got it . . . I figured out how to play that scene. The one that's been giving me all that trouble." He kissed her passionately. "Thanks." "Thanks for what?" Penny had wanted to know. "What makes it worthwhile," the other actor's dewy-eyed wife said, "is knowing you're needed. That's what I'm here for. He *needs* me."

Penny came home and cried, or rather kvetched, on Meredith's shoulder. "I don't want to be like that, I don't want ever ever *ever* to get like that woman." "You won't." "If I spend my life out there, I will. I'll need full-time, four-goes-a-week analysis. I'll go crazy. Will you give me discount rates because I'm a friend?" "Are you kidding? It's not your scene, so forget it. Cal's a big boy. He can cope." When she had gone out again, a few months after the movie was finished, he was, unexpectedly, contrite. "I was a mess, I know. It won't be like that the next time. It was my first time, the director was a schmuck.

Next time I'll be able to handle it." "Cal, listen, I've been think-
ing . . ." He had listened, stunned, to the news that she had taken a
full-time job at Princeton University Press, that she was planning to
live all year round in her parents' house. "I can still come out and
visit," she said. "Visit! I thought we were married." "There are a
million ways to be married. You hate New York, I hate L.A. so—" "I
don't *hate* New York. There just isn't any work there. . . . What about
our kids?" "What kids?" "The kids we're going to have." "We'll mail
them back and forth." "Pen, I'm serious." "Do you seriously want to
have a child now? On what we're both earning?" "Not now, but
eventually . . ." "Let's talk about it eventually, when it's a real
thing."

Her thirty-fifth birthday fell on a Tuesday. Looking at herself in
the mirror at home, at her plain face—bright blue eyes behind large
rimless glasses, straight blond-brown hair fastened with a tortoiseshell
barrette—Penny had suddenly seen, as though ten years in the future,
that same face, thinner, perhaps, more lined. She saw herself and Cal,
forever childless, forever having absurd fights by telephone, immersed
in careers that would falter, stagger. She would become a spinster by
proxy. Cal would, she felt certain, never marry any of the gorgeous,
dopey kids that drifted into and out of his life.

Their marriage was idiotic enough, was based on so many years
of irrational connections, that she doubted it would ever, by the usual
conventional means, come asunder. But who knew. Luckily no one
was asking her to lay bets either way.

As she was leaving Meredith's apartment, the phone rang. Mer-
edith had an answering service, but, since the phone was near the
door, Penny picked it up.

"Is this . . . I wondered if Penelope Howard was there, by any
chance?"

"This is she."

"Oh, I'm so glad I got you. . . . This is Jerry Gardener."

"Oh, hi!" It had been three weeks since they had initially met.
Penny had assumed her suggestions for revision must have met his
approval since he had not called back.

"I'm sorry I didn't get back to you sooner. I wanted to sit down
and digest your suggestions, and well, I have. Could we meet and
discuss it?"

"Sure . . . were you thinking of any special time? Next week is
pretty free for me, if you don't mind coming out again."

"You wouldn't . . . I realize this is a bit late in the day, I tried you earlier at your office but you'd already left . . . I thought we might meet this afternoon, say five, perhaps?"

Penny hesitated. "Sure, that would be okay."

"You sound a little uncertain."

"I was just planning on seeing another movie, but I can . . . I'm sure there's a later show."

"It needn't take that long. . . . Would you like to come here?"

He lived in the East Seventies, on a quiet, tree-lined street. It looked like an old but solid building, not unlike the ones on Meredith's block but better kept up. A uniformed doorman announced her through the intercom.

A little girl let Penny in; the youngest one, she assumed. It was a hot day and the child was clad only in a lavender bathing suit and clogs. She was extraordinarily beautiful, so much so that Penny was, at first, stunned, almost as though she'd come to the wrong house.

"Hi," the girl said. "I'm Jasmine." She looked at Penny inquisitively. "You have the same shoes as me."

"Yes," Penny said, moving into the capacious hallway. It was lined with drawings tacked up on a large surface of dark brown cork.

"I have eighteen pairs of shoes," the girl confided. "But some are from Stacey. She lent me some once her feet got big. Mine are still size-four. What are yours?"

"Eight," Penny admitted.

"Boy, you have big feet." The girl seemed more impressed than critical. "Mom says I sound like a horse when I wear these, but I like the way they sound, don't you? I like to go clomping around. . . . Do you want to see Daddy?"

"Yes, I had an appointment with him," Penny said.

"He's in his study." Penny followed her down a long hall. The girl pushed a large soundproof door open, without knocking.

Jerry Gardener was on the phone. He was sitting on a leather couch, half-reclining, a pillow under his head. Penny sat down in a chair near a fireplace. When she looked up, the girl had disappeared.

"Your daughter is beautiful," she said when he hung up.

"My stepdaughter," he said. "Yes, alarmingly. She's very un-selfconscious about it still, but I don't know how long that can last."

"She looks the way a friend of mine used to look at that age," Penny said.

"What became of your friend?"

"She's a psychiatrist."

"Oh, the one you stay with in the city?"

Penny nodded. "She's always trying to look dowdy so her looks won't interfere. She says she can't wait for her hair to get gray."

He had the manuscript on a low teak table directly in front of him.

"You didn't find my suggestions too stringent?"

"It's not that." He looked at her carefully. "It's just . . . I think you're trying to turn it into a novel, which wasn't exactly what I intended. Or maybe it's also that I don't think I could do that, especially with a female protagonist."

Penny tried to gather her professional identity around herself. "It's just that you never have her think at all about the difficulties, which must have been enormous, for a woman scientist in that era. She thinks exactly like a man."

"And you don't think that's possible? I thought feminists insist that too much has been made of those distinctions."

Why was he so certain, at a glance, that she was a feminist? Was he saying it as a compliment, or the reverse? Penny cleared her throat. "It's just, even if she's an exception, which she definitely is, she must be aware of that, aware of all she's giving up by making science her whole life. That can't have been an easy decision then, if it ever is."

"I hadn't really given a lot of thought to her personal life," he said. "I just wanted her to be a conduit for certain ideas."

"Then making her a woman was a mistake," Penny said crisply. "You can't avoid feminist overtones if you place those ideas in the mind of a woman scientist."

"I didn't want to avoid them . . . I just didn't want to belabor them."

There was, suddenly, a tenseness between them. He seemed like someone who disliked backing down, on principle. Penny disliked it also. "Right now we know nothing about this woman, beyond her thoughts on this given day," she said. "Nothing about her past, her family, her future. She's too abstract."

"Then you're misunderstanding the book," he said, his voice louder. "I don't want scenes of her turning down lovers and telling her parents she must have a career or die."

"I wasn't suggesting that." She was beginning to feel angry herself.

"Clearly, my intent wasn't to write a feminist tract. If you insist on forcing it in that direction, I'll have to take it elsewhere."

"Fine . . . that decision is up to you."

They sat, glaring at each other.

"Has anyone else read the manuscript?" he asked, after a moment.

"No."

"A second opinion might be helpful."

Penny flushed. "I've been at the press four years, Mr. Gardener, and my opinion is considered sufficient to make decisions like these. If you want to go over my head, you're welcome to. You can request another editor, if you like."

The phone rang. He picked it up. From what she heard of the conversation, Penny gathered it was his wife. She took a small pleasure in the fact that she was evidently giving him a hard time about something. "How can I?" he was saying. "I can't possibly . . . Of course, I thought Stacey . . . Look, I'm in the middle of a conference . . . I understand. It's fine. It'll take as long as it takes. I'll see you whenever. Great."

Penny tried to keep her expression impassive rather than ironical when he turned to her again. "Where were we?" he asked.

"You wanted another editor," Penny said. "Or a second opinion, in any case. Would you like me to take the manuscript back or do you want to resubmit a clean version?" She was so angry, she was afraid her hands were shaking as she reached for it.

He put his hand on top of the manuscript. "I think we're misunderstanding each other."

"In what way?"

"I *don't* want another editor. I think your comments are excellent, very perceptive, well taken . . . It's just, I'm not a novelist. I don't want to try to do something I'm incapable of doing. But I'll try." He cleared his throat. "Would you like to go out to dinner."

"Pardon me?"

"I thought I might take you out to dinner?"

"Why?" She was still roiling inside, but tried to keep this from showing.

"I was peremptory just now and I—I'd like to make it up to you, that is, if you're free, if you'd like to."

"I'm going to see a movie downtown," Penny said, disconcerted.

"We can eat near the theater," he suggested. "Wherever it is."

It wasn't until she had downed a glass of white wine that Penny felt relaxed enough to say what she wanted. "My job may seem like nothing to you," she explained, leaning forward. The lights in the restaurant were dimmed. His face looked softer, less critical. "The pay is lousy; university presses are burial grounds for women . . . but it suits me in so many ways. I like living in the country. They're just beginning to give me some responsibility, to let me work on books they consider important, like yours. . . . If you'd insisted on another editor, it would have been terribly damaging for me. I feel men should have the sensitivity not to wield power so recklessly."

He listened with a sympathetic expression. "I really wasn't thinking in terms of that. . . . It's just I get defensive when I feel I'm being attacked."

"I wasn't attacking you."

"I see that now . . . But your manner is rather . . ." He hesitated. "You seem so sure of your opinions."

"I'm sure of some of them." She stared at him intently, the wine softening her mood, making her feel dreamy and relaxed. "What if I'd been a man—would you have said the same things, felt the same way about my being 'sure of myself'? "

"Maybe not. . . . It's harder for most men of my generation to take orders from women."

Penny laughed. "Those were suggestions, not orders!"

"Okay! Look, I'm trying to be honest, since you are."

"I don't think it's honest to hide behind 'men of my generation.' "

"Don't you think we're all influenced by the way we were brought up?"

"Maybe . . . But one can try to transcend all that." She smiled.

He smiled back. "I am trying, Penny."

The dinner was good. Penny wondered if it was worth trying to make the movie. She glanced at her watch.

"What's it called?" he asked.

"It's an old one. *The Umbrellas of Cherbourg.* It's a musical."

"Would you mind if I went with you?"

"No, only—"

"Only what?"

"I didn't think men liked musicals," Penny said.

"I don't see them often, but I enjoy some of the old ones."

"Where's your wife?" she couldn't resist asking.

"She has a board meeting. She thought she'd be able to come home in between, but she wasn't able to."

The movie was strange, slow, stylized. Penny sat motionless in her seat, still staring at the screen as the credits came on at the end. Finally she turned to Jerry. "Goodness, what a terrible ending!" she said.

"I thought it was beautiful."

"Beautiful?" She was incredulous. "In what way?"

"Well, they both ended up with sound, good people whom they were fond of." He looked puzzled. "How did you want it to end?"

"I wanted them to rush off madly together, of course," Penny said, laughing nervously.

"But what about their families?"

She looked at him, into his thoughtful blue eyes. They gazed at each other for several moments. "You aren't very romantic, are you?" Penny said finally.

"I thought I was."

They walked out of the theater in silence. When they were outside, it started to rain. "When there are children, it's not that easy," he said. "People don't just rush off . . . unless they're completely irresponsible."

"Oh," Penny said.

"When you have them, you'll see . . . it changes things."

"I don't think I'll ever have them," she said wistfully.

"Yes, you will," he said. "Someday."

In the cab he took her satchel, which contained the books she had been carrying, and set it between them. They rode mainly in silence back to his apartment. As he was about to get out, they turned to each other and started to speak together.

"I'm going to be in San Francisco next month," he said. "But I'll speak to you before I leave."

Penny was going to San Francisco also, to visit her sister. She just said, "Okay . . . thanks for the dinner."

"I enjoyed the evening."

Lying in bed, she wondered how to interpret the whole evening, the way the mood had shifted so suddenly from tenseness and anger to a certain sympathetic warmth, as though they were old friends. She thought of his remarks about children and how they changed things. Weren't she and Cal just as tied to each other without them, or was there some mysterious difference which she would never know about? "They have good, sound people they're fond of." Was that what it all came to, at forty-five or however old he was? Just the web of familiarity, ties too knotted to undo?

The main reason for her trip to San Francisco was to see an author who was working on a book for the press. He had been promising a first draft for several years, and Penny's boss thought a visit might make it clearer how close he actually was to finishing. But, really, she wanted to see her sister, Helen, who had been living there for over a decade, first with her husband and now with her six children, several of whom were already in college. Helen had married young, converted to Catholicism to please her husband, George, and had a child a year with barely a six-month interval in between, starting when she was nineteen. It horrified Penny. As a child, Helen had been a skinny tomboy who climbed trees, caught fish, was a better horseback rider than anyone in the family. Eight years older than Penny, she had been the rebel, the one who went all-out about everything, who, at sixteen, ran off to Las Vegas with a local hood, a gorgeous Italian boy who'd spent the summer in their hometown.

To watch her sister leap from teenage escapades to a claustrophobically sexist marriage to a heavyset Irish lawyer fifteen years her senior amazed Penny. Yet Helen had thrown herself into Catholic motherhood with the same zest and enthusiasm with which she had leapt fences on her favorite horse. Now, her husband was out of the picture, finally married to the mistress he had kept throughout most of their marriage, and Helen, at forty-three, was in law school, penniless but still cheerful and undaunted. "I still have this completely unjustified feeling I'm going to conquer the world," she told Penny who called her long-distance to announce her impending trip. "Sure, stay. It'll be a madhouse, but you know all about that."

"I may visit Cal on the way out," Penny said. "He's doing *Richard the Third* in Camden."

"Pen, did I tell you? They showed *The Thief of Baghdad* last week, and we all stayed up, just to see Cal. He looked so dashing!"

"What did you think of the movie?"

"Well, it was . . . listen, there are worse things on TV. He was great though. And he's doing Shakespeare? I guess his career is really taking off, huh?"

"Kind of," Penny said. "Listen, we'll talk when I get out there."

"I may be in the middle of exams, but sure."

Penny debated inwardly for the next month about whether to tell Cal she was coming, and finally she decided against it. She would go for the dress rehearsal so that if, by chance, he spotted her in the audience, he wouldn't be able to claim she had wrecked his concentration and thus garnered him bad reviews.

Just before she left, she called Jerry Gardener.

"Listen, I got your revision of the first three chapters," she said. "But I don't think I'll be able to read them right away. I'm going out of town."

"Where to?"

"Well, I decided to sneak out to see my husband in *Richard the Third.* And then I have to look up or track down one of our authors in San Francisco."

"When will you be there?"

"Next week . . . I'm staying with my sister."

He laughed. "This appears to me one of those unlikely coincidences of which life is composed . . . I'll be out there the same week, visiting my brother. Shall we meet for dinner?"

"I guess we have to," Penny said. "Bow to fate or whatever. I could bring my sister and you could bring your brother. We could fix them up."

"It's an idea. . . . What's your sister like?"

Penny thought. "She's forty-three, intense, lively, has six kids, not a penny to her name, and a huge ramshackle house on Nob Hill . . . Would that suit your brother?"

"Well, he's a dreamy, vague scholar who writes articles on seventeenth-century religious history, the kind who wears one blue sock and one brown, and doesn't notice."

"It'll either be a match of the century or a disaster," Penny said.

"Most things are. . . . Well, anyway, putting them aside, there's nothing to stop us from meeting."

"Nothing at all . . . Since neither of us is available, we have no problems." This was in between a hope and a belief.

"True . . . Lack of availability is a virtue not to be overpraised."

He took her number and Penny hung up, wondering why, by phone, they fell so easily into this jocular familiarity. He reminded her of someone, she decided; it must be that. She felt as though he knew everything about her, and thus she had no fear of being judged or put down, as she so often had with men she didn't know that well.

Penny had never been in a play, not since her brief appearance in a third-grade skit, in which she'd managed to muff even her one brief line: "Tell Captain Wesley the Indians have already attacked the fort." But watching Cal was like being on stage herself, in spirit if not in body. By now she could tell, from whatever seat in the theater she was sitting, exactly what his mood of that particular night was. She knew, from the way he lowered his voice, whether he was having trouble with it. Even when he didn't speak, she understood by his expression when he was totally into the part, and when he really lost himself and gave a line a completely new reading, it was as though he were, at that very moment, discovering the meaning. During those moments, Penny's heart would thump as loudly as if she were up on

stage herself. She would wait, breathlessly, for these moments of in-
spiration to fade, when he would begin "acting" again.

He was good at the dress rehearsal. Once, years ago, one of his
friends had had the lead in *Richard,* and she remembered him and Cal
arguing over how it should be played. Cal had said he thought
Olivier had overdone it by making Richard too much of a villain, too
crabbed and Machiavellian, that it would be more powerful and
interesting played straight. "Otherwise it's saying that only insane
people are evil," Cal had said, "whereas in fact most evil people are
as dull as dishwater." Penny could tell he was still acting out a varia-
tion of that. Instead of accentuating Richard's physical deformities,
he portrayed him as someone who pretends they don't exist, except
when it may be useful to play on people's sympathies.

The audience seemed responsive; the house was full. Penny's seat
was far to the left, almost at the back. Even when Cal's eyes swept the
audience as he came to take a bow, she knew he hadn't seen her.

She stood outside the theater, wondering what to do. There was
a chance that he would be angry at her for having seen the show
without having told him ahead of time. Perhaps it would be easier
just to return to her inn and catch the plane she'd scheduled for San
Francisco in the morning.

Back at the inn, she undressed, got into bed, but found she
couldn't sleep. She stood near the window, looking out at the row of
small houses. It was quiet, just a few streetlights burning.

I want to see Cal. Then go see him. Quietly, Penny got dressed
again, in jeans, a shirt, and sandals, and went downstairs. She asked
the man at the desk if he knew where the local theater group was
staying.

It turned out that they were housed in a dormitory on campus,
only a few blocks from the inn. Penny decided to walk.

Although it was nearly one-thirty when she arrived, the building
was ablaze with lights and people were roaming around outside, sit-
ting under trees, talking. She asked a young man who was standing
near the front door if he knew where Caleb Howard's room was.

"Yeah, he's on the second floor, three doors down from the left,"
he said. He didn't seem to find it odd that someone was appearing at
this hour of the night.

Penny stood in front of the door, then knocked lightly. She heard
some sounds, then Cal's voice. "Who the hell is it?"

"It's me, Penny," she said softly.

"Penny?"

He opened the door. He was in shirttails and jeans, obviously put on in a hurry. Behind him, in bed, Penny saw Karen, half sitting up, smoking. Karen waved. "Hi there, Penny."

"Hi there."

"I thought you weren't coming," Cal said. He had the good grace to look flustered.

"I'm en route to California," Penny said. "I thought I'd . . . Listen, this seems to be an inapropos moment."

"Not at all," Cal said. "Come in . . . We're talking about Karen's wedding. I mentioned that, didn't I? She and Dan are getting married next week."

"Congratulations," Penny said. She came into the room.

"Do you think I'm crazy?" Karen said. Penny saw she was wearing one of Cal's T-shirts. Her short, curly, red-brown hair was even more boyish looking than when Penny had last seen her two years ago in L.A. At that time Karen had been living with one of Cal's friends, a would-be director named Jamie Kelly who had eventually left the movie business completely and moved back East. Penny had run into him once as she was leaving Meredith's house. He'd become a stockbroker and lived in Scarsdale, the father of twins. Karen was one of the few women Penny had ever met in California who wasn't an actress. Her father had been a screenwriter, and she had tried a couple of screenplays and had even collaborated on one with Cal, which had never gotten produced. Penny couldn't remember the idea for it, only Karen bursting in one morning saying that she had an inspired idea for the third act. "She's smart," Cal's comment had been. "But she doesn't have staying power. That's her problem."

Penny sat down on the edge of the bed. "Who're you marrying?" she asked.

"Dan Underwood. . . . He's a sound man."

"Sound men are hard to find," Penny couldn't resist saying.

"Cal thinks he's dumb," Karen said, glancing at him. "He's just quiet, that's all. I mean, he's not intellectual or anything, he's not *articulate,* but he's solid."

"I think it's a great idea," Cal said. "Everyone ought to get married by the time they're thirty."

"I'm thirty-one," Karen admitted. She turned to Penny. "You don't regret it at all? Marrying so young? I mean you don't think it's impinged on your freedom or anything?"

"No," Penny said. "I don't think so. I guess—"

"Of course you and Cal are different," Karen rushed on. "You've always been my role models in a way."

"In what way?" Penny wondered.

"Well, like the way you're both so independent. You both have your own thing. You never, like, gave up everything for each other the way some people do."

"True," Penny said.

"We just never see each other," Cal said.

"You're seeing each other now," Karen said. "And you're really involved with each other's careers."

"We are?" Penny and Cal said in unison.

Karen looked taken aback. "Well, yeah . . . Like Cal's always talking about how proud he is of you. . . . It's like he really respects what you're doing. And Dan does too, respect what I'm doing, I mean. I couldn't marry a man who just wanted a wife. You know what I mean?"

"Those are the kind to stay away from," Cal said.

"They're the worst," Penny said. Suddenly it was as though she and Cal were allied in making fun of Karen. When had that happened?

"What I think is really important in marriage," Karen said solemnly, lighting a joint, "is that each person is, like, himself, or herself, or whatever . . . But also, you know, more than that. Like Dan loves birds. He gets up at five to go bird-watching, and I never would've done that if I hadn't met him. I would've known birds *existed,* but I never would have gotten up at five and stood around watching them. And, like, if he got run over tomorrow, I'd never do it again! But when we do it together, it's like we're sharing each other's world. You know?"

"I could never marry a woman who got up at five to watch birds," Cal said.

"Sure you could," Karen said. "You mean, if you'd met someone you loved in every other single way, just that one thing would wreck it for you?"

"That's right," Cal said. "I'm a very intolerant person."

"No, you're not, Cal," Karen insisted. "You're one of the most tolerant people I *know!* . . . Lots of my friends don't like Dan, just because he seems a little strange and quiet and all. And you just accept him like he is."

"I'm not marrying him though."

"That's true," Karen said reflectively. She looked at Penny. "Anyway, I figure in some ways I'm doing it for my mother. I mean, you owe them something, don't you think? And, like, I have this one friend Anna—you met her, you know—she finally decided to get married, and then her mother got run over two months before the wedding! If she'd known she would've done it in the spring . . . But how could she tell?"

"I have an early plane to make," Penny interjected. "I guess I better get back to my inn."

"Isn't that a darling inn?" Karen said. "I was going to stay there, but Cal said why spend all that money . . . Listen you guys, I could, like, bunk up with someone down the hall. I know Nancy has a free room."

"That's okay," Penny said quickly.

"Let me walk you back," Cal said, putting his sneakers on.

"I'll send you an invitation to the wedding," Karen said. She sank back into bed, pulling the blankets up over her ears.

"Thanks," Penny said.

She and Cal walked in silence halfway back to the inn.

"You have to admit it was a setup," Cal said finally.

"In what way?"

"Well, you just come out, without warning."

"Cal."

"Look, she's nervous . . . and I don't blame her, frankly. He's an asshole. They'll last three weeks."

"I thought he was so solid and sound and respectful of her career."

"What career?"

"Isn't she still writing screenplays?"

He shrugged. "It was just a farewell fuck. She's turned thirty, she's feeling manic . . . What could I say? Get lost?"

Penny sighed. "I don't know."

"Frankly, she's driving me crazy. We spend four hours every night analyzing all the guys she could've married but didn't. Most of them sound even worse than him." He looked at her. "Anyway, I thought you never got jealous. What happened?"

"I'm not jealous," Penny said. "I just think she's a fool."

"So? If my sex life consisted of fucking people who weren't fools, I'd have to be celibate."

Penny smiled. "There are worse fates."

Cal smiled back. "What are they?" He reached over and took her hand. "I'm glad you came, Pen. Really. Did you see it? What'd you think?"

"You were good."

"I'm glad you saw it tonight. Tonight I was good. I've been lousy up till now. The production is a mess, though. You have to kind of close your ears when half of them are speaking their lines."

"Lady Anne was good . . . What's her name?"

"Isabel? She's a bitch. But she's okay . . . At least she's done Shakespeare before."

"I thought Karen broke her leg."

"She did . . . Didn't you see the cast? They're removing it the day before the wedding."

"I didn't look under the covers."

They had arrived at the inn. Without asking, Cal went upstairs with her. He reached for her the moment she closed the door behind him.

"I don't know," Penny said.

"Don't be so fucking stubborn. I didn't know you were coming!"

"Look, I just can't do it with you an hour after you've done it with her. Okay?"

He looked at his watch. "It's three hours."

She laughed.

"Let me just stay, okay?" he said softly. "We don't have to do it . . . I'm really bushed, anyway. Let's just be together. It would mean a lot. I always sleep well when I'm with you."

Penny sighed. "I have to get up early."

"That's all right. I'll drive you to the airport. We can bird-watch on the way out."

"It's not *that* early."

They lay together, his arms around her waist, his breath on her neck, and before she could think about the evening, about all that had happened, Cal had fallen asleep. It was true. For some reason he slept well whenever she was with him. Maybe she was some talisman from his childhood, like a teddy bear that you couldn't throw away even when one of its eyes was missing and its stuffing was coming out. Penny thought of all those years of secret, forbidden sex in his room, with his older sister practicing the piano downstairs. She remembered how even then Cal would fall asleep afterwards in just that position, hugging her from behind, and she would lie awake, listening to his sister stiffly and conscientiously practice Bach's *Italian Concerto.* Cal's breathing, his smell would seep into the music, and always after that, Penny, hearing Bach, would become sixteen, wondering why God, in whom she then still believed, had chosen her as the receptacle for this unique, inspired love which made even sewing Cal's costumes for the senior play seem like a divine mission.

Fall 1970

Heather was in love, the first of her seventh-grade class to be struck, singled out by the diabolical blade of Venus. Each day she came home dreamy-eyed, conveying the latest stage of their mutual infatuation. "Today he stared at me all day!" "Today he asked me if I wanted to go to the pizza place with him." The "turning point," however, was the fateful Wednesday when her admirer, Adam Worshowski, chose to formally declare his affections. Walking her to the bus stop, he waited until she was about to board the bus, then blurted out, "Did I ever tell you that I like you very very very much?" and then ran, blushing, down the block. "Three *verys!*" Heather announced proudly at dinner.

"What's he like, sweetie?" Nira wanted to know. She was eating alone with the girls. Adlai was at a meeting.

Heather shrugged. "I can't describe him exactly . . . You'd have to meet him."

"I'd like to."

The romance progressed to an actual "date." They went to the movies. Heather, who related each step of the relationship with precision, informed them that she had taken his arm and placed it around her shoulder "just to give him the idea." They had kissed "a trillion times," according to her diary, which she generously left open on the dining room table. She tended to refer to her diary as "my work of art."

Finally Nira had a chance to meet her daughter's love. It was at a school fair to which she went one Saturday morning with Posey and Heather. Adlai was busy, and the baby remained home with their seventy-four-year-old baby-sitter, Esther Hanks, who lived on the other side of the building. Adam Worshowski turned out to be a small, dark-haired boy with an appealing gamin-like face. He came up to Heather's shoulder. "Hi, cutie," he said, squeezing her affectionately, an attention which Heather tolerated with delighted good grace. He introduced his two younger brothers, Ralph and Martin, age ten and eleven, to Posey, who eyed them evenly and decided the older one—"the intellectual," according to Heather—was the one she preferred. He rewarded her with a bunch of flowers which she carried around for the rest of the day.

"I'm in love too," she announced when they came home.

"You can't be," Heather snapped. "It takes more than a day."

"Not always," Posey said. "Does it have to take more than a day, Mom?"

Nira tried not to be overcome by the irony of being turned to as an expert on these matters. "Well, maybe real love takes longer," she said, "but you can feel a certain initial attraction right away."

"See!" Posey said, taking this as confirmation.

"Well, I thought you meant real love," Heather said. "Not just flirting with someone."

"I wasn't flirting with him," Posey said.

"You were so."

"I was not!"

"Mom, wasn't she flirting? You saw her."

"I think she was being—she liked him and she wanted to let him know it. . . . Anyway, flirting isn't such a terrible thing."

"Yeah," Posey said. "So I was? What's so bad about that? I have to practice, don't I, for when I meet someone I really like?"

"I thought you were in love with him," Heather said.

"I am," Posey said quickly, "but I'll probably never meet him again. He's not even in my class."

"What did you think of Adam, Mom?" Heather inquired.

"He seemed nice," Nira said, hoping that wasn't too pale and overused an adjective for the occasion.

"I don't mind that he's shorter than me," Heather said. "It's not his fault. Boys just don't grow till they're fourteen or fifteen. There's nothing they can do about it."

"Listen, kids, I'll see you later," Nira said. The day had been half eaten away by the fair. She was achingly eager to get to Jerry's. Enough of pre-teen love! Time for the real thing.

"When's later?" Posey wanted to know.

"Dinner time."

Jerry claimed his girls, as far as he knew, were not yet interested in boys. "I think they're going to be late bloomers," he said.

"That's okay," Nira said. "Why rush things?" She looked over at him. They were in bed, naked. It was "afterward." "Who was the first person you did it with?"

He smiled, remembering. "A housekeeper my mother hired one

summer to look after my younger brothers. She was Spanish. She used to come into my room while I was studying and give me these languorous, sidelong glances. Finally we ended up in bed. She was married, but her husband was back at home in Guatemala."

"Did your mother ever find out?"

"Not exactly, but I think she suspected. She started making remarks about how Spanish people were unreliable, stole things, never bathed. When I'd get furious, she'd say, 'Well, you're too young to know about these things.' " He looked at her. "Who was your first?"

"Adlai."

"You mean, you've only done it with me and your husband?"

Nira was pleased at his surprise. She had thought her lack of experience was somehow engraved on her like a scarlet *A*. "I'm a product of my time," she apologized. She hesitated. "How many women have you done it with? All together, I mean?"

"God, I don't know . . . thirty, maybe."

"Thirty!"

"Does that seem like a lot?"

"Yes! . . . When was this? While you were married?"

"No . . . I'm monogamous, basically. Oh, I had a few 'things' while I was with Claire, but most of the women were before I got married."

"What were the few 'things'?" Nira wanted to know.

"Just classic out-of-town things where we'd had a fight and I wanted revenge or just to feel a sense of myself sexually. One-night stands. Nothing to write home about."

Nira laughed. "I wouldn't think so! . . . I should have done all of that, at some point in my life, anyway."

"You're doing it now."

"Am I? Does this count?"

"Of course . . . Why shouldn't it count?"

"But you're just one person. It's not so different from marriage. I'm not doing insane, reckless, irresponsible things with seedy, disreputable people."

He smiled. "Maybe you can work up to that."

"We don't even go to motels," she said. "I always thought real affairs had to take place in seedy motels with broken TVs in the corner and porno movies you could rent at the front desk."

Jerry laughed. "My apartment isn't seedy enough?"

"It's messy . . . That's different. . . . Do you remember them, the one-night stands, I mean?"

"Sure, I remember them."

"Describe one of them."

"Okay . . . Here's one you'll like." He looked thoughtful. "She was a woman lawyer I picked up in a bar in Chicago. We went back to her place. The sex seemed okay to me, but she wasn't satisfied. Finally she said she wanted me to spank her. I tried, but I guess my heart wasn't in it somehow. Anyhow, it didn't 'work.' At the end she said, 'I can tell you're an amateur. Otherwise you'd know; you never hit in the same place twice.' " He laughed.

The women in Jerry's past, disturbing and anxious as they made Nira when she thought of them, were as nothing compared to her obsessions about whomever else presently shared his bed on non-Saturdays. There were the phone calls he left unanswered, the vague unexplained references to social events he attended during the week or after she left on Saturday. One afternoon, as she was about to climb the steps to his apartment, she saw, retreating down the street, the blond in the straw hat whom she used to spy on his porch in the summer. Nira stood stock-still, gazing at the woman's retreating figure. There are many blonds in straw hats. Why assume it's the same one? Nonetheless, impelled by panic and fear, Nira bolted across the street and ran practically down the block only to retrace her steps in order to see the woman from the front. But it was impossible to tell, even then, if it was the same woman. Passing her, gazing surreptitiously at the pretty face, the serene gray-blue eyes, Nira's heart pounded. Perhaps if she said her name aloud, just as a test. But what *was* her name? Damn, what was her name? It had been some odd, androgynous, waspy name. Blythe? Brooke? Only as she had finally finished retracing her steps, only when Jerry was making love to her, did the name suddenly spiral, unwanted, across her consciousness: Paige. But wasn't it good she hadn't remembered? Did she, in fact, want to know?

"There's a word for what you're going through," Fay had told her when they had dinner.

"What is it?" Nira asked anxiously.

"It's called 'getting in over your head.' "

"I thought it was probably called something," Nira said. "You've set my mind at rest."

Earlier in the evening, Oscar, Fay's husband, had appeared at the table with a real French bread which he had bought that morning in Paris and brought home with him on the 711 he took weekly back and forth. "Taste that," he told Nira. "Now tell me, where in New York can you get bread like that?"

"It is good," she admitted, helping herself to another slice. Jerry claimed to find her too thin—a perfect excuse, if not to gorge, then to indulge in occasional extra helpings and midnight snacks.

"You know something?" he said. "It's worth the trip over just for this bread. I mean it."

"I don't know about *that,*" Fay said. "Some things might be worth that, but bread?"

"What would be worth it to you, Nira?" Oscar asked suddenly.

Nira blushed. All she could think of was Jerry, being in bed with him, stroking his body, sucking his cock, lying on top of him and hearing his heart pounding as she pressed close to him while he was inside her. "I—I don't know," she stammered.

Oscar grinned. "It must be something really good," he said.

Later she confessed to Fay that her first thought had not been about food. "The weird thing is," she added, trying to explain, "I don't think I've ever been physically in love before. You know? I mean, most people go through this when they're teenagers or when they're in their twenties, some just totally, all-out physical thing where you couldn't care less if he's a Republican or bathes once a month or buys *Penthouse.* . . . Remember the way you used to feel about the worm farmer?"

Fay smiled fondly in remembrance. "I remember, I remember. . . . How about with Adlai, though? In the beginning."

"It wasn't the same. . . . I feel with Adlai it was more 'like at first sight' or maybe recognition. We got along. We sort of rescued each other. We both grew up thinking of ourselves as oddballs, dreading no one would ever love us. But it wasn't passion. We used to stay up all night—but talking, not making love."

"Maybe that's a better foundation for marriage, though," Fay suggested. "Physical passion tends to . . ." she gestured.

"I don't know," Nira sighed. "It's funny. I feel like I don't know anything anymore!"

Clearly her new self was evident to other people, evident without confessions or any outward signs of which she was aware. Suddenly friends whom she had always assumed, upon lack of any evidence to the contrary, were faithful to their husbands, came forth and admitted otherwise. "I never told you before, Nira," Fiona explained, "because you always seemed so happy, so *married.*" Fiona, easy-going, down-to-earth Fiona, with her precocious twelve-year-old twins, had done it with a security guard in Queens, where she lived, and admitted cheerfully she didn't regret it for a moment. Her only regret was that he had no heat in his apartment and that he'd been transferred to another job in Brooklyn.

The most unexpected of these confessions came from her shy, soft-spoken cousin Evie, who had evidently had rapturous sex in Salt Lake City for seven years with the husband of her best friend. "It was a perfect setup," she said, her voice as low and musical as ever. "I was at home. He came over every day after Larry left for work."

"Didn't Larry ever return unexpectedly? Just for his umbrella or something?"

"Never."

"Did he ever find out?"

Evie nodded. "Only because I told him."

"Why did you?"

"I don't know. Guilt, maybe. . . . It was over by then so it didn't seem to matter. I knew he'd had lovers too. You know what his only reaction was? 'How could you do it with someone who was the husband of your best friend? I thought you were a feminist.' " She laughed.

"Didn't that bother you?" Nira asked.

"No, not really," Evie said. "Rachel's not interested in sex. She's told me that nine thousand times. We've been friends since high school, remember. She's of that you-do-it-for-his-sake school. So I felt I was doing her a favor in a peculiar kind of way. He didn't have to 'bother' her so often." Picking at her chef salad, she added, "Sex with Larry is so . . . It's an effort of will, for both of us. And with—my friend" (She wouldn't give his name though she claimed Nira didn't know him) "we couldn't get our clothes off fast enough. Do you know what I mean, Nira?"

"Yes," Nira sighed. "Yes, I know."

Usually she came home Saturdays feeling like giving all her worldly possessions to the poor, wanting to help old ladies across the street, feeling so sated physically that it was almost a spiritual feeling, the way Joel claimed he felt after transcendental meditation. On the day of the school fair, she was late and, running into the building, bumped into Adlai, who was evidently also returning from wherever he had been. They looked at each other and laughed nervously.

"I had trouble getting a cab," he said.

"Me too," said Nira hastily. If such a perfunctory excuse was good enough for him, why not for her?

They stood in the slow-moving elevator, suddenly desperately out of conversation, like two people who only meet every decade or two at a relative's funeral.

"I didn't expect it to rain," Adlai offered.

"No," Nira said, seizing this inspired tidbit gratefully. "It was sunny this morning."

"How was the fair, by the way?"

Oh, the fair! Of course, the fair seemed a thousand years ago. "I met Heather's boyfriend," she related.

"What was he like?" Adlai asked, genuinely interested.

"Little, cute . . . kind of a flirt. I don't know how long she's going to hang onto him."

"Well, at this age, that's probably just as well."

"True."

You will never have that with anyone else, she told herself censoriously, trying to be her mother who, had she known, would surely have taken such a tack. She had been far more miserable with Nira's father than Nira knew she would ever be with Adlai, but she had felt divorce was an option only for maniacs or women whose husbands were bankrupt, alcoholic, and congenitally incapable of fidelity. Even then you should think it over.

It was not only women friends who approached her with confessions of past or present misdeeds. That very night, at a dinner party, Faith's husband, Curt, with whom, in a fifteen-year association as couples, Nira had never had more than a three-minute conversation about anything, took her aside over drinks and asked, evidently eager for her reply, if she thought men and women could be friends.

"Well, yes," Nira stammered. "I don't see why not. I mean, it doesn't seem to happen that often, but that doesn't mean it's not possible."

"I suppose the danger," he said, refilling her wineglass, "is that so often friendships between men and women take on a sexual overtone."

Nira gulped down more wine. "Sure. I suppose that could happen . . . But would that have to be bad? I mean, couldn't it be a nice thing?"

He looked briefly off into the distance, his eyes opaque behind heavy tortoise-rimmed glasses. "It's bad only if one person has to reject the other."

"What do you mean?"

"Well, if one is content to keep it as a friendship and the other wants more. . . . Do you find that's a problem?"

She was an expert? Nira tried to look detached, as though they were discussing some political upheaval in a country many miles away. "I think it's easier if both people feel the same way."

"It's also easier if both people are married."

"I guess." Was he propositioning her, or were they just discussing an abstract topic? Ought she be able to tell the difference? "Why is that easier?" she couldn't help asking.

"If one person isn't married, eventually that person wants more."

"It couldn't be the other way around?"

"It rarely is."

It was clear he was thinking of what probably applied to his own life: single girls. Nira instantly thought of Jerry. Once he had said something about how he needed to "recover" from his marriage. He had described how the woman with whom he had had the summer affair in La Jolla, upon hearing of his separation, had appeared suddenly in New York, wanting to move in with him. "That was the last thing I needed," he said. "But it was hard explaining that to her." Nira had been unable to help identifying with the forlorn woman who had, ultimately, trekked back to La Jolla, suitcases unpacked, hopes dashed. "I didn't invite her, Ni," Jerry said, clearly wanting to justify himself. "One day I opened my door and there she was!" Like me! Nira had thought. God, how many times had he opened his door and found desperately eager or willing females, suitcases in hand, idiotic romantic fantasies trailing around their brows?

She wondered if, for Jerry, the advantage she presented was that she was married and not, therefore, looking to be rescued, not, at least on the surface, desperate. So far he hadn't looked much below the surface, or perhaps she was just as glad only to have him see her as she was able to be for a few hours each Saturday—relatively gay, spirited, sexy. That was truly how she felt most of the time with him. But she was aware that she censored a lot, that she had never told him of the moment she had run headlong down the block to look at the face of the blond woman in the straw hat, of the sick plummetings in her stomach when the phone rang five or six times and he would finally say angrily, "Damn that answering service. They're supposed to pick it up after two rings."

Her motives that first day, when she had come to see him after getting the job, had been, as she saw it now, so pure, so sensible, and so totally unlike the reality. She had seen it as a fail-safe situation. If Adlai left, she would have someone. If he didn't and just "fooled around," she wouldn't have to feel simply the cringing wife, desperate to hang on to her husband at any cost. She would have her own moment of pleasure—to be enjoyed both for its sake and to hold up in memory during the week, to bolster her self-confidence.

But in fact, it now seemed to her she had simply put herself in a worse position. Now there were two men, instead of one, that she felt anxious about losing, though in completely different ways. She was no less anxious about losing Adlai because of Jerry. But her anxiety was based on motives that she would have hesitated to reveal to a close friend. As a husband, Adlai stood between her and so many fears—the fear of financial insecurity, the fear of being alone, of being unable to cope. Being married, for all its disadvantages, meant never having to worry about having a date on Saturday night or New Year's Eve. It meant giving life an illusion of continuity, which she had seen even in the lives of her parents who had screamed at each other non-stop for fifty years. To break all that, to have to start afresh, didn't gleam before Nira as a shining vista. And to have to start afresh because you had been booted out in favor of someone who probably was smarter, nicer, more relaxed or relaxing seemed even more daunting and formidable a prospect. To have to start all over trying to be charming, trying to be a good listener. I can't! she would think frantically, watching Adlai regard himself in the mirror with that new amused geniality. Let him just be having a fling. Let her be a dopey secretary. Please.

But losing Jerry would be as bad, maybe worse, because she loved him. She was waiting and hoping for "that part of it" to go away, to simmer down, wanting what she remembered nostalgically as the peacefulness of not even understanding what romantic sexual love was. Romantic love had always struck her, right up to that day she had climbed the stairs to his apartment, as a myth, an aberration, something people insisted existed, like the myth of women instinctively adoring their babies or men being naturally aggressive. And now she realized it was a real thing! It *did* exist. Oh, let him take years to "recover" from his divorce. Maybe he never would. Maybe he would remain a permanent bachelor. But that seemed unlikely. He had once said he thought he was "the married type," that he envied his married friends, that he wanted that security and stability. Hopeful man! What security? What stability?

She took him to her parents' country house in the Berkshires. Though her mother lived in Florida most of the year now, she kept the house for summer use, not bothering to rent it in between. It was the Saturday before Thanksgiving. Jerry said that for Thanksgiving he was taking his children to San Francisco, where his brother still lived. Nira and Adlai always spent Thanksgiving at the home of Adlai's college roommate's mother. She was French and wealthy, a widow now, and Thanksgiving with her reminded Adlai of being with his own family, but without any of the tensions.

"Do you mind if I drive?" Nira asked. She and Adlai rarely used their car except for weekend trips. "I only got my license last year."

"Sure, I hate driving."

"I'll try not to drive off any cliffs," she joked, thinking of *Jules and Jim*, which she had reseen a few weeks earlier.

He just made a gesture, somewhere between what if you do and try not to. He seemed in a moody, depressed state which Nira couldn't figure out and didn't feel able to ask about.

"Do you hate holidays?" she asked, turning onto the Taconic Parkway.

"Not in general. This year . . . ." He stopped. "Do you mind if we don't talk for a while? I feel kind of wound up."

"Okay." She did mind, actually. The trip, as she had envisioned it, would be full of genial, drifting conversation as they wound along the tree-lined roads. Turning to him half an hour later, she saw that he had fallen asleep.

I called him in September, she thought, glancing back at the road. That means we've been seeing each other two months. She wondered how well they really knew each other. Sex created and prevented intimacy in about equal measure. Created the illusion of it. But wasn't intimacy as much those low plateaus—knowing all those petty details of the other person's everyday life and thoughts—as the intensity of physical pleasure? She thought of his work life. She knew the rough outlines of it, though she understood very little about it. It was "cancer research," which meant he had a lab, he had to get grants, he wore a white coat, he went to meetings, he had other people working for him, and, if they did publishable work, his name appeared on the paper. She knew he was dissatisfied; he felt he was becoming too much of an administrator, when he had gone into science originally, so he said, because he felt he wasn't good at working with people and preferred abstractions. He found the other scientists at the institute hard to talk to, too limited in their interests. If they were brilliant, science was their world, their only world. If they were scientific bureaucrats, they were bogged down like bureaucrats everywhere in the minutiae of budgets, hirings, and firings. If he had it to do over, he would choose academic life with its long vacations. . . . Yes, she knew some things, but it was still remote, veiled. She won-

dered if there were aspects of his character that he consciously chose
to conceal from her, as she concealed things from him, things he felt
she wouldn't like, that would make her respect him less. They said
men wanted women to respect and admire them, and women wanted
"simply" to be loved. She hid from him all she felt was unlovable in
herself, yet maybe those were the most basic things about her—her
panics, her rages, her sense of confusion about life.

She knew that her being a mother had some significance to him.
Perhaps because his wife didn't seem to enjoy that role or was inade-
quate at it, he always smiled with pleasure when Nira repeated things
her daughters had said, or brought him compositions they had writ-
ten at school or drawings. It was not that she was not genuinely
proud of them, but that she saw herself doing it as a way of saying to
him that she was indeed a good mother, if not such a terrific (or
faithful) wife.

"I'm sorry . . . Have I been sleeping a long time?" Jerry stretched
and opened his eyes.

"About an hour. We're almost there."

"I haven't been getting a lot of sleep," he said, without elab-
orating.

Why? Because Ellen—damn, why did she always block that
name—Paige was insisting she sleep over during the week? Cut it out,
kid. Concentrate on the driving.

Her parents had an old house, ten bedrooms, Victorian-style.
They had talked for years about renovating it and had even built a
tennis court. But it was rarely in good shape. Leaves were piled all
over it; the net was torn. Her father had had money when she and
Joel had been growing up, but he had spent it extravagantly and
generously, giving to causes he believed in, traveling, buying artwork,
none of which had turned out to have much value after his death.

"Is this where you used to work?" Jerry asked as she pulled into
the driveway.

"Yes . . . I haven't for years. But the stuff is all there."

"I'd like to see it."

"I'll show you . . . It's in a separate house. Their land goes on for
about ten acres."

The studio her father had had built for her was about half a mile
from the house. He had built it when Nira was in college, and she
had driven up, sometimes during the week, sometimes on weekends,
through the first ten years of her marriage. Since his death, three
years ago, she hadn't been there at all.

They got out of the car. Nira looked over at Jerry. He was wearing tan corduroy slacks, a heavy, rust-colored sweater, no jacket. He looked boyishly handsome, lean, his sandy hair ruffled by the wind. Suddenly there seemed something slightly portentous about this trip, a version of bringing your boyfriend home to meet your parents. She knew that she wanted him to know something of her origins, but she wasn't sure why.

"Why don't you come up anymore?" he asked as they walked to the studio, the autumn leaves crackling under their feet.

"I don't do artwork anymore," Nira said. "It was a dead end."

"Why?"

"I was fooling myself. For fifteen years I was putting all my energy, everything into making these things . . . just for my father! It was crazy. If I'd been selling them, okay."

"Why didn't you try to?"

"I was scared . . . Oh, I tried a little. But it was humiliating, the whole thing of dragging your slides from gallery to gallery, sitting there while contemptuous people made slighting remarks. And maybe I knew deep down I didn't have the talent to make it."

"It isn't just talent. . . . It's perseverance."

"I know. Okay, I didn't have either. . . . If it hadn't been for my father, maybe I'd have stopped doing it altogether. But he paid me for them! He pretended to be my patron. He'd 'commission' things. It was sick." She found herself getting upset talking about it.

"He must have been very involved with you."

"He was obsessed with me." She stood still, looking at him, trying to explain. "I don't know. It was so many things. Somehow, by the time I was born, he'd turned against my mother, his work didn't satisfy him . . . I was going to be an answer to all of that. And I wanted to be. I spent my life desperately trying to please him, to be what he wanted. When he died it was like—I didn't know what had been him and what had been me."

Jerry put his arms around her. "There's a lot of you left." He stroked her back. His body felt warm and comforting.

"Talking about him makes me upset." Nira tried to bring her voice under control. "There's something I never told you. When he died, I had a breakdown. I was in a mental hospital for four months."

"That's nothing to be ashamed of."

"It was so awful, Jerry! It was like *One Flew Over the Cuckoo's Nest* squared. Insane sadistic doctors, nurses forcing people to have shock treatment. I can't describe it. I'd spent years reading articles about what it was like, but even having been there, I can't believe it. They took people who were sick and desperate, and did everything in their power to destroy them totally . . . and succeeded in a lot of cases."

"Not with you."

"No . . . I got out in time. I escaped actually, with the help of a woman friend. It was a funny thing. She's an old friend, but we haven't been that close for years, just kept in touch. She was the only person who believed me about how horrible it was. She lent me the money, and I took a cab to the train station and escaped. They have this strange rule that if they find you or track you down within three days, they can bring you back to the hospital. But after that, they can't. So I spent three days in this odd monastery in upstate New York that Susan had heard about. It's all so odd that it happened to me, I mean, like another life."

He had been listening with a curious kind of undivided attention. "My wife had a breakdown," he said quietly. "She was in a hospital too."

"Was it when you were married?"

"No, after . . . I used to visit her. It was incredibly depressing. She seemed so—out of reach."

"It was good you went, though. That means a lot, no matter what the person is like. . . . After I got out, friends said, 'I feel ashamed not to have visited you,' and it's true. A lot of people are scared in some way."

"I went . . . well, her family lives in Europe now and they wouldn't have come anyway. They don't 'believe' in mental illness."

"Did you know . . . I mean, did she seem at all unstable when you married her?"

He frowned. "I haven't thought about all this in so long, or talked about it ever, really . . . Yes, she seemed confused in some way. She'd had a difficult childhood, a lot of conflicting expectations. I did hesitate. And then some friend of mine, a doctor, fell in love with a woman who'd had two breakdowns and been institutionalized three times. He married her anyway, and he said to me, 'Look, I love her and she's the only person I want to marry. So she's mentally ill? Some people are physically ill.' And I thought, if he can do it, I can." He made a wry half-smile.

"Do you regret it?"

He had been talking so openly that Nira was taken aback when he said, "Regretting things is a waste of time."

"Can't one learn, though, from past mistakes?"

He had a pained, confused expression, as though the whole conversation had drawn him back into a past he would rather not think about. "I think what I've learned is that when I marry again, I have to choose someone with a stronger"—he gestured—"center, somehow. Someone who doesn't look to me for everything. There was so much rage and competitiveness in Claire under the surface because she didn't have anything of her own. When I had any success, it threw her so. It was like I was stabbing her in the back."

Nira was silent a moment. "I was getting like that," she said. "That's why I got the job." What had pierced through her were his words "when I marry again." Not "If I marry again," a vague possibility, but a fact: someday he knew he would marry again. And at this very moment, as they stood in this windless chilly field, somewhere his future wife existed. Maybe she was writing a letter, about to board an airplane, studying for her midyear exam in Social Studies. She was there, she existed, and could Nira, by pressing a button, have erased this person she didn't know from the face of the earth, she would have done so without a moment's hesitation.

"You're a survivor, though," he said smiling, as though to break the grimness of the conversation. "No matter what you went through when your father died or early in your marriage. . . . You'll make it."

"I hope so," she said. "Oh, I hope so, so much, Jerry!"

"If you married again, what would *you* do differently?" he asked.

Nira felt alarmed. She had never told him about her fears about Adlai. "I'm not going to," she cried. "I'm happily married."

"In every way?" he said wryly. "That can't be so or we wouldn't—"

"No one's happy in *every* way," she said defensively. "But we're as happy as anyone can be. The thing with you is just . . . It's just not having done all this when I was younger, the way most people do. Finally it caught up with me. It's just sex." Oh, you liar. You dopey, transparent liar.

She couldn't tell, from his expression, how much of this he believed. "No, I'm glad in a way," he said. "Because, well, eventually I will have to find someone, you know, someone I can really share my life with. I just wanted to make sure you understood that."

"Oh sure," Nira said. "No, I know that. This is just like a fling." She was afraid she might cry.

"And what then?" he asked gently. "After that?"

"I don't know." She turned from him angrily. "I can't figure my whole life out," she said. "I just . . . this is for now."

He took her hand and held it tightly. "Let's see your artwork," he said.

When she'd been in the hospital, Nira had had fantasies of burn-
ing down the studio, of destroying everything she had worked so hard
on for so many years. She had envisioned, with satisfaction, the whole
building and everything in it blazing to the ground. And for a year
after she had gotten out, she had not even visited her parents' house
for fear she might actually be tempted to do it. But the impulse was
gone. She felt a certain curiosity, even, about how her artwork would
strike her.

At one time she had admired very much the work of a woman
sculptor named Marisol who did large wooden figures in groups,
often whimsical and humorous in conception, with painted faces,
hats, and objects attached to create a mock semblance of reality.
Nira's statues had been made of wood also, but on a much smaller
scale. Some of them were like fantasy scenes reduced almost to doll-
house size, Victorian families wandering in prehistoric landscapes.
She had learned at Parsons to paint realistic backdrops with great
skill, and now, so many years later, she was struck with mixed plea-
sure at the professional quality of what she had done. They were not
terrible. Some of them were good.

Jerry walked around, examining them all carefully. "You might
have made a go of it," he said. "I don't know. It's not my field. But
this isn't the stuff you see in Greenwich Village art shows."

"No," she agreed, staring at one of them. "It's funny, now I can't
even go to art shows. It starts up such a conflict in me about what if
this, what if that. I want to blame my father for forcing me to waste
all those years, but no one was forcing me . . . It was a choice. And
maybe it got me through those early years with the kids, having a
separate place to come and be alone with my fantasies. It wasn't
harming anyone."

"Why was it a waste?" he said.

She shrugged.

"Look, I might switch from research into teaching . . . But I
don't think the years I've done research have been a waste necessarily.
It was a transition. I needed to go through it."

"It's different," Nira said. "You were getting paid." She was
startled at the bitterness in her voice.

"So? Where did that leave me? Look, I see your point. I do think
being paid for what you do matters, but it's not the only thing."

Nira frowned. "I do hate that, that thing women do—"

"What thing?"

"Well, I see how my mother blamed my father for the fact that
she didn't have a career, and how I, at times, blame my father for

falsely, excessively encouraging me, or I blame Adlai for not having said: 'This is a dead end, cut it out.' It's a dodge. Yet one falls into it so easily, wanting a scapegoat."

"Well, men do it about women too," Jerry said. " 'I could have been a great whatever if I hadn't had to support the wife and kids.' Beasts of burden. That's what my father used to call men."

Nira laughed. She reached out for him. "You've been so good, Jerry, coming up here with me like this. There were so many ghosts. I mean, you can't really lay them to rest, but . . . maybe because you weren't a part of it. Whatever."

They hurried back to the big house, impelled both by the cold rain that had started and the sexual urgency that had sprung up, in part, through the talk. She wanted suddenly to get away from words and see him again more as he seemed when they were in his apartment: the lover. This is my lover. It reduced him somehow, gave him a purpose which, in its seeming single-mindedness, she liked. I'm here because I want to get laid. But she knew that wasn't the only reason, or even the main reason, and probably never had been.

She brought him into the bedroom she had had as a teenager. Her mother, though she had seldom used the house after Nira's father's death, had changed nothing. Occasionally a cleaning service came in, once a year at most, but on the walls were the same Matisse posters her father had bought in Paris, the photos from her eighth-grade school trip to New Paltz, churning butter with her best friend of that era, Michelle Potts, the wooden man she'd ordered from a catalogue who could bend obligingly into a table or stand, holding a discarded skirt or pair of socks.

Jerry took his clothes off right away and lay on the corduroy-covered bed, watching her with an expression of amused expectation. Usually she was the one to undress as if in a marathon. Her period was just ending. She had deliberately not worn a Tampax, but had a sanitary napkin in her underpants. Nira yanked off her jeans and underpants in one hasty gesture, as much to conceal the pad as to hurry to him. She still felt self-conscious when he stared at her in that intense way when she was naked, although she knew her body was fine. She and Adlai had always made love in the dark or with their eyes closed.

He was lying on his side, his penis erect, his hand outstretched for her to join him. God, he was so beautiful! "When I marry . . ." But she forced that from her mind and flung herself into his arms. They did it too fast and it was painful, perhaps because of her tenderness from her period. Adlai disliked doing it until her period was totally over—it was the fact of the blood rather than the smell that struck him as distasteful, he said. "I love being inside you," Jerry said, his hands gripping her so tightly it hurt. "Oh Nira, God . . ."

The room was almost black, though it was just mid-afternoon. Nira, exhausted as much by the driving, their long talk, the intensity of the sex, fell into a deep, heavy sleep which seemed to go on for days, as though she had been drugged. When she woke up, she felt frightened and couldn't remember for a moment where she was. Then she saw the wooden man, the paper face she had painted for him smiling genially at the foot of the bed.

"Jerry?" He wasn't in bed with her.

"I'm in here." He was in the living room, dressed. Nira saw it was past six.

"God, I'm sorry," she said. She stood naked in the doorway. "It's so late! Do you have to get back or something?"

"No . . . Do you?"

Nira thought. "We were going to go to a dinner party . . . do you want to stay over? I could call Adlai and tell him I'm here and that I'd be back tomorrow. I used to do that a lot, when I came up here to work."

"Won't he be suspicious?"

"I don't think so. It's a party with some people we hardly know. It'll be huge. He'd just as soon go without me."

A little later Nira sat on the kitchen stool, a blanket wrapped around her. "I'll drive in if you think I should," she said to Adlai. "But I feel like I want to . . . It's the first time I've been out in so long. It stirred up a lot of things."

"Of course," Adlai said. "Stay . . . I'll be fine."

"Will it be okay with the kids?"

"Sure."

"Will you remember to tell Mrs. Gunderson that if she gives Jas the sweet potatoes, not to give her creamed corn too? The doctor really thinks she's been gorging on sweets. Tell her carrots are okay. She likes those too . . . And make sure she boils the nipples. They looked awfully grungy."

"I did it when I came home."

"Oh thanks," Nira said. "Are the other two okay?"

"They seem to be . . . Listen, Po wants to speak to you so I'll sign off."

Nira waited a moment. Then she heard Posey's high, excited voice. "Mom? Listen, promise you won't be mad?"

"What is it?"

"Promise first!"

"I promise."

"Well, you know the place Heather went to have her bangs cut? Near school?"

"Yeah?"

"Well, we went there today and I had them cut too!"

"How do they look?"

Posey sighed heavily. "Not that great. They're all curly."

"Isn't that the way they're supposed to be?"

"No! I wanted them exactly like Heather's."

"But hon, everybody has different hair. Your hair is curlier. Anyway, it'll grow in."

"The doorman thought I looked cute."

"I'm sure you do."

"Mom, we did one other bad thing that you won't like. We painted our nails red. *And* our toenails . . . And—this is the worst—we painted the baby's nails too."

"Po! Why?"

"We thought she'd look nice . . . but she smeared it all over. We tried to explain to her how she shouldn't touch them till they were dry, but she didn't understand."

"Hon, she's seven months old!"

"So? Babies understand lots of things . . . When will you be back?"

"Tomorrow."

"Are you at a friend's house?"

"No, I'm . . . I'm at Grandma's."

"Oh . . . Are you there all by yourself?"

"Yeah."

"Well . . . Have a nice time."

"You too, Po."

"Good night, sleep tight, sweet dreams!"

"Good night, sleep tight, sweet dreams!"

"Good-bye!"

"Good-bye!"

Posey made loud, stagey kissing sounds. Nira made them back. Then she hung up.

For a few moments she sat shivering in the kitchen. She realized she was bleeding onto the blanket. Hurriedly, she went into the bathroom and took a long, hot shower.

In the morning the sun came out. Nira had slept fitfully, perhaps because of her long nap. She sensed Jerry had also. He seemed to always be moving around, trying to find the right position.

After breakfast, they took a long walk in the woods. He had gotten silent again. Maybe if she knew him better, she thought, she could interpret what kind of silence it was. Sometimes he seemed preoccupied and worried, but reluctant to share whatever it was with her. Other times, like the night before, when they'd listen to music on her parents' phonograph, it had seemed a more contented, shared silence in which she didn't feel locked out.

"Is it working out with your daughters?" she asked, just to say something and partly because he mentioned them so seldom.

"In what way?"

"I just mean . . . well, you feel like you can still maintain a relationship with them only seeing them once a week? Are they happy?"

He was silent for a long time. She had the feeling of having encroached on something. "It's a disaster," he said suddenly. "It's terrible. I have to do something . . . I think I'm going to steal them."

Nira looked at him in horror. "What do you mean?"

"She's not capable of looking after them in the most minimal way. They don't eat properly. They haven't been to school in weeks." He grabbed a branch and broke it. "I thought something was wrong. They never seemed to have homework when they visit me, but I thought it was just—well, maybe they'd done it on Saturday or whatever. Then one Monday they stayed over an extra day, and the teacher said they hadn't been in school since October. I guess they didn't want to tell me because they knew how angry I'd be."

"I don't understand," Nira said. He had started walking faster. She had to hurry to keep pace with him. "What does she do with them?"

"They stay around the house with her. She doesn't . . . I don't know if it's some kind of weird revenge on me or if she's just so up in the clouds she doesn't know or care what's going on." His face darkened. "But it doesn't matter. I'm just going to take them."

"How?"

"I'll kidnap them . . . I'll change addresses and have an unlisted number. They can live with me."

"You mustn't!"

"What do you mean?"

"You mustn't just take them from her like that. Try to explain."

"Explain! She's not a person who listens to *anything*. She's stoned about twenty hours of the day."

"But if you just take them . . . you'll destroy her. You said she'd had a breakdown."

"What about *them?* Look at the way they're living! They're *my* children. Think about it. Imagine they were yours. What would you do?"

"If you do that, you'll be a criminal," Nira said. She felt so upset, she was shaking. "You *can't* just steal them."

"I'll do whatever I want. I'm not asking for your approval or advice."

She felt as though he had struck her. Stop identifying with his wife, she told herself severely. Just because she had a breakdown doesn't mean she's you. She's a different person. "I just meant," she said finally, "that maybe they mean a great deal to her. What you're saying by taking them is you don't trust her at anything. Isn't she going to be devastated at that?"

"But what about them?" he said. "What about their lives?"

The anger had drained from his voice, but he still sounded removed.

They drove back in silence to the city. Nira felt as though his anger had passed from his wife to her. She drove with her hands gripping the wheel, petrified. When she let him off, he was going to turn to her and say, in that flat, detached tone, "I never want to see you again." She steeled herself while her stomach clenched into a hard ball of fear.

But when he got out, he just said quietly, "I'm sorry if I wasn't that talkative. I just . . . you're right. Perhaps if I talk to her."

"Will I see you Saturday?" She couldn't refrain from asking, although usually it was just assumed.

"Saturday?" He looked blank. "Sure, well . . . I felt mixed up for a second. I guess this is the first Sunday we've spent together." He kissed her lightly, before he left the car, leaving the taste of his mouth with her.

Over your head, over your head. Fay's words echoed in Nira's mind as she drove away. This is supposed to be a fling. She had always so much envied people who had some kind of inviolable, built-in reserve about human relationships, wives who confessed that, after twenty years, there was much they never discussed with their husbands and never would, people who drew invisible, perfect lines. It seemed to Nira that the high points in life for her had been those moments when someone opened up, shared, invited her into their souls. She was always waiting for those moments, and the rest seemed just trimming. But it was dangerous with him, to feel this close after two months. She could only hope that it was like a fire. She would pass through it, and then out of it. There was another side.

Nonetheless, that night the remnants of their conversation converged into a nightmare from which she awoke terrified and soaked in sweat. It was the middle of the night. For two hours she lay in bed, awaiting daylight. As soon as it was eight, she went downstairs, on the pretext of getting something from the drugstore, and called Jerry from a phone on the corner. She knew he got up early.

"Jerry, listen, I had such an awful dream . . . and I woke up wondering: what if Adlai were to divorce me and take the children? Could he? Because of my having been in the hospital? And because of you?"

"Of course not," he said. His voice was patient, kind. "First of all, why would he want to? He's not a monster. Your children are so attached to you."

"But could he, legally?"

"Look at how they gave Jane and Stacey to Claire!"

"I don't know," she said. In the bright light of day, her fears seemed exaggerated, crazy. She watched a neighbor from their apartment building pass by and stare at her. It was windy and she had worn a coat that wasn't warm enough. "I'm sorry I called," she said. "It was just the dream. It got me so scared."

"I shouldn't have brought it up Sunday," he said. "I didn't mean to upset you."

"It's okay." Suddenly everything seemed calm and orderly again, people hurrying to work, efficient.

"Where are you calling from? I can hear noises in the background."

"The street corner . . . I was afraid to do it from home."

There was a brief pause.

"Nira, I was going to ask you . . . This Saturday I . . . the daughter of a friend of mine is getting married. It's not too far—Scarsdale. Would you like to come with me?"

She was taken aback. "Sure . . . What sort of wedding is it? Fancy?"

"I really don't know. I—I haven't seen them in a long time."

"Is it a good friend?"

"At one time, yes. . . . Then why don't you come around noon? It starts at two."

Apart from Fay's, Nira hadn't been to a wedding in years. She and Adlai had married at City Hall. At the time she'd been in rebellion against "all those conventions," had boasted to friends that her wedding dress was drip-dry. Now, fifteen years later, the conventions no longer seemed as absurd. Or maybe it was just that disobeying them wasn't the thrill it had been. She wondered, though, throughout the week, what friend of his it was. He didn't seem to have many friends, but then, neither did Adlai or any of the men she had known. She wondered if he and his friend had fought over something, and if the wedding invitation was a kind of peace offering. Once that had happened with her, and she had been glad that the other person had searched for a way to mend a quarrel whose point or purpose was so faded in time.

For this wedding, the wedding of someone she didn't know, Nira dressed more elegantly than she had for her own, in an off-white silk dress with a high collar and a full, floating skirt. There was something formal about it, their appearing as a couple. How would he introduce her? Or was he inviting her because it was just an awkward occasion where the presence of another person would make it more palatable? She remembered her brother saying that he always took a woman on vacations because he knew it wouldn't be enjoyable otherwise. He took women he had had affairs with years earlier, just for the companionship.

"You look pretty," Posey said as Nira fastened her earrings in place. They were opals, a present from her father who had always claimed that her mother did not receive gifts gratefully enough. See, Daddy? I'm grateful! You're dead and I'm still wearing them.

She told Adlai she was going shopping with Fay, checking with Fay ahead of time to make sure she would be unreachable. "I feel, now that I'm working, I should have some new things," she said, which was true.

"Is that new?" Adlai asked of the dress. "I like it."

"I got it two years ago, but I never wear it much. I'm always afraid it will get dirty."

"That style suits you."

"Thanks." He had good taste in women's clothes, and always bought her tasteful, attractive presents on her birthdays. "Are the earrings too much?"

"Not at all."

"When are you going to take me to have my ears pierced?" Posey wanted to know. "You said you would."

"I will," Nira promised.

Posey gazed at her thoughtfully. "You look like you're going to a party."

"We are tonight," Nira said. To Adlai she added, "I thought this way I wouldn't have to bother changing if it runs late."

In fact, she felt she ought to buy new clothes for work, but what she was earning scarcely justified it. Taking a cab to Jerry's, she felt irrationally lighthearted, cheerful. The weekend before, in the country, seemed far away. Who cared about his former wife? None of that mattered. It had nothing to do with her.

When she arrived at his apartment, she was startled to have the door opened by his older daughter. "Oh hi," she said. Had she gotten the day wrong?

"Are you Nira?" the girl asked. She still had that imperious, quiet detachment Nira remembered from that awful evening over the summer.

"Yes."

"Daddy said we should meet him at the corner in five minutes. He's getting the car."

His younger daughter, Stacey, was sitting at the kitchen table, drawing. She was wearing an elegant white dress with embroidery on the collar. "Why are *you* coming?" she asked.

Nira laughed. "I don't know."

"I never was at a wedding," Stacey said, continuing to draw.

"Yes, you were," corrected her sister. "When you were four, Aunt Sylvia got married."

"I don't remember," Stacey said. She looked up at Nira. "Have *you* ever been to a wedding?"

"Well, I was at my own." She looked at the drawing, a beautiful, vividly colored scene of animals grazing in a tropical forest.

"You got married?"

"She has three children," Jane said impatiently.

"She does?"

"We had dinner with them over the summer . . ." Jane looked at Nira with amused condescension. "She has the most terrible memory of anyone you'll ever meet."

Stacey looked up. "Oh, was that you? You look different. You had that baby."

"I still do," Nira said.

"I could baby-sit for you. Do you need a baby-sitter?"

"Well, I—"

"She's only eight," Jane said. "She's too young."

"I usually use this woman in our building," Nira said.

"I baby-sit already," Stacey said eagerly. "I get paid and everything, only I split it with Georgina because she's the one who really knows the baby. It lives in her building. Is yours a girl or a boy?"

"A girl."

"Girls are the best . . . Boys cry too much."

"How do you know?" Jane asked. She gave her sister a shove. "We have to go. Daddy's waiting."

The three of them walked down the stairs.

Stacey sighed. "First up, then down . . . I wish Daddy didn't have so many stairs."

"He can't help it," Jane said. "He's poor." Then to Nira she added. "He's not really *poor,* but the thing is, Mommy has our old apartment and it has more rooms. But Daddy said he doesn't need so much room."

Jerry was wearing a gray flannel suit. He looked more formal and Ivy League-ish than usual. He was even wearing a tie, paisley. The car was a slightly shabby-looking VW. Nira got in the front next to him. "The girls decided to come at the last minute," he explained. "Carla said it would be all right."

"Who's Carla?"

"It's her daughter who's getting married."

His children were quieter than hers would have been. At one point they began to sing together. Their voices formed a screen of sound, hung like a curtain between them and the adults. But there was an awkwardness for Nira in his having brought his children. How had he explained her to them? Or didn't he? Children, her own anyway, seemed to bound so indiscriminately from the conventional to the unconventional. Sometimes they seemed to require endless, elaborate explanations for the simplest things, and at other times accepted things which adults would have balked at totally.

Despite the similarity in age, his daughters seemed to her different from her own. They had a quiet kind of enclosed quality together, talking back and forth, commenting on things. A trip like this with Heather and Posey would have been much noisier, with a lot of demands for adult attention and interaction. In fact, usually Posey sat in front with Adlai, a privilege that meant a lot to her. She was allowed to find good music stations for him to listen to, to pay for tolls, to check things on the map. And in the backseat, Nira would sit with Heather who would try to engage her in "adult" conversation.

Halfway there, Stacey announced that she had to go to the bathroom. Jerry pulled over at a snack bar and all of them disappeared into the available facilities. When they got out, Jerry was not there yet. The three of them moved over to the candy counter.

Stacey looked up at Nira. "Do you have any money?"

"Sure . . . what do you want?"

"Saltwater taffy."

"It'll make your fillings come out," Jane warned.

"Not if I chew it in the back."

They waited, all chewing on the candy, for Jerry.

"Did you wear a long white dress when you got married?" Stacey asked.

Nira shook her head. She touched the collar of her dress which protruded above her coat. "Something a little like this."

"You know what Mom wore?"

"How could she know?" Jane asked. "She wasn't there!"

"She wore a white dress with big, pink polka dots . . . You know why?"

"Why?" Nira asked, fascinated.

"Well, you know people getting married—"

"—brides," Jane intervened.

"—wear white because they're not supposed to have had any boyfriends except the person they're marrying."

"That's not the way it goes," Jane said, exasperated. "You're getting it wrong."

"It is," Stacey said. But she looked uncertain. "That's what Mom said."

"You can have had boyfriends," Jane said. "But you're not supposed to have had sex with them. The white is for purity," she explained to Nira.

"Yeah," Stacey said, cheerful again. "That's what I said . . . So anyhow, Mom said she didn't believe in that and she *had* had boyfriends. She said the pink spots were for all her boyfriends."

Nira laughed, delighted at this detail which she knew Jerry, even if they had an affair for fifty years, would never have mentioned.

"She had pink shoes to match," Stacey added. "Did you have boyfriends before you got married?"

"Not too many," Nira admitted.

"I'm going to have a lot," Stacey said. "My dress is going to have lots and *lots* of pink spots."

"I'm not even going to wear a white dress," Jane said. "I think that's dumb. I'm going to wear a purple dress."

"You can't," Stacey said. "They don't let you."

"You can wear whatever you want," Jane said. She turned to Nira. "Can't you?"

"Sure," Nira said. "You can do whatever you want."

"Hi," Jerry said, appearing suddenly in front of them. He smiled at her.

"Hi," she smiled back, pleased yet startled by the realization that in a funny way she felt more at ease with his children than she did with him.

The wedding was at a church. They arrived a little late and sat toward the back. Nira sat between Jerry and Jane. Stacey was on his other side. The girls were grave and well-behaved. There was no scuffling or whispering, as she knew there would have been with her daughters. They gazed straight ahead with solemn, attentive expressions.

Going to a wedding where you didn't know the people who were getting married was odd, Nira thought. You didn't have any of those complex, mixed feelings about hoping it would work out, wondering if they were suited. The couple getting married were young. The girl looked about twenty, the groom maybe a few years older. She wasn't extravagantly pretty, but had a round, cheerful face, heavy eyebrows. He was barely taller and wore thick, black-rimmed glasses. He seemed to have a slight limp.

After the ceremony the wedding party gathered in front of the church. There were about a hundred people.

"Is it over?" Stacey whispered.

"Of course," Jane said.

"I didn't hear her say, 'I do.' "

It was true that the vows had been exchanged so quietly that they had been barely audible. "*I* heard them," Jane said.

There was no formal receiving line, but the bride and groom were standing with what looked like his or her parents just outside the church. "Let's go over and say hello," Jerry said.

They passed in front of the couple. Nira saw a middle-aged man, either the bride or groom's father, glance at Jerry angrily and walk away. The bride noticed and frowned. She smiled at Jerry. "I'm glad you could come," she said. She looked at Nira and the children. "Is this your wife?"

"This is a friend of mine," Jerry said. "Nira Goldschmitt, and these are my children, Jane and Stacey."

"Oh, aren't they darling?" the bride said.

The girls stared up at her uncomfortably.

Jerry cleared his throat. "Where's Carla?" he asked.

"She hasn't been at all well," the bride said. She hesitated. "Are you coming back to the house? She'll be there."

"Will it be all right?" Jerry asked. He indicated where the older man stood now, at the far side of the lawn. "Your father won't object?"

"No, no, that was . . . Mother would like you to come."

"Okay, we will then."

Nira looked at Jerry, puzzled by the exchange. They greeted the groom more briefly and passed onto the edge of the lawn. In the car, driving to the house, Stacey said, "The bride had a moustache."

"It wasn't a moustache, really," Jane said. "It was *like* a moustache, though. . . . If I had one, I'd take it off, wouldn't you?"

"Yeah, I would," Stacey said. "But maybe her husband loves her anyway."

"Of course he loves her," Jane said. "They just got married five minutes ago! Do you want them to get divorced the same day they get married? He'd better love her now!"

"Did you think she was pretty, Daddy?" Stacey said.

Jerry, preoccupied, didn't hear.

Nira touched his shoulder. "Stacey wondered if you thought the bride was pretty." It was the first time she had touched him all day—this day, usually reserved for nothing but touching. But she felt awkward even touching him in the most casual way in front of his children. Perhaps because of that, the light touch started a haze of sexual feelings in her, which continued throughout the ride. She wished suddenly that the children weren't there, that they could stop somewhere on the way back. She wanted him, and to have to wait another week seemed suddenly unbearable.

"I think she's nice-looking," Jerry said.

"Would you marry someone with a moustache?" Stacey asked.

"Which of us do you mean?" Jerry said.

"Oh Daddy, come on! You! Of course *she* would marry someone with a moustache."

"I'd have to give it some thought," Jerry said. "Do you have someone in mind?"

"Mom's boyfriend has a moustache," Stacey said. "But he might shave it off. It tickles."

The bride's house was not large. Most of the guests were in the living/dining room. Near the window was a table with a large punch bowl and a few platters of sandwiches.

Nira became separated from Jerry. She stood in the corner, sipping punch. She always felt awkward at large parties, even when she knew some of the people. She saw Jerry off in a corner, talking to a small, fragile-looking woman with dark hair. Who were these people, anyway? And where was his friend? She felt angry at him for bringing her and then leaving her there, stranded. She thought of his former wife with her pink spotted dress. Had she been good at parties? Had she mingled and flirted and been bubbly and effervescent?

"Are you a friend of the bride or the groom?" a man asked Nira. She turned. He was middle-aged, evidently of the generation of the parents.

"I'm . . . well, I'm here with a friend," she said. "A friend of the bride's."

"Me too . . . that is, my wife is a friend of Carla's from college."

"Who's Carla?" Nira asked.

"Janet's mother."

"Oh . . . who's Janet?"

He laughed. "She's the gal who just got married."

"The person I came with knew them a long time ago," Nira explained. "And I've only known him a fairly short time."

"Your boyfriend?"

"Sort of."

He smiled. "Still deciding, huh? Why not, you're young? Look, I got married the first time at twenty-two. Can you believe it? That's why when I see young kids like this who don't know up from down deciding to rush into things, well. . . . They'll regret it."

"*I* got married at twenty-two," Nira said.

"Oh." He looked puzzled. "You're divorced?"

"No, I—"

"Separated?"

She laughed nervously. "I'm not anything," she said. "That is, I'm married, but . . ."

"We're all married but, honey. That's how I met my wife. She was married but, and I was married but. We put both our buts together and . . ."

"I need to go to the bathroom," Nira said. "I'll see you later."

She pressed her way through the crowd. She couldn't see Jerry. When she came to the end of the hall, she saw the bedroom. Probably there was a bathroom there. She entered hesitantly, then saw that, on the bed without coats, a woman was lying down. Her eyes were open and glanced across at Nira.

"I was looking for the bathroom," Nira said.

The woman raised one thin arm and pointed. "Right in there."

Nira went to the bathroom. When she emerged, the woman was lying in the same position. "Are you okay?" Nira said. The woman's skin was dead white and her limbs looked like sticks. Yet she had a pretty face and large, dark eyes that had a watchful, almost frightened expression.

"I'm okay," the woman said very softly. "Do you think you could get me a glass of water?"

Nira hurried to the bathroom and brought back a glass half-filled. She stood and watched as the woman raised herself up to drink. From this close, it was clear she was wearing a wig. It had slipped just slightly, and its heavy abundance was too much of a contrast to the woman's sharp-featured, delicate face. "At least I only have one daughter," she said with a slight smile. "I don't know if I could go through this again."

"Is it your daughter who got married?" Nira asked.

"Yes. Janet." She lay back again, sinking into the pillow.

"I'm sorry. I don't know anyone," Nira said. "I'm here with a friend, Jerry Gardener, and he—"

The woman smiled. "You're Jerry's friend?"

"Yes," Nira said. "My name is Nira."

"I'm Carla."

"Oh," Nira said. She felt trapped by the woman's steady, inquisitive stare.

"You've known each other a long time?" Carla asked.

"No, not that long. . . . He, um, he might do a book for my husband on the history of science. My husband's a publisher. He publishes—well, mostly books on art, but some in other fields too."

"He didn't mention that you were married."

Nira's heart was thumping. "Yes, yes, I am."

The woman kept staring at her. The brown eyeshadow around her mascaraed eyes made her eyes almost hypnotic.

"Would you like me to call your husband?" Nira said, trying to break the intensity of the mood. "Does he know you're not feeling well?"

"I've been ill for a long time," she said. "Ten years. He knows."

"You'll be all right, then?"

She nodded. "Be happy, Nira," she said. "That's the main thing . . . The rest of it doesn't matter."

"I'll try," Nira said.

She came out of the room feeling exhausted, trembling. Jerry was standing at the other end of the room with his daughters. "We were looking for you," he said.

"Could we go?" Nira said. "I feel funny."

"Sure, the girls are exhausted. They've been up since five, evidently."

In the car Jane and Stacey fell asleep instantly, entwined in the backseat, using each other's bodies as pillows.

"That woman," Nira began. "The bride's mother . . . She seemed very ill. She was lying in the bedroom all by herself and—"

"She's dying."

"Is it cancer?"

"Yes . . . She's had it a long time, had a lot of remissions, but I think, well, this may be it."

There was a pause.

"Who is she, Jerry?"

"She was my first love," he said.

"She's older than you, isn't she?"

"Ten years . . . I met her when I was twenty-two. Her husband went to college with me."

"He seemed so angry when he saw you outside the church."

"We had an affair for three years. It must still be painful for him."

"How did you meet her?"

"At a party . . . Scott was about to go away for the summer, to do research at MIT, and I gave a party for him, a farewell party. I'd never met Carla before. She was very beautiful then."

"She still is."

"She was always pale, but she had wonderful long, black hair, parted in the middle, just loose. She was wearing a white dress . . . at one point she came up to me and said she wanted to see some drawings I had in the next room. We went inside and I began talking to her about them. She kept staring at me the whole time in this kind of mesmerized way. Finally she reached over and put her hand on mine. She said, 'Jerry, I'm a very simple woman . . . and I think life can be very simple.' " He laughed mirthlessly. "Three suicide attempts later, it seemed things weren't that simple, after all."

"Why did she?" Nira asked, seeing it in her mind like a movie— Jerry at twenty-two, serious, explaining the painting; the pale, long-haired woman, her impulsive, sensual gesture, wanting him, touching his hand; the guests and her husband in the next room.

"I couldn't . . . I tried to leave. She knew I had to, but each time she went to pieces."

Nira remembered her terrible, sad, piercing look. She had known she was dying. She sucked in her breath. "Could we pull over somewhere?"

"Sure." He cast a worried glance at her.

Sitting there, the seat belt around her, Nira felt anxiety sweeping over her. She hadn't felt that since before her breakdown; she had forgotten the feeling. *Oh shit.* She touched her hands to her cheeks.

Her fingertips were icy cold. When they came to the rest stop, she undid her seat belt quickly and got out of the car.

"I better stay with the girls," Jerry said, glancing back at them. They were still asleep.

"I won't be long," Nira promised, and rushed off. In the ladies' room, she stood near the window, staring at the wet floor strewn with paper towels. She tried to take long deep breaths. Look, people die, affairs don't last forever, and life isn't just. Which of those things didn't you know before today? It isn't that. It isn't a matter of knowing. What then? I don't know. You're yourself. You're not her, not his wife, no one but yourself. Okay? Sure. None of that worked. They were truisms which passed through her mind and vanished. Nira closed her eyes.

Sometimes, when she felt tense, she tried closing her eyes and thinking of the most soothing, peaceful thing she could remember. What came to her mind now, standing in the shabby, smelly ladies' room, was her mother-in-law's garden in Devon. She remembered how they had walked down a pebbled path, her mother-in-law in a straw hat carrying a basket, occasionally stooping to clip a few flowers, all the time talking on about her garden, how much work it was, how satisfying, giving the names of all the flowers. Adlai said that his childhood memories of his parents were of his father silent and his mother babbling. He found her babbling irritating, but to Nira, whose mother had been painfully shy, it was soothing. The words flowed on, unimpeded. There was no need for response beyond an occasional nod or question. She could no longer remember now the names of any of the flowers or, in fact, anything of what they had said, but she remembered how protected, how warm she had felt, how relieved that Mrs. Goldschmitt accepted her so totally, didn't mind her being American, called her the daughter she had always wished she'd had.

Nira felt someone touch her shoulder. Opening her eyes, she saw a young teenage girl with bad skin and a Mickey Mouse T-shirt looking at her with a concerned expression. "Are you okay?"

"Oh yes, I'm okay," Nira said. It had worked. Walking back to the car, she felt calm, her breath came normally.

Jerry was sitting where she had left him, behind the wheel, gazing off into space. Where was he? What garden? Everyone doesn't need that. But he looked concerned when he saw her. "Are you all right?"

"Yes." She looked at him. "I felt bad about Carla," she said inadequately.

"She's had a difficult life," he said. "For a while she thought she might leave him, but I guess she never quite made it. I used to send her money after I moved to New York. I tried to stay involved in her life, but . . ."

"Her daughter seemed fond of you."

"She's settled down now, but she had a tough time growing up. Once she needed an abortion and I gave her a name and lent her the money. I think she's always remembered that. Her father was somewhat on the moralistic side, very stern."

Suddenly Stacey said something in her sleep. Nira and Jerry turned around, but she had just turned into another position. "She's like me," he said. "She sleeps fitfully. . . . I spoke to Claire, Ni, about what we talked about last week, my having the children, at least more than I do now . . . she said definitely for the summer, maybe through part of the fall. She's going to Europe. It's funny. I could tell she really in some way doesn't want them. She looked so relieved when I brought it up, maybe because I didn't do it in an accusing way. I just said I thought it was only fair she have her freedom some of the time the way I do, to set up a new life. She kept nodding. She has this way of saying, 'Yes, yes, yes . . .' But you were right. I think if I'd confronted her and called her a lousy mother, she would have just hung on to them for dear life . . . It's all strategy, basically."

"No," Nira said. "You were thinking of her feelings."

"I'd like to look at it that way but, frankly, I do think she's a lousy mother."

"You might be too, if you had no job and no self-confidence and—"

"I never stopped her from getting a job. My mother worked all her life. I'm not like that."

"Well, maybe she needed more encouragement. Look, Jerry, I don't know. But I'm glad you've given her her freedom, as you put it. I hope she knows how to use it. Did she ever do anything, professionally?"

"She wrote poetry . . . She had a few poems published, actually. But then she decided they were terrible and burned everything. She was like that, terribly intense about everything."

"Well, next time you'll marry a placid, relaxing, bovine person," Nira said dryly, "who'll cook you hot dinners every night."

He laughed. "I'd settle for cold . . . Anything but take-out Chinese food for another ten years." He looked pensive. "But if the girls do come to live with me, my life will change, that's for sure."

"In what way?"

"Well, a lot of my spare time will have to go to them . . . And eventually I will have to think of finding a mother for them."

Nira grimaced. "God, what an awful way of putting it!"

He looked startled. "Why?"

"Like you were hiring someone."

"That isn't what I meant . . . I just don't want a parade of women passing through their lives. They're disoriented enough as it is."

A parade of women. Damn. They looked at each other. Jerry leaned over and kissed her gently on the mouth. They both hesitated, partly because of the children sleeping behind them, and then their mouths opened and he pulled her into his arms. "Come back with me, after I drop them off," he said softly.

"I can't," Nira said, wanting him so much she would have made love with him right there, in the front seat of the car, children or no. "We have to go to a party."

They kissed and kissed. "We better stop," Nira said breathlessly into his neck.

He stroked her hair, touching the opal earring which hung just below her ear. "I love you," he said.

After the conversation they had just had, the words cut through her like a sword. "Oh Jerry," Nira said, pressing her face against him. They held each other, their hearts beating together. Then they pulled apart, almost formally. He started the car. Nira fastened her seat belt.

"Hey, this is the first Saturday we haven't had sex," he said, smiling.

"Well, sex," Nira joked.

"Terribly overrated."

"Boring, actually. If you've done it once—"

To their laughter, the children finally woke up.

"Are we there yet, Daddy?" Stacey asked. "At the wedding?"

"The wedding's *over*," said Jane. "Don't you even remember?"

Stacey yawned. "That's right . . . I do remember," she said. "Only she forgot to say, 'I do.' "

Fall-Winter 1981

"I was fantastic," Helen said. "I have to say it. I have to give credit where credit is due. And you know what the secret is, Pen?"

"What?" Penny asked. She had arrived by plane that morning, but Helen had just returned from her law school classes a few hours earlier. The two children who were still living at home, the others being off working or at college, were upstairs watching TV. They were sitting over coffee in the gigantic shabby kitchen of the house Helen had bought and partially renovated after her divorce.

"I'm mellow, I'm even-tempered, I see right from wrong, I don't get flustered. I mean, take this kid who's on the case with me. Every time we lose a point, he crumples. He's a real mama's boy, just like George. He's been told he was wonderful, a boy-genius, since he was born, and if the world doesn't agree, God forbid, he's a basket case. Whereas I—I've been through such idiocy, such shit . . . this all seems like nothing. After life with George, I could argue in front of the Supreme Court and it wouldn't faze me a bit. You know what I ought to be, though? A judge."

"You'd be great," Penny said, smiling. She liked the image of Helen sitting erect and stern, banging her gavel. Her boyishly short hair was streaked with gray, but she had the same impish, daredevil smile as when she'd been a girl.

"What's odd," Helen said, "is I like working within the system. Don't ask me why. Because it's definitely not mutual. The system couldn't give less of a damn about working within me. It's screwed me up every inch of the way. But I still get a perverse kind of pleasure in knowing all the laws, all the angles; I guess fooling them at their own game is what it boils down to."

"George had that," Penny pointed out.

"George had that, but George, let's not forget, was a manic, a case unto himself. I mean, what else can you call a man who on his own *honeymoon* calls his mistress long-distance to tell her it's a great hotel, screws everyone in sight for fifteen years, and then sues his wife's lover for alienation of affection . . . *and* wins seventy thousand dollars?"

"It is a little hard to believe," Penny said. "I mean, his winning, apart from everything else."

"George could sue the State Department and win," Helen said. "No, I have to give him credit. All those odd little quiverings of feelings for justice and mercy and sensitivity to others, which we all, at least part of the time, think about, mull over, even if we're not acting on them every second—they don't *exist* for him! He doesn't believe in them. If George decided gravity didn't exist, he could climb out a window and just sit, suspended in midair indefinitely."

"That he found someone with seventy thousand dollars too!"

Helen grinned. "*I* found him. He just sued him."

"What I don't understand, really, is why you couldn't counter-sue. If he'd had all those girlfriends for so many years."

"Sweetie, he covered his tracks. They all went into hiding. I had women who'd told me every act that had taken place. There was this one totally off-the-wall kid on our block who used to come over every day and tell me all about it. I don't know, maybe it was relieving her conscience, God knows. . . . When I tried to get her or any of them to go to court, they all hid under the covers, you should pardon the expression."

"The perfect crime," Penny smiled.

"Life is the perfect crime. And the proof of it is, now that he and Bethie are finally joined, conjoined, or whatever, *now* who does he call on his honeymoon?"

"Is that like, what is the sound of one hand clapping?" Penny said.

"No, that was a real question . . . Who did George call on his honeymoon with Bethie?"

Penny shrugged.

"Me!"

"Come on."

"I mean it. I swear . . . Either George has no sense of irony at all or the most well-developed one I'll ever run into. He actually went back to the same damn place we were at twenty-four years ago, and he called me. He said, 'Helen, you won't believe this, but they have the same desk clerk. That guy with the twitch. He's still there. He asked after you.' There was this desk clerk who used to flirt with me like crazy. . . . We were talking and I heard Bethie come into the room. I heard him say to her, 'It's Herman,' and to me, 'I'll speak to you about the tax shelters when I get back.' "

"And does he still call you?" Penny said, incredulous. "Even after the honeymoon?"

"Not only calls! He sends flowers on my birthday, takes me out to dinner. When I got into law school, he sent me a malachite ashtray you could take a bath in."

"Is it guilt?"

"Guilt, insanity, who knows? There will, unless God is more of a practical joker than I think, only be one George. And for that, we can all gratefully say our prayers at night and count our blessings. No, the weird thing, Pen, is that I have now become, the Other Woman. After being married to someone who was not faithful for a single *week* of our marriage, suddenly he thinks I'm wonderful."

"Well, maybe that's the solution," Penny mused.

"To what?"

"To marriage . . . I mean, now you have him, in a way."

"Phooey. I don't have him and no one ever will. And I don't want him. I love the irony of it, but what do I have? You can't screw a malachite ashtray."

"I've never tried . . . So what do you do, then? Or don't you have time?"

"No one has time. That's not the point . . . Well, I went through my prescribed phase of selective promiscuity, and now I'm easing into . . . God knows what."

"What was it like? You make it sound awful."

"Not at all. . . . Do it sometime. It really has a lot to recommend it. And let me tell you, all those people who say that in the dark they're all the same, and if you've seen one you've seen them all . . . those people are *wrong*. I am here to tell you they are dead wrong."

"In what way?"

"In the dark they are all totally, *totally* different. They smell different, they look different, they do it differently. It was really fascinating. I was so surprised—I mean, sometimes not in a good way—but I consider it to have been a valuable learning experience. I even see George's point of view in a way I never did when we were married. I mean, I don't think I could do it *and* be married. That's where I'd still part company with him . . . But I can totally see the thing of savoring and enjoying the variety."

"And you didn't ever fall madly in love?"

"A bit, now and then. But not in any hideous way. It passed . . . I guess if I love anyone these days, it's still Bernie."

"You're still seeing him?"

"Well, he was a little stunned by the seventy-thousand-dollar thing, as well he might have been. But he has more where that came from. He still talks about our getting married. He adores the kids. What can I say? What will be will be."

"So, you aren't interested in meeting anyone else?"

"Sure, I do all the time."

"No, I ask," Penny said, "because this man I know has a brother who lives out here, and he thought you might want to meet him."

"What man?"

"He's one of our authors. He's done a kind of historical novel about eighteenth-century science. It's wonderful, really . . . and, well, he mentioned that his brother lives in San Francisco."

"Does the brother have any other identifiable traits?"

"I'll ask Jerry when I see him."

"Jerry?"

"The author, the man I just mentioned."

"Aha, the plot thickens . . . how come he's out here?"

"To visit his brother."

"The light descendeth, in a vague kind of way. Don't tell me we're going on a double date? I don't think I can quite face reverting totally to adolescence."

"No, I just thought I'd check with you. It's all terribly vague."

The phone rang. Helen answered it. She beckoned to Penny. "It's for you."

Penny picked up the kitchen phone. "Hello?"

"Penny? It's Jerry Gardener. I hope this is an all-right time to call."

"It's fine." Helen was clearing the dishes and putting them in the dishwasher. Penny looked up at the cork bulletin board with all the scattered scraps of paper—phone messages, school calendars, Helen's exam schedule, movies.

"How about dinner tomorrow? Will you have time before you go back?"

"Sure . . . Do you want to bring your brother?"

"That's a bit more complicated than I indicated. I'll tell you about it when I see you . . . why don't we meet at the restaurant in my hotel? It seems pretty decent."

"I thought you were staying with your brother."

"I'm visiting him, but he doesn't like anyone to stay overnight in his apartment. He has a big thing about privacy."

They set a time to meet. Penny told Helen before she went up to bed.

"Dinner at his hotel?" Helen said suspiciously. "Hey sweetie, I thought I'd told you the facts of life twenty years ago."

"It's not like that," Penny said, laughing. "He's just a nice person. He's not available, anyway. He's married."

"That's the non sequitur of the year."

"Listen, I'm not *that* naive . . . He's not, seductive, or what have you."

"Okay, well as long as there aren't little men with violins and candlelight."

"What if there are? Should I run to the ladies' room and hide? I thought you were just counseling selective promiscuity."

Helen looked at her, head to one side. "I guess you don't seem old enough."

Penny smiled. "When will I be?"

"Probably, to me, never . . . You just still seem so, I don't know, fragile, untouched . . ."

"Come on, give me a break."

"Okay, I know . . . I'm just overdoing the big-sister bit, for a change. Tell him I'll be waiting up for you with a rolling pin in my hand."

"I'll be sure to."

Although they joked about it, Penny knew it was true. Helen would always, even when they were seventy and seventy-eight, regard her as too young, not quite ready for life, in need of protection and looking after. It had been the tenor of their childhood relationship, when the eight-year gap between them had seemed several generations at least. To Penny, Helen had always been the ultimate authority on everything, knowledgeable about sex, books, ways of dealing with parents, unafraid of challenge and conflict. All the battles with their parents had been fought by Helen with such intensity that, by the time the same issues reappeared in Penny's life, they were too exhausted to struggle. And Penny had never had Helen's gift for inviting or inciting conflict, pushing issues to the edge and over. Maybe it was from watching Helen, but she had learned, instead, the art of watching safely from the sidelines, calculating other people's reactions and working around them. Their parents died in an automobile accident, driving to Penny's high school graduation. Both in their forties, in perfect health, they were killed instantly in a freak accident on a sunny day when a two-ton truck careened off its course and sent their small Volvo tumbling into a river hundreds of feet below. After that, Helen had been literally the only person for Penny to turn to, other than Cal. And for Penny, Helen had always been there, rock-of-Gibraltar like, no matter what disasters her own life was going through; ready to listen, to commiserate, to boss. Maybe that was why there had always been so much friction between Helen and Cal. It was as though both of them, in different ways, wanted to dominate her and control her life, from love, from feeling they knew what was best for her. And with both of them Penny felt she shrank somehow when she was with them, became in fact childlike and dependent and clinging. It was a relief to her, despite missing and needing them both, to have them three thousand miles away.

The restaurant did have candlelight and violins. Penny did not run to the ladies' room. Maybe this is a seduction. Maybe I will go to bed with him, she thought. Why not? She had never indulged in random affairs, not only because of her personality, but because Cal had always seemed so eager for her to do it to justify his own escapades. She felt she was not good at judging men. Clear-cut, out-and-out philanderers she could usually pick out, but she always assumed all others were like her father—quiet, genial, lusting-only-in-the-heart types.

"Do you never stay with your brother?" she asked as they sat down. Jerry Gardener looked handsome in a seersucker jacket, slightly tan but tired also, with wrinkles around his eyes. She was conscious of a date-like feeling to the occasion, she herself in a deliberately chosen, flowered cotton dress with a scoop neck.

"He's . . . Well, it's a peculiar story. He was a monk for about twenty years."

"Was your family Catholic?"

"No, it was an Episcopal monastery. Russ was always a little strange, very solitary. He used to spend hours and hours building model ships. He learned calligraphy at eleven, drew hand-painted manuscripts. I guess his idea was partly to live a very quiet, unworldly life . . . But it didn't work out that way. When he finally left, he told me a lot of it had just been brutish, backbreaking labor, getting up at five to pray, weeding the garden. He was terribly embittered for a long time."

"And now?"

"Now he has a doctorate in religious history and teaches, and is, within certain confines, content—as far as I can tell. We don't talk much about many things. . . . He never wants me to stay with him." He frowned, as though still puzzled by that. "Here we shared a room for almost twenty years when we were growing up!"

"Is he younger or older?" asked Penny, trying and failing to imagine a date between Helen and the ex-monk.

"Younger." The violinist was hovering near their table. Penny glanced up at him. "Do you have any favorites?" Jerry asked with a slightly ironical smile.

"No." The image of Helen drifted past. Penny smiled at it and then at him.

"You look so pretty tonight. Is it due to getting away from work?"

"Maybe, though I like my work. It's not . . . I mean there are pressures, but it's basically something I enjoy."

"I feel that too, now, about what I do . . . I mean there are lots of committee things, but the teaching and having time to write make it worthwhile. I've never been sorry I switched."

Penny looked up at him. "Do you come out here mainly to see your brother?"

"Mainly . . . though I did something else today. Maybe it was a mistake. My first wife lives out here. I went to see her."

"Why was it a mistake?"

He didn't reply for a long time. "She's . . . well, never exactly found herself in any way. She never remarried, doesn't work, kind of drifts . . ."

"How does she manage financially?"

"Her family has money. She gets jobs and then, if anything goes wrong, if someone speaks to her harshly or whatever, she quits. She was talented in a lot of things, but she never got it all together, somehow."

"Why was it a mistake to see her?" Penny pursued.

He looked off in the distance. "I don't know. It shouldn't be, after so many years. We've worked out the thing with the children pretty well. Or at least I raised them, and she drifted in from time to time. She's been there, but never as a solid presence with a home, an apartment, a life . . . but whenever we're together for longer than half an hour, she starts getting very hostile. It's like smoke starts coming out of her ears! I can just see her expression change. Her voice gets very low, so low I can hardly hear what she's saying. . . . It makes me very tense and—"

"Guilty?" Penny suggested.

"No, I mean, I don't feel responsible for her fate . . . I created a new life for myself. She could have also. I haven't prevented her from finding a new man or a new job. She just didn't do it. It's funny, though. Almost everything I know about her comes from Nira. They've gotten friendly. When I'm out here, if Claire's in New York, she stays at our house. She tells Nira about her boyfriends, all kinds of things she'd never tell me. I think she admires her in a way."

"Doesn't it make you uncomfortable?" Penny said.

"No . . . Why should it?"

"Does Nira tell her private things too?"

"Not so much, probably. She feels sorry for her basically. She's
. . . She reminds me of you a little, Claire. I thought that the first time
I saw you. She has a certain waif-like quality, somewhat tentative—"

Penny shuddered. "Waif-like?" She wondered if being out here
for just two days had already made her shrink that much, back into
childhood.

He looked taken aback by the intensity of her reaction. "I didn't
mean it in a derogatory way . . . just the way you have of being
vehement, and then suddenly, totally retreating."

Penny felt struck down, almost speechless. "That's awful. I feel
terrible I give that impression."

He looked concerned. "I'm sorry. I truly didn't mean it in a
critical way."

"I know. That makes it worse, somehow."

"Which is it that you mind? That I said you were vehement or
the other?"

"The other! I *want* to be vehement. That's my goal . . . Or at
least strong. I have such contempt for people who look to others all
the time about how to live."

"Isn't contempt a pretty harsh word?"

"Yes."

There was a long silence.

Jerry reached out and touched her hand. "Can we start again?
Why don't we go for a walk after we eat?"

"Okay."

They had dessert and coffee, and the conversation eased into
more general topics. As they walked out of the restaurant, Jerry said,
"Would you mind if I just went to my room a minute? I want to see if
I have any messages on my answering service."

"Okay, sure." They got into the elevator together. Penny felt
confused. It seemed to her there had been nothing especially seduc-
tive about his manner during dinner. He had been friendly, inter-
ested in stories about Helen, but there were no innuendos or sidelong
glances. She sat in a chair while he called his service. Then he put
down the phone and turned to her.

"So, should we take a walk?"

Penny looked at him in surprise. "Aren't we going to go to bed
together? I thought that's why you brought me up here."

He looked embarrassed. "No, I . . . I didn't really . . . I'm happily
married," he stammered.

"Oh." She felt suddenly rejected and humiliated by her inaccu-
rate assumption.

He sat down next to her. "I guess I've been flirting with you.

Was it that? You're beautiful, and you, well, I won't say it again that way, but at times you seem a bit . . . as though you're looking for something. And your marriage seems so—"

"Yes," Penny said, remembering the scene with Cal and Karen. "It is. Oh, it's dumb. I have such a dopey marriage."

They sat in silence a moment.

"We don't have to go for a walk," Jerry said. "Do you want to just talk? Either one is fine with me."

"Let's just talk," Penny said. "Is that okay?"

They lay back on the bed. Jerry put his arm around Penny. She rested her head on his chest. She could hear his heart beating. "The trouble is, I'm just not restless as a husband," he said.

Then what are we doing here? Penny wondered. Aloud she said, "Are you really happy together?"

"Well, I'm . . . We have problems, like anyone. We've had difficult times. A few years ago something happened that was very painful, but—" He broke off. "I don't have the heart or the energy to start again. I'm almost fifty."

"That's not so old," she said, though she had thought he was younger.

"No, but to start a whole new life, to readjust to a new person, to explain yourself again, justify everything. And you build up so many ties. I feel I've helped her raise her children, she's helped me."

"Has that worked?" Penny asked. "I heard that can be so difficult, stepchildren and so on."

"It's a total mess. . . . Her husband lives in England, but he still feels he has the right to decide what schools they should go to, and Nira somehow feels she has to knuckle under for all sorts of reasons . . . and then there's a lot of friction with her and my younger daughter, Stacey, who's a hard kid to deal with anyway. Nira and Jane get along amazingly well, almost better than she does with her own children, they always have. But Stacey keeps threatening to run away, to live on her own, to stay with her mother, who doesn't want her and couldn't keep her. It's better now, but . . ."

Sitting next to him, Penny began wishing she had not, so abruptly, raised the issue of seduction. Maybe it would have happened naturally if she hadn't felt obliged to discuss it ahead of time. She could tell he was attracted to her. That men always wait for women to make the first move was one of Helen's beliefs. "I don't know what to do about my marriage," she said, feeling sleepy and relaxed. "Do you think I should have affairs? Everyone else does." The room was overheated, almost stuffy.

"Well, can you handle it?"

"Handle what?"

"Whatever consequences may arise."

"What do you mean?" Penny asked nervously.

"Well, you know, people fall in love and—"

"Do they still? I thought most people just did it."

"That's what my wife thought when we met. But things have a way of getting out of hand."

Penny gazed off in the distance. "It's a pity you're that happy. Otherwise you'd be perfect."

He smiled. "In what way?"

"Well, you don't seem grossly womanizing, you know, like you wouldn't remember my name in the morning and that sort of thing."

Jerry leaned over and kissed her. "I'd remember your name in the morning, Penny."

Penny reached up, she touched him lightly. "Let's do it, just for tonight. I mean, it can't kill us, can it? Just for once. Would you like to?"

"Of course I'd like to, but . . ."

"Nira won't know, you don't have to tell her."

"I certainly wouldn't tell her. That isn't the point, really . . . But I just, I'm not sure how I can square this with my self-image as a good husband. I know it sounds corny, but that means a lot to me, being straight."

"You've never been unfaithful?"

He hesitated. "Once or twice, but nothing . . . They were just one-night stands."

"So, that's what this will be." Penny smiled, feeling excited and on the verge of victory. "I've never had a one-night stand."

Jerry was smiling. "This wouldn't be that."

"Why? We don't have to do it more than once."

"We'd want to."

"How do you know?"

"Because things take off, they spiral—" he gestured. "And before you know it . . ."

"But couldn't they just fizzle? I thought that happened too."

"I just don't feel comfortable with it . . . I don't think you know what you're getting into."

"How bad could it be?" Penny said. "Just one time. Are you afraid I'll fall in love with you?"

"No, it's not that. Look, why don't we just be friends? Really, I think we would both regret this a lot."

"Okay."

But she thought she was going to cry, she wanted him so much. She felt like Rock Hudson in one of those Doris Day comedies. Was he just a terrible tease? Bringing her here, lying with her in his arms, talking in that soft, caressing voice, and then saying, No, I'm not available, you can't have me. It's not fair! Penny thought miserably. If I were a man and he were a woman, I could just start making love to him. Damn being a woman! It's awful! Whoever set it up like this ought to be taken out and shot immediately. Look, just get up and take your clothes off. I can't, it's not my personality. Forget your personality, just *do* it! He doesn't want me. Those were all excuses. He just plain doesn't find me attractive. The image of him looking in horrified distaste as she removed her clothes kept her rooted to the spot. Finally, steeling herself, she looked up at him.

He was gazing down at her with a dreamy, intense expression. "You're so beautiful," he said, sighing.

"Would you kiss me?" she asked. "Or don't you think I can handle that either?"

He moved down to where she was slouched against the pillow and kissed her lightly. Penny kissed him back, touching his lips with her tongue. She leaned against him and they kissed some more. His mouth opened and he brought his arms around her, down her back, caressing her. When they pulled apart, he said, "Okay, I give up."

"Unconditional surrender?"

"Definitely."

She unzipped her dress and tossed it on the floor along with her panty hose, then watched as he finished taking his clothes off. In the dark they're completely different, Helen had said. They look different, smell different. His body looked older than Cal's, who always kept himself in perfect shape, lifted weights, worked out at gyms. He got into bed beside her.

Penny had thought they would lie together naked, caressing each other, getting to know each other's bodies, getting used to the idea that this was happening. She was startled when Jerry flung himself on top of her, entered her immediately, and began making love to her. Somehow, mentally she felt ten minutes behind what was going on, still lying in his arms listening to him discourse in that calm, rational, convincing-to-her way about how he wasn't restless as a husband. It was like some movie where a crucial scene has been cut. How did they get from there to here so rapidly?

But it was happening! He was moving inside her, kissing her, seeming to have found—or had it been there all along?—a feeling of passion and intensity that she wanted desperately to share. But couldn't. Oh help, Penny thought miserably. I'm doing something for which women are stoned to death in small Near Eastern countries, and I'm not even enjoying it! She could hardly remember once, in twenty years, that she had not come when she and Cal made love, and now having an orgasm seemed like some impossible, extraordinary feat that she could no more have performed than she could have juggled eight oranges while riding a unicycle.

Something of her confusion and anxiety must have communicated itself to Jerry because he reached down and started caressing her, trying to help her catch up with him. But all her bravado had fled, just when she needed it most. Where was it? Down in the hotel lobby? Somewhere she couldn't reach it, far far away.

"Jerry?"

"Yes?" His voice was so tender and gentle, her heart flipped over.

"I just don't think I can do this."

"Okay," he said a moment later and withdrew.

Penny lay in his arms, too mortified to speak. She couldn't remember when in her life she had felt more humiliated. Well, maybe it doesn't count as adultery, she tried to console herself, if I didn't come. In a remote way that cheered her up slightly.

"I'm sorry," she said, touching his cheek. "Will you survive?"

"It's okay . . . Really."

"It isn't even that it's adultery," Penny said. "I don't know what it is."

"Maybe it's really just as well," he said.

"I feel like one of those girls in fifties' novels who wanted to be technically virgins . . . Am I now technically a non-adulteress?"

"It takes more than one time to make it adultery," he said.

"Really? How many times does it take?"

"No, what I mean is, I think occasional sexual escapades are one thing. What no one wants their spouse to be doing is falling in love, finding someone who's more—"

"Cal's found dozens of women who are more . . . whatever than me," Penny said. "But it's true. I've never felt he really was 'in love' with any of them. Maybe infatuated, though. . . . Do you think your wife is faithful to you?"

Jerry laughed. "I hope so."

"You just hope? You don't know?"

"How can anyone know? I think basically she is. There was one summer when she may have . . . I don't know. She used to come home pretty late, a bit high and flustered."

"But you didn't force the issue?"

"How?"

"Hire a private detective or whatever."

"No . . . What would be the point? That only makes sense if you're looking for evidence for a divorce case. I wasn't."

Lying in his arms, Penny began feeling attracted to him again. She tried to force Helen from her mind. "Apart from your being married," she said, "would you want to have an affair with me?"

"There is no apart from my being married, Penny. I'm married."

"No, I mean just . . . Say, Nira suddenly was run over or vanished into thin air?"

He pulled her closer. "Of course I would, then . . . I think you're wonderful. There are lots of things I can talk about with you that I can't with Nira—my work, my writing. But—"

"Jerry, listen, I know this is an awful thing to say, but, could we try it again? Please? I won't stop in the middle this time. I promise."

This time she slammed a door as hard as she could in the face of all her doubts and anxieties. She didn't try to come—that still seemed somehow impossible to her—but she let herself want him and move with him, and she didn't try and stop herself from crying out as he finally collapsed on top of her. She knew by then that it was too late. Despite whatever had happened or hadn't, she was in love with him.

Afterward, lying in his arms again, Penny felt a strange kind of manic excitement—whether from this realization or just the fact of it having happened, of their having weaved their way through so many false starts and missed connections. He had wanted her; it had really happened; she was here! She felt deliriously, idiotically happy. "Can I stay all night?" she asked.

"Of course."

"My sister will kill me," Penny snuggled against him, half-asleep. "I guess I should call her. She'll think I've been murdered or something."

"The phone's right here." Maybe out of politeness, he vanished into the bathroom while Penny called Helen. She saw by the bedside clock that it was two-twenty.

"Pen, my God, what happened? Where are you?"

"Listen, I'll see you in the morning, okay? I just wanted you to know I was safe."

"See you in the morning? What are you talking about?"

"I can't explain now . . . But I'm fine, everything's terrific."

"Listen to me . . . Are you in trouble? Just say 'sister' in your next sentence and I'll come to where ever you are and pick you up."

"I'm fine . . . Really. Promise not to worry?"

"Promise not to worry?"

"Helen, I'm thirty-five, okay? I feel extremely happy."

"Oh Christ."

"I'll see you around ten."

"I'm not going to sleep all night."

"Take a Valium. There are some in my cosmetic case. And hot cocoa. That'll do it."

When Jerry returned, he asked. "Did you get her?"

"She thinks I'm twelve years old!" Penny exploded.

"You look like twelve years old sometimes."

"How old am I going to have to get before she sees I can take care of myself? She probably thinks you drugged me and slung me over your shoulder and had your way with me before I could open my mouth."

He laughed. "It's funny. With all the women I've ever been seriously involved with, they've been the ones to make the first move."

"That's what Helen says . . . She says women always do."

"I thought she thought—"

"It doesn't make perfect sense . . . She has a lot of theories about things."

Penny slept fitfully. She hadn't slept in the same bed with anyone in a long time. The night with Cal she had slept, but that was different. Basically she was used to the solitude of her bed at home. Having a body next to her, the smell, the warmth, the closeness, was strange. In the middle of the night she woke up and found he wasn't there.

"Jerry?"

He came out of the bathroom. "I feel funny," he said. "I can't breathe!"

Penny panicked. Was he going to have a heart attack? "Maybe we could open the window," she suggested.

"You can't," he said. "I tried. They're jammed shut . . . and the air conditioner's broken."

Wanting to comfort him, Penny reached up and took his hand, drawing him back into bed with her. Touching him, it was as though a fire that had been guttering fitfully suddenly burst into a whoosh of flame. The darkness, the disorientation of being in a strange place crumbled the last shreds of her inhibitions, desire defeating conscience with scarcely a struggle. He kissed her hungrily everywhere, her breasts, shoulders. She felt electrified, dazzled by the fact that this was happening, that they were really there together, naked, alone. He guided her hand down to his genitals, and she stroked him slowly, wonderingly. He was already hard; she wanted him. There seemed no point or possibility in pretending. They made love greedily, hastily, but this time she shared that greediness. She clasped her legs around him as he gasped, his mouth open on her neck, coming a moment after she did.

"This is what I was afraid of," he murmured as she started vanishing into sleep.

Half of her mind tried to follow that thought and then abandoned it before she was certain he had actually spoken. When she opened her eyes again, it was morning and he was asleep beside her.

At breakfast he seemed nervous, totally different from the night before. He ordered rye toast and, when the waitress brought it, got mad at her and said he'd ordered whole wheat.

"I guess I must have a criminal mentality," Penny said cheerfully. "I don't feel at all guilty."

For a moment she thought he hadn't heard her. "Well, I do," he said finally.

"How come?"

"I don't know." His manner was curt and abrupt, as though he were angry at her.

They ate breakfast mainly in silence.

"So, I'll get the manuscript to you as soon as I can," he said in the same distant, abstracted way.

"You already did give it to me," Penny reminded him. "I haven't had time to read it yet."

"Oh, of course, I forgot . . . well . . ." He cleared his throat. "I hope you enjoy the rest of your stay in San Francisco."

"I think I probably will," she said, trying to smile.

"We'll be in touch."

He shook her hand. Penny looked after him as he walked away to the elevator. Was this how it was done? She had never committed adultery before and thought perhaps she didn't know the rules yet. Did you pretend the next morning it hadn't happened? Was that part of it?

"Men are strange," she announced to Helen upon her return.

"If it's taken you this long to figure that out," Helen said, "I should never let you out of my sight."

Penny gave her an abbreviated description of the night's events. "I don't regret a minute of it," she said defiantly. "It was an educational experience."

"You sound suspiciously detached," Helen accused her. "You're not in love with him or anything classic like that?"

"I could be," Penny admitted. "But he's not available . . . so there's no problem."

"Well, if he keeps on being not available like he was last night, maybe that *could* be a problem."

"It was a one-night stand."

"Doesn't sound like it."

"Why not?"

"You spent half the night talking, he practically faints dead away from guilt—"

"Do you think that was it? The hotel room was a bit stuffy."

"Bernie was the same way the first few months . . . I think unless he'd had a signed permission slip from his wife, he thought he should be drawn and quartered."

"I thought people weren't guilty anymore."

"Jewish husbands not guilty?"

"Jerry's not Jewish."

"They're all Jewish when it comes to adultery . . . except the Georges of this world, and who knows? Maybe George had his occasional twinges."

"I think I want to have an affair with him," Penny announced.

"What is it with you intellectual girls? Don't you save any brain-power for your life? Why him?"

"He's a nice person."

Helen just raised her eyebrows.

"Well, what do you want? Should I pick someone up who works at a gas station? You always said I was too much under Cal's thumb, and I should do something to retaliate, and a life without sex has no meaning . . . so I'm just taking sisterly advice."

"I take it all back. From everything you've said, he'd be more trouble than he's worth."

"If you met him, you'd like him, really. And his wife sounds awful. She's never there. She's always off with this business she has, designing clothes. She has affairs. She doesn't get along with his children . . . I feel sorry for him. Something happened in their marriage evidently, something painful. He wouldn't say what it was, though."

"Oy . . . you mean, he actually stooped so low as to feed you that 'my wife doesn't understand me' garbage?"

"No! You're making him sound like a stereotype."

"Wives *always* understand their husbands," Helen said grimly. "That's what they're fleeing from: the cold, merciless light of understanding. Better the foggy mist of sexual hopes."

"Am I a foggy mist?" Penny wanted to know.

"Probably . . . You probably sit there and listen, with that wide-eyed, eager expression. You know what would help a lot, Pen? If you stopped parting your hair in the middle. It makes you look like you've just stopped wearing braids, but you were afraid to take the next step."

"To you!" Penny said. "To him, I'm a seductress, a woman of the world . . . Anyway, I did what you said women had to—I made the first move."

"*He* got you up to his hotel room. *That* was the first move."

"That wasn't a move," Penny insisted. "He just needed to find out if he'd gotten any messages on his answering service."

"Bullshit . . . suddenly at eleven-thirty at night, he has a burning desire to call his answering service? Next thing you'll be telling me, there weren't candlelight and violins."

"There were," Penny acknowledged. "But he didn't *put* them there. They just happened to be there."

"Just wandered in out of the rain, huh?" Helen snorted.

"I thought you'd be proud of me . . . except for the stopping in the middle part."

"That was the one sensible thing you did all night."

Penny helped herself to another honey bun. "I admire his mind. He's a wonderful writer, a feminist even, in a sense."

"Those are the worst," Helen said. "Did he actually have the gall to call himself a feminist?"

"No! But his book—"

"Forget his book. He just tossed in some little feminist overtones to make it saleable.

"My sister, the cynic," Penny said, loving her.

"Call it what you will. I am merely wise in the ways of the world, my dear. . . . Marry George for a few years and you will be too."

"You can't stop me from doing anything I want to," Penny said.

"True," Helen sighed. "Okay, jump in . . . but remember, I'm refusing all middle-of-the-night phone calls when you meet his wife and discover she's pregnant with their millionth child and he told you they never have sex."

"He never said that . . . and she's forty something."

All day Penny found herself wondering about Jerry Gardener's wife. She sounded so self-assured and sophisticated, coming home high from having been with a lover, flying off to Paris to start her own business. Penny imagined her as the kind of woman who would wear a felt hat turned down dashingly at the brim, who would have one of those real leather attaché cases with a gold monogram. Two children, two stepchildren, that beautiful apartment on the East Side. I hate her, Penny thought. God, how awful, to hate someone I've never met!

Helen was right. This had been a mistake. It hadn't been a one-night stand, and it didn't look like it would be much of anything else. The trouble was that suddenly she felt like being sexually involved with someone. Had it been seeing Cal again and realizing how hurt she really was by his lovers, no matter how lightly he did it, no matter what "fools" they were? She did mind, horribly, and always had and always would. And, as though retrospectively, the pain of that recent night with him came back to her—his arms around her, Karen's scent clinging to him, his needing her in that same childlike, demanding way he always had; her needing him. She didn't think of Jerry Gardener as a revenge; but in some way his seeing her as desirable had stopped the pain of Cal, had taken away, however fleetingly, that inner image of herself as the neuter, the sexless, brainy, self-controlled girl who'd read *Moby Dick* in two days and written Cal's history essay for him because he didn't have the time or the energy. With Jerry Gardener she was, instead, some echo of his waif-like first wife. Curious that, where everyone else saw her as so efficient and organized, he chose to join her with someone who was drifting and vague. The other side of the coin, the person she might have been, but hadn't let herself become.

She found the author who had promised them the manuscript. He was a Japanese man, small but imperious looking. "You have come to track me down?" he said, smiling genially.

"Not track you down," Penny said. "We just wondered how it was coming along. I'm out here visiting my sister and I thought, if part of the manuscript was complete, I might take it back with me."

"It is complete," he said. He handed her a black box. "It has been complete for a year, but I wished to let it rest before it entered the world."

"Oh," Penny said, wondering how much longer he would have let it "rest" if she hadn't appeared.

"I am sorry for any inconvenience," he said. "You will find it needs no editing. It is a perfect manuscript."

"How convenient," Penny said. "That will save me work."

"Yes," he agreed. "You should not have to work so hard."

She had tea in his garden. An Oriental woman, housekeeper, mistress, or wife, hovered in the background, rarely speaking.

"I am glad you came in person," he confessed. "I do not trust the mails."

"My sister lives out here," Penny said.

"You have many sisters?"

"Just one."

"I, too—just one." He pointed in the direction of the house. "My sister."

"I thought that might have been your wife."

"No wife."

"I'm sorry," Penny said. "That is, if you would like one—"

"I have had three . . . Time to stop, no?"

"Why, necessarily?"

He leaned forward. "With my work I have perfect judgement. With women I have no judgement."

"Do you have children from any of your marriages?"

He held up six fingers. "And grandchildren. Eighteen! Are you impressed?"

"Very."

"I tell you, it is strange—the grandchildren are the best part. Not the wives, not the children . . . but the grandchildren. Unexpected, but true."

"And your sister?" Penny asked. "Has she ever been married?"

"No, she is in love with me." He announced this calmly, with neither pride nor regret. "She is like another wife. She protects me from my fourth mistake. She is my watchdog."

Penny noticed, when the sister reappeared, that she did indeed have a watchful, suspicious expression, as though afraid Penny might have ulterior motives in coming to see him. "She seems very . . . attentive," she said when the woman had made her cautious disappearance again.

"Very . . . Perhaps I should have married a Japanese woman. All three were Occidental."

"It's not too late to try again," Penny said.

"You are proposing?"

"No." She laughed. "I am married."

"But no ring?" He gestured to her hand. "Why no ring?"

"I don't like rings."

He nodded. "Yes, you see, it is that spirit I have always admired in American women . . . that lack of convention. And yet it has always gotten me into trouble. Led me down the garden path, as you say?"

She took the manuscript carefully, as though it were a Ming vase, and put it in the backseat of the car she'd rented for the week. "Thank you for the tea."

"Thank you for the company. I like you. That is good. I like the no-ring. Very American, very honest." He put his head to one side. "In the event of your divorce, you will let me know?"

"I'll send you a card," Penny promised.

"I need a fourth mistake," he mused. "Life with my sister is so calm."

Penny spent the rest of the day walking around San Francisco. She had arranged with Helen to return home two hours before her flight left for New York. If she could get away early, Helen promised, she would come home first. If not, she would meet Penny at the airport.

Penny packed and sat in the empty house, reading the paper, and then she dozed off, waiting for Helen. The phone rang. She went into the kitchen to answer it.

"Helen?"

"No, this is her sister, Penny. She's at school now."

"Penny! How about that? Hi, it's George."

"Oh, hi, George."

"Listen, what a terrific thing that you're there. Out for a visit?"

"Right. I—"

"Pen, you've got to do me a favor, will you, honey? It's Helen's birthday next week and I'm going to get her this gorgeous robe I saw in a store in Hong Kong. But I can't remember her size. Will you go up and check? Look in her closet?"

"She's a ten," Penny said, not having to check. She and Helen had always been one size apart.

"You're a doll. How does this sound to you? It's light green—for her eyes, you know—pure silk, the real McCoy, with a high collar, what they call a Mandarin collar. She looks great in that style, doesn't she?"

"Yes," Penny said, remembering. "She does."

"Did she tell you she made law review? What do you think of that? Six kids, forty-three, and she ousts all those little snot-nosed kids right out of college. I wasn't surprised, mind you. What a woman! Are you proud of her?"

"Yes, I am," Penny said. "Very."

"There's no one like Helen," George said. "Believe me. I know. I've been around a lot. No one . . . She's going to look gorgeous in that robe, I know it. She deserves a robe like that. It costs three hundred dollars, but a friend of mine's going to try and get it for me at a discount. Do you think she'll like it? It's sea-green. That's what they call it."

"I think she will," Penny said.

"So, how's life, Pen? Still married to that actor?"

"Yup."

"No kids, still?"

"Well, he lives in L.A." Penny said. "So it might be—"

"Have them," George said expansively. "Have them anyway. Kids are great."

"Well, but our income has always been a little uncertain," Penny said.

"It is? Helen never told me that. How come? Hey, listen, you want to have a kid? I'll lend you some money. Just tell me how much you need."

"That's generous of you—"

"Listen, it's nothing. Business is good . . . It'd be a pleasure. You just tell Helen and she'll send me the bill. No, wait—let me give you my address. Have a kid. You'll love it. You're like Helen. She's the greatest mother ever. You'll be too. I can tell. You girls were made to be mothers. Did you know Helen never even had anesthetic? Those babies just slid right out. She has perfect hips. Born for it."

"George, I'm going to have to hang up," Penny said. "I'm flying back to New York this afternoon."

"Well, I'm glad I got ahold of you . . . Don't tell Helen about the robe, okay? I want to surprise her."

"I won't."

"She's going to look fantastic," he said. "I know it. Sea-green is her color. It's the mermaid in her." With a laugh he hung up.

At five Helen had still not appeared. Penny put her suitcase into her rented car, locked the house, and set off for the airport. As she was checking in, Helen came running up. Bernie, her lover, was with her. He was tall and round, bearded, an affable, shy man with rimless glasses. As Penny recalled, he had six children of his own and an alcoholic wife, who ran a health food store and had inherited two million dollars from her maternal grandfather.

"I'm sorry, hon," Helen said. "I couldn't get away. Are you okay? Did you get the manuscript?"

"Yeah . . . Should I become the fourth wife of a Japanese historian who lives with his sister?"

"Does that require an answer? Pen, you remember Bernie?"

"Hi, Bernie," Penny said. She went with them to have a drink before the plane.

"By the way, George called." she said, sipping her daiquiri. "He has a surprise for you for your birthday."

Helen looked from Penny to her lover. "I'm so glad both of you actually know George. Because no one else would believe in him. Whenever I describe him, I can tell everyone thinks I'm exaggerating or even making it up. What's the surprise this time? Did I tell you what it was last year?"

Penny and Bernie shook their heads.

"A fur coat . . ."

"What kind?" Bernie asked. He let the foam settle on his beer and drank.

"It wasn't mink, it wasn't ermine, it was some fluffy, soft, little brown animal."

"Beaver?" Penny suggested.

"No."

"Chinchilla?" offered Bernie.

Helen raised her hand. "Nutria, that was it . . . A nutria jacket. Now George knows, or might have picked up the information in fifteen years of marriage, that I despise furs, object to them, hate them. I told him I was going to take it to a thrift shop and sell it. He said, 'Fine, just don't take anything under twenty thousand.' I mean, this from a husband before whom I actually had to go down on my knees to beg for a dishwasher. Can you picture that? *Me,* on my knees?"

"Not for a dishwasher," Bernie said, smiling.

Helen snorted. "Great. You mean, you can picture me on my knees for other things?"

"I can't," Penny said.

"George loves women to go down on their knees for him," Helen said, bemused. "The symbolism of it incites him to amazing acts of kindness and humanity . . . like washing the dishes. . . . So I wonder what it'll be this year. A yacht? An island in the Adriatic?"

"It's *my* money," Bernie said. "I'm glad he's using some of it on you."

"Isn't it Shirley's, really?" Helen asked.

"Her grandfather's, if one wants to be precise."

"That is what I call recycled money," Helen said. "It's like Monopoly. George was always great at Monopoly. He beat all the kids. When he didn't, he cried." When she went off to go to the ladies' room, Bernie said, "She's wonderful," and finished his beer.

"I wish George would get out of her life," Penny said.

"He never will," Bernie said. "He'll probably come on our honeymoon with us, if we ever have one."

"Do you think you will?" Penny asked.

"Sure. Someday, if I could only find someone for Shirley. She's not a bad wife, really. Do you know anyone?"

"Would she be interested in a thrice-divorced Japanese historian?"

"Could be . . . She likes little authoritarian men. Is he short?"

"Diminutive."

"Her first husband, the one who died the first year they were married, was five feet two. Give me this guy's number."

"Won't she let you go unless she has someone else?" Penny asked. "Is that it?"

"Partly . . . Also, apart from wanting to murder me and all those classically wifely sentiments, she has this thing about Helen. She feels she should have gone to law school and done everything Helen's doing."

"Why doesn't she?"

"She'd rather complain about the miseries of being thwarted."

"The pleasures of martyrdom?" Penny suggested.

"Precisely . . . What's George's present *this* year? Did he say?"

"A sea-green silk robe. He says Helen looks beautiful in green."

"She does," Bernie said, looking dreamy. "It's her eyes."

Helen hugged Penny as she was about to pass through the screening booth. "Beware of men who write feminist books," she whispered.

"Beware of ex-husbands who buy nutria jackets," Penny whispered back.

She waved at Bernie, who took Helen's hand and stood with her, smiling, his fingers entwined with hers, as Penny hurried toward Gate Eleven.

"I'm very pleased," Penny's boss, Judson Benedict, said. "It's as good as you say." He had read the manuscript by the Japanese historian, which Penny had gone over during her first weekend back. To her surprise, it was as close to perfect as the author had promised.

"Worth waiting for. I'm afraid if you hadn't bearded him in his den, we'd have had to wait another ten years."

He had just informed her that she was getting a raise and a promotion: to associate editor. Penny knew it was no more than she deserved, but she was surprised. Nothing happened without reason, no matter how irrelevant. "It was a good trip," she said. "I had a chance to visit my sister and . . . Mr. Gardener was out there at the same time. We had dinner together." Trying—in whose eyes?—to put a professional gloss on it.

"Yes, oh, I meant to mention that. Mr. Gardener seems very pleased, Penelope, *very* pleased with your suggestions on his manuscript. We had a little trouble with him on the earlier books, or book, I should say. I wasn't here when we did the first one. I gather he can be rather . . . Well, anyway, it's a peculiar book, and I'm not sure myself how I would have handled it. But if he's happy, then I am."

Penny took a breath. She wondered, hesitated, then said, "When did Mr. Gardener speak to you?"

"Oh, it was some time back. I've been meaning to mention it. Then you went away. It slipped my mind."

She was relieved. Not that it would have made her promotion undeserved, but it would have given her an uneasy feeling to feel his praise had been, in whatever sense, for services rendered. Prompted by that, she read his revisions that night. She had been putting it off because of the encounter in San Francisco, the fact of it as well as the awkwardness of the way it had ended, the way he had kissed her in the hotel room that morning and said, "I'll say good-bye to you here," as though CIA-men were ringing the lobby. Coming home on the plane, she had thought of it again—the reversals of mood; her tendency to misread his intentions. She wasn't sure who had been to blame. Just a confusion of motives on both sides?

Setting the revised portion of his book on the floor, Penny felt pleased. Not only had he made the book better, but he had taken all of her suggestions, the very ones he had so balked at when she had first presented them, had even taken them further than she would have dared suggest.

"I think it's wonderful," she said, having waited to call him from the office the next day. "I like the idea of their being twins. It explains a lot. And her anger when he fails to give her credit when the spokesman comes from the Queen. That's good. That's what I meant."

"I put it aside for a week," Jerry said. "And when I reread your suggestions, I could see what you said was all necessary. . . . Well, I'm so pleased! You seem like someone who doesn't mete out praise that unstintingly."

Penny laughed. "I mete out praise all the time," she said. "It's the lack of clarity that bothers me."

"Yes." His pause made her remark seem more meaningful than she had intended, almost an accusation. "I've gone ahead and done some more work. I thought perhaps—could I bring it out Saturday? I have to go to my office then."

"You can bring it to my parents' house," she said, giving him the address.

Another pause.

"How was the rest of your stay in San Francisco?"

"Oh, it was fine," Penny said. "It was a successful trip, all told." Suddenly everything she said seemed a double entendre. Get off the phone!

"Was your sister angry at you?"

"Angry?"

"You were afraid"—he stopped, as though fearing she didn't want any reference to that night—"she'd be waiting up for you with a rolling pin."

"She said, 'Beware of men who write feminist books.' "

To her relief, he laughed. "Quite right. . . . Is two o'clock all right? On Saturday?"

Penny went horseback riding every Saturday afternoon, usually from one to two or three, but decided she could do it slightly later in the day, after he left. In the winter there were few riders; she never had trouble getting the horse she liked best.

She was surprised, on Saturday, to see Jerry Gardener in jeans and a duffle coat. Somehow he had always seemed an urban type to her, whose main exercise might be taking the dog for a walk or strolling in a leisurely way to classes.

She brought him inside the house.

"It looks gigantic," he said, looking around. "You live here all by yourself?"

Penny nodded. "I only use the downstairs, really. It was my parents'. They bequeathed it to me when they died."

"And you don't—you could sell it and get a good price . . ."

She tried to explain. "I really love the country. I just like the quietness. I don't even mind being here all by myself. Everyone thinks it's crazy, and it is, probably. I like owning a house, too, and having land . . . I don't think I could live in the city."

"It gets pretty oppressive," he agreed.

"I thought you were a city type," she said.

"I suppose I am now, by default. But I grew up in the country. I miss it." He paused. "Well, my wife is talking about buying an apartment in Paris, so who knows?"

"Why there?"

"She and her friend Fay have a business, and most of their sales are in France. Fay's husband does a lot of business there too, so the three of them thought having an apartment there would make sense. It's true. Nira has to travel there pretty often—"

"Maybe she has a French lover," Penny suggested. "Tucked away somewhere."

"It's possible."

"You sound so casual . . . Wouldn't you mind?"

"Yes, I'd mind. But she's a free agent." He sounded angry. "Don't *you* mind about your husband?"

"I told you I didn't."

"That's hard to believe, that's all."

There was a tense silence. Penny stared at him, then smiled. "If she leaves you, you can have an affair with me."

He laughed. "That wouldn't be fair to you . . . Penny, listen, I've felt bad about what happened. It was my fault. I think I was giving out a lot of crossed signals."

"I don't regret it . . . Do you?"

"Not at all."

She tried to smile. "So, no problem." She went into her study/bedroom, which was near the kitchen, and returned with his manuscript. "By the way, thanks for putting in a good word for me with Benedict. I got a promotion . . . and a raise."

"Not on my say alone?"

"No, but it helped." She hesitated. "I was glad you did it before San Francisco."

"I wouldn't have done it afterward."

She smiled.

"No, I mean . . . There was no connection—" He looked embarrassed.

"I know." She handed him the manuscript box. "Just keep on going," she said. "It's so much better. I was really relieved. You seemed so—obdurate at first."

"I tend to be . . . But then, so do you."

"Yes," she agreed. "That's why we'd be a terrible combination."

"Do you think so? I don't. We'd work it out. . . . What I meant to say before was just, I don't feel it showed a tremendous amount of strength of character on my part."

"Which you pride yourself on?" she said teasingly.

"To some extent. Anyway, it seemed taking advantage of your situation, my being married, you—"

"*I'm* married!" Penny exploded. "Listen, cut that out, okay? I've been married twice as long as you. *You're* just a rookie."

"But your marriage is so—"

"Stop that! I have the marriage I want. I'm as married as you are. I'm not some guileless, dopey single girl."

He was regarding her seriously. "You do have a certain guile-lessness."

"I don't . . . You're dead wrong. I'm terribly calculating. I plan everything out. Please don't start that waif-like thing again . . . I just hate it when men do that!"

"Do what?" He looked taken aback by her outburst.

"That idealizing of women, seeing them as types . . . the inno-cent, the guileless one. It's all just total garbage! I wanted to go to bed with you and I did, and I don't want to hear another word of phony apologies."

He put up his hand. "Not another word."

"Hey, my sister went out with your brother," Penny said, taking herself in hand. "Did you know?"

"No, how strange. When?"

"A week or so ago. . . . Want to see her letter?" She went back into the study and showed it to him. Helen had written:

"Dear Pen,

An oddity of the last week was my 'date' with your writer-friend's brother. He called unexpectedly, and I thought, what the heck. Did you know he'd been a monk for twenty years? Just what I need! Anyway, he's incred-ibly handsome, wonderful blue eyes and, I guess, enough stored-up libido to start a forest fire. Who'd have thought it and all that. No, seriously, it was interesting. He's very peculiar in many of his views. I guess at this point I don't have the intensity for what he's looking for. I'm not sure he's too clear about it either . . . Is your friend that good-looking? If so, I understand.

Sorry, by the way, about being so heavy-handed about the big-sister bit. It's just you came home looking so idiotically radiant. But you can handle yourself (she said nervously).

Hey, and George's sea-green robe is out of this world! He got my size right for a change. Bernie says I look like a Chinese empress. What would we do without men? (If you have an answer, call collect. Otherwise—)

Much love,

Yr affectionate sister."

"That's very unexpected," Jerry said, amused. "I never thought he'd call her. He'll probably never mention it to me."

"Don't you talk about personal things?"

"Not much. . . . Your sister sounds nice, perceptive."

"She is." Penny glanced at her watch. "Look, I have to go."

"Where?"

"I go horseback riding every Saturday, and Sunday too if the weather's good . . . Want to come?" She threw this out cavalierly, assuming he wouldn't know a horse from a cow.

"Sure I'd like to," he said. "I haven't ridden in years. But I used to, when I was growing up. My parents had a lot of land, and they kept a few horses."

"You don't seem the type."

"You put *me* down," he said, "for typing women. And you do the same with men. What 'type' am I supposed to be?"

"You know . . . urban, scholarly, intellectual, in bad shape physically, maybe an occasional game of tennis or squash."

"Thanks." He got into the car beside her. After a moment, he said, "I used to be a damn good squash-player actually, until my heart attack."

"When was that?" She felt bad for teasing him.

"A few years ago."

"Do you still play?"

He shook his head. "If I play the way the doctor says I have to, it's no fun. If I play the way I'd like to, I'll die . . . It's pretty clear-cut."

She thought of his saying, "I can't breathe," in the hotel room and felt, retrospectively, alarmed. "What brought it on?" she said, driving down the road which led to the stables. It had snowed two weeks earlier, but most of the snow had melted by now, leaving the ground sodden and black.

"A lot of things . . . My father died at fifty-five of a heart attack, so I suppose it's partly heredity. But also, there were a lot of family problems at the time. My older daughter was extremely depressed, suicidal really."

"How old was she?"

"Seventeen."

"Did she actually try and do it?"

"Yes."

Penny kept her eyes on the road. Finally she said, "I tried to, when I was around that age."

He turned to her in surprise. "I'm sorry."

"It was such a long time ago. I—" But she found, to her surprise, that her voice was shaking.

"Was there any special reason?"

"My parents died in a car crash going to my graduation. I guess—well, I must have felt responsible, somehow. I didn't in any rational way, but . . . They were in perfect health and—" They were at the stables. Penny stopped the car and sat for a moment, shaken by the unexpected exchange. He was staring at her, but in a sympathetic way. "We're both all right now," Penny said suddenly. "And that's what counts, isn't it?"

"Right." But he seemed withdrawn, not speaking, as they went to select their horses.

Penny liked the ride through the meadow. It was far off the main road, through a large apple orchard, past a small stream which bordered on the woods. There was a path through the woods too, but in the winter she preferred being out in the open.

He rode well. She stopped glancing at him anxiously when they came to an abrupt turn. "It's lovely in autumn," she said. "When the apples fall on the ground. I love that smell, when the horses step on them. It's like perfume."

They didn't talk much, but she felt a relaxed, pleasant kind of intimacy in sharing this with him and was glad, after the tense moments of the morning.

"My daughter did a lot of riding at one time," Jerry said.

"The one who was depressed?"

"No, my younger daughter, Stacey. She's more athletic in general. Now she's a terrific skier, goes almost every weekend . . . Jane is more like me, living in her head."

"But she's better now?"

"Yes, it all passed. She has a boyfriend. They're living together." He hesitated. "She'll always have problems. But I hope if she marries someone who can look after her, who'll be protective. . . ." His voice trailed off.

Penny noticed that he referred much more often to his own children than to his stepchildren. Maybe that was always true. Blood ties, whatever.

Back at the house, she handed him a towel. "There's a shower down here," she said. "I can use the one upstairs."

In fact, she hadn't used the upstairs bathroom in months. The tub was dusty and the water came out slightly rusty at first. Penny washed herself with the bar of soap that had been there for over a year, pine-smelling. She felt conscious of her body because he was in the house with her, and thought of him downstairs, washing himself. Guileless, sure.

She came down the stairs as Jerry was leaving the bathroom.

"Those are nice photos," he said. "Over the sink. Did you take them?"

She nodded. He looked clean, his hair slightly wet from the shower. "I'm sorry it's so cold in the house," she said. "I keep it down to 65."

"I don't mind."

She walked over and put her arms around him. "I'm being calculating," she informed him. "I want you."

He embraced her, but hesitantly. "Penny, I think we should make up our minds what we're doing."

"Why?"

"Well, there's an inconsistency in—"

"Consistency is the hobgoblin of petty minds," Penny said. "Or something."

Jerry smiled, letting his hand run down her back. "Where do you sleep?"

She pointed to the bedroom. "And I have a down comforter. All the comforts of home."

They threw off their clothes hurriedly and ducked under the comforter. "Your body is wonderful," he said, touching her.

She kissed him everywhere, smelling the same pine scent on him as was on herself. Her body felt limp and relaxed already, from the riding. She lowered herself on top of him, easing him into her. For a moment she lay like that, her head on his chest, listening to his breathing. "It's hard for me to go slowly this way," she whispered.

"That's okay." His arms were holding her buttocks and he helped her move so that they rocked in rhythm together. "My beautiful Penny," she heard him say, but his voice seemed far away. She felt as though they were in the meadow still, the comforter enclosing them like a cocoon. When she came, she arched back, wanting to feel him more, then slumped against him, breathless. His skin felt hot and moist.

"You need a lover," he said after some time.

"I guess."

"I wish so much it could be me . . . if things were otherwise."

"It is you right now," Penny said. "Please don't start in again about your marriage, okay? I get it. I understand. Everything doesn't have to be that . . . precise."

He was stroking her hair, parting it with his fingers. "Do you sleep and work in here?"

"It's odd, I guess . . . since the house has six bedrooms upstairs . . . but I like the compactness of it. Since I got the stove, the house stays warm."

"It's a nice stove."

"What I like," she tried to explain, "is the continuity—that my parents lived here, that my children might if I have any. I know this is going to fit into your image of me as some weirdo out of Emily Dickinson, but at Christmas I get all these ornaments down from the attic. My mother had all these special displays she used to set up, wooden dolls and glass figurines. I do it the same way."

"I understand that. My parents sold the house I grew up in. My father's no longer alive and my mother's in an old-age home so . . ."

Penny stretched. "Do a lot of women proposition you?" she asked.

"No, none that I can think of."

"I thought they did a lot, nowadays."

"Well, if one were single, perhaps . . ."

"Predatory divorcées and so forth. None of those?"

He smiled. "If one wanted to make a thing of it, there are women who give out an aura of availability, but that's about all."

"Did I? Give out an aura of availability?"

"Not at all . . . rather the contrary. A distance, a sense of an invisible line one mustn't cross."

"I thought I was babbling on so much in the car that day."

"You seemed to want to talk . . . That's different."

"What *is* an aura of availability?" Penny wondered. "Parted lips, languorous smiles." She made those gestures, liking teasing him.

He bent down to kiss her. "Right now you have an aura of availability."

She laughed. "I thought I looked formidable and precise."

"Not with your clothes off."

They stayed in bed most of the afternoon. Penny brought in tea and sandwiches on a large enamel tray, apples, honey. They talked, listened to music. Was it better or worse that, in addition to the sexual bond, they got along so well? Worse, the image of Helen pronounced unequivocally. Where other people had a Conscience, she had a Sister.

When they made love again, it seemed more natural. He had stopped, for the moment, justifying and explaining: she had stopped, for the moment, trying to decide whether this was a terrible mistake or the opposite. He smiled as she nestled back against him. "All this sex," he said, kissing her. "I'm not used to it. I'm just a chaste husband."

"Do you and Nira . . . Is that part of your marriage good?"

"Yes. We still . . . That hasn't died out. It's partly just that she travels so much now. When she comes back, it's like taking up a thread that's been broken. We look at each other almost in surprise . . . and then gradually it's okay."

"I think one reason I've never wanted to live in L.A.," Penny said, "is I resent the sexual power Cal has over me when we're living together. It's just there. It isn't that he creates it or even misuses it . . . but I find I start acting toward him the way I did at the very beginning, creeping around silently if he's in a bad mood, feeling terrified and responsible if he's angry. . . . I've gone out there so many times determined to act differently, and maybe I do for a day or two days. And then it comes back."

"Nira had that with her first husband," Jerry said. "Maybe when people marry young, those patterns are set up and hard to break."

"Was it like that with you and your first wife?"

"Yes," he said reluctantly. "I was overbearing or, at any rate, distracted, not there for her a lot when she needed me. I didn't think of it that way. I was tremendously busy at the lab; I had to work long hours. I just assumed she would manage everything at home. I couldn't understand her messiness. I'm not that neat myself, but I'd come home and there'd be piles of dirty diapers all over the apartment; the stench was incredible. That was her only way of expressing how angry she was, I guess. She acted the way you say you did . . . creeping around, glancing at me furtively."

"And you think it's different in a second marriage?" Penny wondered aloud.

"Well, one is usually older, maybe not quite so vulnerable and needy and blind, in good ways and bad. I guess one could set up an identical pattern if the need to was strong enough. I don't think I have, though. . . . It's just these gaps, the sexual neediness they create. It's a different kind of problem. Even if sex isn't quite the pressing issue it was when one was younger."

"You could have a mistress," Penny said. "I could be your mistress." She liked the idea of that, of herself in such an unlikely role.

Jerry smiled. "I don't know if that works for Americans. Maybe because we marry out of romantic love."

"I probably wouldn't be good at it, anyway," she decided, abruptly reversing herself.

He looked dreamy. "I think you'd be wonderful."

"Really?" She tried mentally stepping back, trying to see herself from another angle. It didn't work. "I always thought mistresses had to come dancing out in black lace camisoles with roses between their teeth, beckoning enticingly, that sort of thing." She sat up. "Jerry, really, maybe it would be a perfect solution for both of us . . . so we're American! We still could. It could only be when Nira's away and when Cal isn't here."

"It's a tempting thought, but . . ."

"I think we should, really. We get along. It isn't like we'd be setting up false promises or expectations. We're both married. It seems so even."

"It wouldn't stay that way."

"How do you know?" She felt impatient at his resisting her.

"Because I did it . . . That's how Nira and I . . . She was like you. She thought it would just be a fling."

"I bet she just said that," Penny said crossly. "She probably was trying to snare you all along."

"I don't think so . . . I think she felt her marriage was giving her a lot of problems she couldn't handle and I seemed like a solution. Unattached, available."

"Okay, but that's the point," Penny said. "You *were* available, so it had that sense of possibilities. But if both people are married—"

"You're trying to program it out . . . You can't.

She pounded her fist on his chest. "You're so stubborn!"

He laughed. "And you're not?"

Penny collapsed on the bed again. She stared silently off into the distance. "I don't know what to do about my life," she said, as though he weren't there.

Jerry touched her gently. "Penny." As she turned to look at him, he said, "You go so quickly from one extreme to the other. A moment ago you sounded so sure of everything."

"It seemed . . . But you don't really need me."

"I can't afford to let myself, not in that way. I'm not being altruistic. It's for me. You haven't been through it. You don't know how painful it is, watching a marriage dissolve. I don't want to take that chance, no matter what the odds."

"Okay." She felt as though he were drifting off to sea on a raft, getting smaller. "I started falling in love with you . . . But that's not your fault."

"I started falling in love with you . . . That's not your fault either."

She brightened up. "We can still like each other."

Jerry laughed. "Definitely." He started getting dressed.

Penny lay under the covers, watching him. "And maybe occasionally—"

"Sure. You're such a tenacious creature. Tenacious and tempting."

After he left, she dozed and awoke feeling desolate. The house seemed empty and cold. Penny took a hot shower and then, for dinner, prepared herself a special meal, as though she were a guest, and even opened a bottle of wine. I'm still a nice person and I deserve nice things, she told herself.

The next morning, when she went horseback riding, the owner of the stable handed her a small leather case. "I think your friend dropped this yesterday," he said.

Penny opened it up. It was mainly credit cards, Jerry's driver's license. She put it in her pocket. "Thanks," she said.

But before getting on the horse, she took it out and flipped through it more carefully. Toward the back there were several photos. She looked at them as though for clues—to what mystery she wasn't sure. What did she want or hope or even expect to find? One was of Jerry and a woman Penny felt certain was his wife, perhaps on a honeymoon, on a trip anyway. He was wearing a straw hat which looked like hers, and she was feeding him wine from a Chianti bottle. He looked young and silly. In that photo his wife's face was blurry, turning away from the camera. But there was one of both of them and their children, more a formal portrait where she was more visible. Although the children were mingled together, it was clear which were hers and which his. Hers were dark-haired. The younger one, who looked about twelve, was dressed in a beautiful, long dark-velvet dress and looked grave and impish at once. Her older daughter stood close to her, holding her arm. His older daughter had her hand in his in a proprietary clasp. She was very fair and too thin, squinting into the camera. Penny recalled his saying, "She lives in her head, like me." There was a slightly detached, pained expression on her face. The other blond girl, his younger daughter presumably, sat cross-legged next to the impishly pretty one, looking over at her with an expression that combined camaraderie and envy. She too wore a long dress, but it hung limply on her, and she had the end of her long velvet sash coiled tightly around her finger. Who was the chubby baby, though, that squatted cheerfully in the foreground, her head a mass of curls, her round arms and legs as succulently pink as peaches? He had only mentioned four children. A cousin, perhaps? Penny looked at his wife. Like the daughters, her dark hair was cut short. She looked elegant in her embroidered blouse, but more pensive and pretty in a more unconventional way than Penny had imagined. Though her arm was linked with her older daughter's, her hand was in Jerry's, and she was looking at him, rather than at the camera. What was her expression? What was she thinking?

Penny took the photo out. On the back someone had scribbled: Wedding day, October 1972.

Spring-Summer 1971

"Try and stick it out a year," had been Fay's advice to Nira about the job. Her reasoning was that, given the hiatus, the long time in which she hadn't worked, Nira had to try hard not to appear flighty, not the sort to up and bolt at the slightest provocation. Despite that, after her weekly fights with her boss, Sol Fishbein, Nira fantasized about other offers and leafed through the employment section of *The New York Times,* imagining herself climbing the unstable ladder to career success.

Not that her entanglement with Mystique Sports Wear had been an out-and-out failure. In a way, the fact that they were aiming so low, were so uncertain about what they were doing, gave her a certain freedom. The problem was that Sol never remembered what issues he had backed down on, and often looked with totally innocent indignation at what he concluded was Nira's insubordination. "But you said those buttons were all right," she explained, wondering how an hour-long fight a mere week ago could have so totally slipped his mind.

"These buttons?" His mind always seemed to be elsewhere—where, she had no idea.

"He's had a lot of . . . mental trouble," Murray had explained once when Nira couldn't resist describing her confusion to him. "His father killed himself, he had a breakdown . . . you've got to make allowances, okay, hon? He's a good guy. He just needs to prove himself; he needs to feel he's good at something." His assumption that his partner's "mental problems" would be beyond her ken touched Nira. Did she, then, strike him as so put together and sure of herself? Or wasn't she quite a person to him, since he came into the office so rarely, only to "see how things are doing."

They were friends in a funny way, Murray and Sol. Although they were the same age, Murray acted as though Sol were a younger brother, made allowances for all his mistakes, even when they were costly to the business. When Murray talked on the phone to their clients, he was brusque, abrupt, imperious. With Sol his voice lowered. It became gentle, almost pleading. And Sol, who looked most of the day as though he were on some drug that wasn't working, his eyes darting, his forehead glazed with perspiration, seemed to try visibly to pull himself together when Murray appeared. "Listen, don't tell him about the buttons," he would say to Nira. "It's not the money, but I only want him to know about the good things, okay? He's a worrier. He may not look like it, but Murray has a heart of gold. I'm not kidding. I don't mean just as an expression. He'd cut off his arm for you, if you wanted."

For me? Nira wondered. But she did not let her mind dwell much on either of them. When she was at work, she tried to think of nothing except getting back the expertise, and with it, she hoped, the self-confidence she had had in her early twenties. There were days when she felt she achieved that, when fantasies of doing something more creative danced merrily, mercilessly through her head. And other days when it seemed some skill lost forever, acquired in youth due, perhaps, to nothing but youth and bravado, surely not merely lack of experience and a couple of design courses at Parsons. The more you know the less you know. Was it her father who said that? Someone. A downward path to wisdom. She hoped it didn't apply to everything. At times she felt it might.

It seemed she knew less about children, having three, than she had as a young mother pushing her baby in the park. Less about husbands, having been married nearly sixteen years. Less about love now that she was in it. Less about sex than when, a virginal seventeen, she had mooned over *Lady Chatterley's Lover* and tried to imagine the possibility of orgasms that would make her fall, helpless, at someone's feet.

Summer was coming. Soon, at the end of April, she would have to open the country house. They started going weekends in May. Of course, this summer she would have only a month off, whether she quit before or after August. She would have to hire a mother's helper to stay with the children if she intended to go in for job interviews. And what of Saturdays with Jerry? How could that be rearranged? Nira juggled excuses in her head. A course on something? French cooking lessons?

"I could say I need to take a refresher course in something connected with my work," she mused aloud to Jerry one Saturday. It was close to time for her to get dressed and leave, past four. Outside a light summer rain fell.

"Ni, there's something we have to talk about."

"There is?" His calm, precise tone of voice frightened her.

"Claire's agreed to let me have the children for the summer," he said. "She's going to Europe to see her parents."

"That's nice," Nira said, trying to curl her mouth up into a smile. "When will that be?"

"The end of May, probably, not that far off."

"Will they be staying here, with you?"

"Well, that's the thing. There's no room here, obviously. I was thinking of looking for a new apartment, but then this thing came up . . . You remember how I told you I was trying to get sabbatical leave for a year? To try and test out the teaching thing, to see how I'd like it? Well, they agreed." He looked eager, excited. "I have off till January. So . . . I'm going to rent a house in Princeton. I have a friend that teaches there, Sam, the one who'll teach part of one of the courses with me. He's the custodian of Einstein's papers, but he teaches a few history-of-science courses. I thought it would be nice for the kids, being in the country. The schools there are good."

"Won't Claire want them back in the fall?"

"Maybe . . . She seemed very vague, said she might not be back till October, maybe later. She's like that. I think she wants her freedom again. That's okay."

Nira tried to breathe normally. "That sounds ideal. Did you say you had a house already?"

"No, I'm going out tomorrow to look."

She frowned. "It's sort of a long drive . . . from New York."

"Yes."

"I can do it, though . . . My driving's getting better," she said brightly, as though that were at stake. She remembered a friend who had told her about the session with the doctor at which they had told her she had cancer. She had described how, sensing what they were going to say, she had a peculiar sense of deja vu throughout the whole conversation, even though, in fact, she had never gone through anything similar before. The doctors, misinterpreting this, had commended her on her calmness.

"Well." She took only a small pleasure in the amount of difficulty he seemed to be having trying to say it. "It's not the drive, really." He looked at her, almost pleading, wanting her to help him out.

I won't! Do it yourself. "What is it, then?" Trying to look innocent, unaware.

"I think we should stop seeing each other for a while."

"Okay," Nira said too quickly, a giveaway. "Any special reason?" Maybe, though unlikely, she could get through this acting bright and cheerful, and collapse once she was outside.

"I just feel this whole thing isn't fair to you. I think you should try and talk to Adlai, try and figure out what's going on in your marriage. Otherwise—"

"Otherwise what?" Nira said, feeling the anger shooting up like electric shocks.

"The point is"—he was conducting this like a scientific meeting—"you both are hiding so much from each other. You'll never have a marriage that's worth much unless you're more open."

"We want that kind of marriage," Nira said, wishing neither of them was naked, that they were sitting, upright, in a restaurant. Perfidious skin. "We're both perfectly happy with it."

He frowned. "How can you say that? You've told me so many times how unhappy you feel, how it seems like a farce."

"That's just what marriage is like!" Nira said, trying not to look at him, knowing she was not going to make it out to the street before collapsing.

"It doesn't have to be."

"How do *you* know? Look at yours! You don't know anything about marriage. How can you give me advice?"

"I knew enough to get out when it wasn't working," he said.

"Wonderful. So, now you're an expert? You're a marriage-counselor? I can take care of my own damn marriage, Jerry. It's none of your business."

"Okay." He looked upset himself, which made it harder for her. "I just want you to be happy," he said softly. "And I feel—"

"Oh fuck that!" Nira said. "You want whatever will make *you* happy. If I were lying on the road and you had to run over me to get there, you would."

"Am I that bad?" His voice was ironically but gently aloof. Oh, she hated him! How could he do this half an hour after making love to her? What was wrong with men? After a moment he said, more calmly, "Some of what you say is true. I do want to think of myself, of trying to get my life back in some kind of shape. I need some stability, not only for me, but for the girls. They'll probably be living with me permanently. I don't want them to have a father who's running around crazily with married women. They need my undivided attention. If I keep on with you, they won't have it."

Aha. Her true rivals. Nira recalled them at the wedding—their grave, pale beauty. "Carry me to bed, Daddy." "So, you'll give up sex for their sake," she said. "And live celibately ever after?"

"No, of course not . . . but I do want to give them a settled home, a parent who loves and cares for them in a solid way they can count on. Does that make me a monster?"

"No, it makes you a saint." Nira leaned against the headboard, hugging the pillow in front of her like a shield, for protection. "Jerry, listen, there's something here you're not telling me. Do me the kindness of being honest, okay? Is there some other woman? Someone you'll be seeing out there?"

She had hoped for a "No, don't be silly. You women think only of rivals." Instead, after a long and overly weighty pause, Jerry said, "Yes, there's someone."

"Who?"

"Paige, that woman who used to visit me last summer. She's been away most of this year, in Boston . . . But she has a job in New York now and—"

"Is she divorced?"

He nodded.

"Have you been sleeping with her this year?" Her voice rose, despite herself, threatened to crack. "Did she come in ever to see you?"

"Yes . . . occasionally."

Nira dug a sharp end of her fingernail into the palm of her hand, as she did at the dentist, to distract herself from the pain. "Well, it sounds perfect. A job, a new lover, you've got your kids, a house . . . You really will live happily ever after."

"Are you angry about her having come in while I was seeing you?"

Nira opened her mouth and didn't find words. They had scattered somewhere.

"Look, Ni, you're right to be angry in some ways . . . But you weren't available for *me* either. Once a week isn't—"

"Sure, I was just using you, just getting laid once a week." She leapt to her feet. "You need someone who's there all the time—to wash your feet in hot water and lemon juice every night, to understand your work, to do all those little lover*y*, wife*y* things. Every man needs that." Her sarcasm was like tossing jelly beans at someone armed with a machete.

"That's not what I'm looking for."

"What *are* you looking for?"

He cleared his throat. "Someone to love me whom I can love; someone who'll be there for me in some kind of undivided way."

If you don't get out of here in two minutes, you're going to be a basket case. Nira began getting dressed with frantic speed, not caring if everything was inside out, if buttons burst. The wetness slid down her leg, the smell of sex assaulting her. "I guess we all want that," she said, not looking at him. "Good luck, Jerry—in getting it, I mean."

He reached out for her. "I want you to have it too," he said.

At his touching her, Nira wanted to cry. "I will," she said. "Sure. Why not?"

He held her while she cried, stroking her over and over, and she felt the sexual sparks start up again between them, even after the anger and accusations, like a dead frog's legs jerking even when detached from his body. She ran out of the apartment, not looking back. She didn't want to go home now; she couldn't. And have Adlai see her like this? She called him from a corner phone booth, rehearsing her words over and over. There was a movie she wanted very much to see, she would say. She'd impulsively bought a ticket and was in the theater. Would it be all right if she skipped the evening at the Dawns'? Could he make an excuse for her? She was too tired, not up to it. She would see him later.

But he was out. Heather answered the phone and promised to deliver the message.

I want to die, Nira thought, walking along the park which looked beautiful and fragrant. "Bad things always happen on nice days," Posey had once announced. Die, then. It's easy. It's the easiest thing in the world. All the old fantasies came back to her. She saw herself effortlessly jumping from windows, vanishing. But what she had found in the hospital was that no one really did want to die, even those who had discovered wonderfully inventive, seemingly foolproof methods. Being suicidal meant very little, after all. Just another way of saying something, a way other than words. But having little to do with wanting to leave the earth. Everyone just wanted it to be different, wanted another kind of world. You'll get through this, she told herself, less as a pep talk than as a fact, a mother telling a child, based on experience the child might not have had yet.

The weeks that followed had a zombie-like quality, drifting somnambulistically together. Words from their fight zigzagged through her mind while working, shopping, making love, sleeping. "Running crazily after married women." Were there others, then, beside her? "Yes, occasionally." What was occasionally? Every month? Every two weeks? Phone calls in between? "Who's that woman in the photo, Jerry?" "Well, she's kind of desperate and—the sex is good." "Better than with me?" Her dreams of suicide were replaced by hopes that Jerry would be found dead. Each day she flipped eagerly to the obituary section. "Molecular biologist killed in head-on collision with . . . married woman?" Was he important enough in his field to merit an obituary? Maybe his death would be announced more quietly, in those rows and rows of people who had done nothing significant enough to take up much space? But she failed to find his name there, either. Such unlikely, unnecessary deaths—a girl she'd known, dead at twenty-six of cancer; a friend killed by food poisoning while on his honeymoon in Spain; her childhood friend, a photographer, mowed down by Arab guerrillas while taking photos of birds on a beach in Israel. Why not him? Come on, God, you don't care about justice or sense. Just flip your little lever.

She played the scene again and again in her head. He was driving to Princeton. But who was in the car with him, and how should *they* die? His daughters and Paige? Nira hesitated. No, she would spare them, she decided magnanimously. They would be in the car, but would not be hurt. Only he: sudden death. She would spare him, even in fantasy, hours of agony bleeding on a highway. Thanks, Nira. Just a quickie, one for the road. And his last thought of her.

God was always out to lunch when appealed to. That same God who had failed, generously, to strike her down for committing adultery evidently didn't feel Jerry's crime deserved punishment by death. God was wanton, the only true amoralist. No wonder her parents had been atheists.

For the first time in years Nira found herself consciously missing her father. He would have understood, would have petted and stroked her and called Jerry an unfeeling, no-good bastard. He would have railed against him, pounded his fist, threatened to get his Mafia-connected patients to "give him a little trouble." He would have taken her to a wonderful lunch at The Russian Tea Room and said she deserved, and would get, better. He would have guaranteed it! "You're beautiful, Nira. You look like Anna Karenina in that fur hat. Let me buy it for you." Coming into her room at night when she was a child, and making drawings in the dark with the lighted tip of his cigarette. The time in college she had wanted to kill herself. "Let me die with you, darling. I don't want to live without you." That got you into trouble, kid. Even Adlai had said, apologetically, "I can't love you like that." "I don't want you to." But sometimes, like now, it would be nice. "I will protect you from all harm." Promise her anything, but give her?

Comfort from friends. Fay:

"He sounds like a moralistic prig."

He is, he was!

"Men always do that. They can't just dump on you. They have to invent lofty excuses. . . . What does he know about marriage?"

"That's what I told him."

"Good . . . I'm glad you told him off. All that shit about his kids, trying to win your sympathy."

"I think he's fond of his kids." Why in the name of anything was she leaping to the other side of the net, taking his side?

"Sneaking that little journalist in behind your back."

"But I was having sex with Adlai all year."

"So? You're married. What else could you do?"

"I was enjoying it too."

"Listen, Ni, you're lucky. You're well rid of him . . . I've had men like that up to my ears."

Fay's tough-minded banter was cheering, though Nira knew she would have adapted her story to anything she felt Nira wanted or needed to hear at that time. That's what friends are for, right?

The baby had her first birthday, turned one amidst all this emotional clamor, untouched, fat, radiant. She sat in her high chair at the head of the table, the rubber band of her gold paper crown biting into her double chin. Heather and Posey sat at the decorated table, hats on their heads too, waiting until Nira brought in the cake with its two lighted candles. One to grow on.

"Happy birthday to you," they all sang, including Adlai, from the living room, where he was playing the tune on the piano. The baby, unaware of what was going on, unaware of deserving or not deserving this attention and gaiety, beamed at them all.

"She doesn't know how to blow, Mom," Posey cried, getting up from her seat. "She doesn't get it."

"She doesn't even know it's her birthday," Heather said languidly.

"Blow, baby, blow!" Posey coaxed, bending down to teach her by example. By chance she blew out the candles. "Is that okay, Mom? Now she can't make a wish. I'll make one for her." She smiled at the baby. "I made a good wish for you."

It was an all-chocolate cake, rich, heavy, thick with frosting. The baby, innocent of diets and cholesterol, stuffed large mouthfuls in, letting the frosting smear all over her face.

"I guess she likes chocolate," Heather observed, eating her own slice more neatly.

"She's going to be a chocoholic," Posey said. "Daddy, did you know there are people who are addicts for chocolate? Mom, she's reaching for another piece. Should we let her?"

"Sure, why not?" Nira said. "It's her birthday."

"Eating patterns are set in early life," Heather said. "She'll be fat forever."

"No, she won't," Posey said staunchly. She got up and blew her blower in the baby's face. The baby shrieked with joy. "You're a mess, you know that?"

Nira wiped Jasmine's face and hands with a wet towel. Her crown was askew, toppled royalty. "We'll save the rest for later," she said, clearing the plates.

"I'm going to take her for a ride," Posey offered. "She loves that."

"She's getting awfully heavy," Nira warned. "Can you manage her?"

"Sure." Posey bent down while the baby clambered onto her back, then went galloping around the apartment. The baby's cries rang from room to room. Her fair skin was as rosy as a piece of fruit about to split in the sun.

Later in the day Posey and Jasmine took a bath together. Nira went in to check on them. They sat, naked, their paper party hats still on. Posey had no figure yet, in the feminine sense. Yet her bud-like nipples and thin, stalky limbs were as beautiful, Nira thought, as what was to come. The baby was androgynous in her plumpness, the slit between her legs a decoration. Posey soaped the baby's belly and knees carefully. "She wouldn't take her hat off, Mom," she said. "It might get a little wet, but I figured it was better than having her kick up a fuss."

"I'm exhausted," Nira said to Adlai, stretching out on the bed. The temperature had shot, prematurely, into the eighties. The belt of her skirt felt tight. She had gorged on cake, unthinking.

It was a Saturday, a fact Nira had tried to ignore each time it arrived for the past month. Pretend it's Sunday, there's not that much difference. Did Adlai wonder or care why she was suddenly always available to take the children places if he was busy? He lay down beside her on the bed. Nothing has changed. See? Same husband, same children, same apartment, same job. You are the same person, whoever that person was to begin with.

"It's almost summer," he observed.

"Yes . . . I have to put an ad in for a mother's helper."

"Right."

The pause between them seemed strained, but she had stopped, long ago, trying to decide how much of that feeling came from her, how much from him.

"You deserve a vacation," Adlai said suddenly. "You've been working so hard."

"Yes," Nira agreed. "You too."

"Yes, well . . . And you'll start looking for something new over the summer?"

"What?"

"A new job . . . You'll start—"

"I don't know." Nira looked at the ceiling. "If something comes up." The summer stretched ahead like a wasteland. Who would rent the Richardsons' house this year? Nights with Adlai, sitting on the same porch, sipping wine, the children a year older.

"I want you to have a nice, relaxed summer," Adlai said.

Why was it so hard to talk to men? Nira wondered. When she was younger, she had thought it was because her neediness for their good opinion made her anxious and ill at ease in their presence. With women, not caring half so much if they liked her, she was relaxed and herself, in the good sense, almost always. Fay, acknowledging that men were harder to talk to than women, claimed Nira picked the ones who were even more difficult than the average. It was true. The challenge, definitely. Her heart rushed out to the handsome but mournful ones who were dressed impeccably but looked ill at ease, imprisoned. She, in her fantasy, would come charging up, Princess Charming, and with a delectable, irresistible blend of warmth, sex, intensity, melt down their reserve and make them deliriously happy. Oh, those illusions. You cannot "make" anyone happy. But along the road to realizing that hard fact were the momentary triumphs which, evidently, made it worthwhile, created the impetus to charge, unheeding, toward the next victim.

She did all that was expected of her: opened the country house, found a mother's helper, outfitted the children in summer clothes. Ninety to ninety-five percent of each waking day she thought of Jerry. At first she railed at herself, furious at her inability to tear him from her mind. In which lobe, which section was he imbedded? But then she accepted it. He was there. He would be there for a long time, whether she ever saw him again or not. At times she conversed with him mentally, as though they were not estranged. She asked his advice, as she had in the past, or just described things to him, told him how things were going. At those times he might have been some favorite uncle who lived in another state. The bad times were at night when, not content with occupying her daytime life, he invaded her dreams and she awoke with tears streaming down her face or, once, with her hand between her legs as her body gave way to an unwilled, unwanted orgasm. Look, you take things too seriously. Presumably that has some advantages. This is one of the disadvantages. Ten years from now you will not be thinking of him all the time. He may be a vague memory, something to reflect on in tranquility.

A friend, Alice, passed through New York on her way to a summer vacation in Maine. Three years earlier, after a tempestuous affair, she had left her children and married her divorced lover. Now, she related, that marriage too was breaking up.

"Why?" Nira asked, half-pleased at this story. A morality tale, perhaps.

"It should have just been an affair," Alice explained. "I wanted out from my marriage and I couldn't—I guess it's me, our generation, whatever—I couldn't leave without another man on hold. I made him into something I wanted."

"Was it the sex?" Nira asked tremulously. "Was it so good that it blinded you to his faults or something?"

Alice reflected. "The sex was lousy actually."

"Really? How could it have been?"

"I don't know . . . it just wasn't great sex. But I wasn't looking for sex, anyway. I guess I was looking for—you know, something magical, something that probably doesn't even exist."

Her voice had turned so flat and melancholy that Nira just stared at her. "Are you sorry you did it, then?" she ventured. "Do you wish you'd stayed with David?"

Alice sighed. "No, I guess . . . I'm not sure *what* I wish. I think I wish I'd waited. Seen Uli, but also seen other men. I was too scared! And the dumb thing is, I'd be the same way if I had it to do over. You can't remake your personality."

Walking home, Nira tried to construct a moral—helpful if possible—from Alice's tale of woe. Don't rush into things? Look before you leap? There is a difference between someone you can have a good affair with and someone you will want to marry? But lousy sex? That was strange. Or was that just the bitterness of hindsight? "You're lucky, Ni," Alice had said as they parted, hugging each other. "Value what you have."

"Oh, I do," Nira said.

"David was a . . . Adlai's such a sweetie. Listen, you think out there, there will be piles of marvelous sexy men. Forget it. They all died a few centuries ago."

"No, I know," Nira promised her. "I'm devoid of illusions."

Sure.

They were to leave for the country on Friday, July 12th. Nira packed, made arrangements, took the girls for doctors' appointments.

They were excited. "This year I'm going to teach Jas to swim," Posey said.

Nira was poised somewhere between anticipation and dread. She hoped it would be a relaxed, quiet month, time to focus on Adlai whom, presumably, she had been neglecting on some level. Not in any gross "I'd rather not tonight, dear, I have a headache" way, but in some way. Maybe he had noticed. She had no idea. And maybe Jerry was right. No need to confess but maybe trying to be more honest would be good. Talk about essentials, whatever they were, discover sides of each other that had become submerged under parental and marital duties. It wouldn't be frolicsome, but it might be good anyway. And you've achieved something this year, she tried to reassure herself. You did get back in the work world, you did find something, even if it was imperfect, even if it ended. Jerry had loved her, she felt, which in some ways made it worse, but at least she hadn't been ill-used in any classic way. Yes, he was right. He did need a full-time person, someone to count on. But that virtuous she could not be, even in thought. Let him not find that person, she still begged. Please. Let her be disappointing. Let her hate his kids. Let them hate her. Make her give him VD. You have imagination. Do whatever you like. But don't let him have an ecstatic, fulfilling summer with a perfect person. Okay? You can spare his life, but don't give him a perfect person.

Adlai, with the aid of the doorman, was loading their station wagon. Heather and Posey were sitting in the backseat. The baby was buckled into her car-seat. Nira was to sit in front, next to the baby, while Adlai drove. Midway, she might take over the driving. It was a beastly day, over ninety-five, a good day to be leaving the city. Luckily they had air-conditioning. The back of the car was stuffed with suitcases, toys, baby equipment. Adlai and the doorman discussed the logistics of fitting in the last box of paperback books.

"Uh . . . there's something I forgot," Adlai said, coming around to where Nira was sitting.

"What is it?"

"The camera."

"Wasn't it on top of those books? I thought I put it there?"

"No . . . Ni, would you come up with me and look for it? You might have put it someplace else."

Nira unbuckled her seat belt. "Sure," she said. "Kids, keep an eye on the baby, okay? Po, could you come in front with her till we find it?"

They rode up in the elevator in silence. Inside the house, Nira went to the kitchen where she often placed things that were not frequently used. Adlai followed her. It wasn't there.

"That's odd," she said. "I was sure—"

"Ni." Adlai touched her shoulder.

"What?" He looked sick, as though he might faint. "Are you feeling okay?"

"Yes, I . . . Could you sit down a second?"

"Why should I sit down?"

"No, you don't have to, but . . . Look, I know where the camera is. I just . . . I wanted you to come up here because there's something I have to tell you."

Nira stared at him, uncomprehending.

"I'm not going with you today," Adlai said. "I'm going to England . . . I'm going to be there all summer, till Labor Day."

"What?"

"I'm sorry, Ni. I should have told you earlier. I just . . . I couldn't bring myself."

"But what am I going to *do?*" Nira cried breathlessly. "I don't get it! How can you be going to England for the whole summer?"

Sweat was pouring off his brow. He kept wiping his forehead. "Look, Ni, I'll write you about all this when I get there."

"All *what?*"

"I'm in love." He said it desperately, like someone confessing to tax evasion, or murder even.

"With who?" Her terror was glazed over with amazement. In the moment before he spoke, her mind raced crazily over every woman he had flirted with at a party. The one he'd met at an airport in Seattle and taken to the Brooklyn Botanical Gardens? The girl in the publicity department who, he confessed, had propositioned him on a business trip in Boston, but whom he had nobly turned down—so he had claimed at the time? One of, God forbid, her friends?

"Do you remember Serena Bassington?"

"No!"

"She was, she was one of Jeremy's friends at Oxford and she . . . Listen, I can't talk about it."

"Tell me who she is." The hysteria she had been trying to hold down came bursting out.

He collapsed in a chair. "Well, she was married to Oswald Garth."

Despite herself, Nira burst into uncontrollable, painful laughter. "You're making up these names!"

"I'm not . . . He was a prominent art historian. He was crippled in a car accident. They had four children and he . . . Well, he died last year, and I went to see her, to offer my condolences, and we. . . . I don't know." He jumped to his feet again.

"You're spending the whole summer with her?" She felt like collapsing herself. The air seemed to have gotten thinner. Just getting out a sentence made her chest feel as though it were about to explode.

He nodded. "I have to, Ni . . . I'm sorry. I just . . . I love her."

"You said that." She couldn't bear that word *love*. Couldn't he have substituted, just out of politeness, *infatuated*. "I have a crush on her; I'm smitten with her." Couldn't he at least—God, there should be an Emily Post for adultery—have started off, "I know this is some form of craziness, mid-life crisis." Anything!

"I can't tell you how rotten I feel. But I just have to be with her. She told me it was unfair to you, not telling you. I wanted to, Ni. I've wanted to for months, but you seemed so preoccupied with your job. I didn't want to just add another burden."

Nira buried her face in her hands. "I don't know what to do," she whispered.

"Sweetie, I'm so sorry," Adlai said. "Really."

"How can I drive out there with the kids?" Nira said, the thought of them waiting innocently and patiently in the car pierced her. "Can't you leave next week?"

"The plane leaves in two hours."

"Cancel it . . . Put it off," she pleaded.

"I can't." He sounded irritated. "I've planned it months ago. This isn't an impulse."

Nira sat stunned, unable to take in the information. All that was coming through was: how could she survive this afternoon? "What should I tell the kids?"

"Just say I—tell them I had some unexpected business."

"But if you're not there all summer?"

"I'll call . . . We'll work something out. Maybe they can come over to see me." He looked at her uncertainly.

"No!" Nira said. "They're not going over. That's that. Forget it. You'll see them when you get back, if you get back." She liked the sound of her tough, hardhearted voice. It was like another person unexpectedly appearing and coming to her aid.

"I feel so awful about the girls," he said softly.

"But not awful enough to cancel?" Nira looked at him with contempt.

He ran after her as she ran to the door. "Nira, forgive me, please." He clutched at her, like someone begging for a loan.

"Oh God." Nira fell on him. Contempt and anger gave way to confusion, grief, and terror. She got into the elevator and waited as it stopped to let on extra passengers on the fourth floor. I don't know if I can do this, she thought. You can. What if I crash the car? I don't know, I don't know.

The girls looked up as she opened the car door. Posey was feeding the baby animal crackers. "I think she needs to be changed," she announced.

"We don't have time," Nira said grimly.

"There's pee dribbling down her leg," Posey said.

"I can't help it," Nira said. She got into the driver's seat.

"Where's Daddy?" Heather asked, putting down her book.

"He's not coming." Nira started the car, turned on the air conditioner, and started across the park.

"How can he not be coming?" Heather said.

"He's just not," Nira snapped.

"Where is he going? Is he going to stay all by himself in the city?"

"He's going to England."

"How come, Mom? Why's he going there?" Posey wanted to know.

"Because he's in love with someone!" Nira said, not wanting or even trying to lie. "He's in love with someone and he wants to spend the summer with her."

There was a stunned, appreciative silence.

"How can he be in love with someone?" Posey wailed. "He's married to you."

"Is she his girlfriend?" asked Heather. "Does Daddy have a girlfriend?"

"She's his girlfriend," Nira waited, then moved behind a truck that seemed stalled. "And her husband died, and she has four kids, and her name is Serena Bassington."

Posey giggled. "Is that really her name?"

"She just said it was," Heather said angrily.

"How come he picked someone with such a funny name?"

"I don't know," Nira said. She paused. "I have a funny name."

"Mom, this is serious," Heather said. "Is he going to marry her?"

"Hon, I haven't the faintest idea . . . I just heard about it five minutes ago."

"Daddy's a shit," Posey said.

"He is not," Heather said loyally. "He can't help falling in love with someone."

"Why not?" Posey said, echoing Nira's thoughts. "Why *can't* he help it? She had a husband . . . I bet she's mean and ugly."

"Why would Daddy like her if she was mean and ugly?" Heather questioned. "Mom, do you have a picture of her?"

"No," Nira said.

"What does she look like? Is she pretty?"

"I haven't any idea."

Posey leaned forward, her breath on Nira's neck. "What are we going to do, Mom? Are we going to try and get him back?"

"How?" Nira asked. "What would you suggest?"

Posey thought. "We could fly over and bring him back."

"You are the dumbest person in the whole world," Heather said in exasperation. "She just said he's in love with her. He doesn't *want* to come back."

"Doesn't he want to be with us?" Posey said. "Doesn't he want to see us all summer?"

"Maybe he'll send for us once he gets there," Heather said.

Just let him try, Nira thought.

"Mom, listen, I have a great idea," Posey said.

"What?"

"When does Dad's plane leave?"

"In about two hours."

"Well, let's drive to the airport and buy tickets, and we can all fly over with him."

"Posey!" Heather heaved an adult sigh. "If he wanted us, he'd have taken us." She sounded bitter. "He doesn't want us."

"Do *you* think it's a good idea, Mom?" Posey pursued.

Nira found that tears were flowing down her cheeks. "I don't know, hon."

Her voice was so shaky that the girls noticed.

"Are you okay?" Heather asked anxiously.

"I don't know."

"Maybe we should pull over at a snack place," Posey suggested.

"Yeah," Heather said quickly. "That's a good idea."

Nira nodded. "Tell me if you see a sign."

They drove in silence until Posey cried, "There's one, Mom . . . there!"

Nira pulled over. She sat, weeping, her head on the steering wheel. Posey patted her neck. "Don't cry, Mom," she said softly.

Heather handed her some Kleenex. "Daddy'll come back," she said faintly, unconvincingly.

"Look, Mom," Posey said. "The baby's crying too."

Nira looked up and saw the baby, still buckled in her seat, tears streaming noiselessly down her face. She fell on her, and the two of them wept in each other's arms, like lovers, like parents whose child has died. Heather wedged them apart.

"We'll all feel better when we've had something to eat," she announced briskly in the voice of her English grandmother.

"Yeah," Posey echoed. "And something to drink too . . . But let me change Jas first."

Nira stood by, silent and drained, while the baby was changed. The four of them found an unoccupied table and ordered ice cream sundaes.

"Did you know about it all along?" Heather asked tentatively. "That Daddy wasn't coming with us?"

Nira shook her head. "He just told me before . . . Remember when he said he couldn't find the camera?"

"Boy, is that a crummy thing to do!" Posey said, delving past the whipped cream to the chocolate ice cream underneath. "No warning, even!"

"I guess he felt guilty or something," Heather deduced.

"I guess," Nira said.

"He should," Posey said with hearty vengeance. "I hope he feels so guilty he has a rotten summer. I hope she drowns and all her children too!"

"That's not nice," Heather said. "She might be a nice person."

"I don't care," Posey said.

"I wonder what she's like," Heather mused. "What do you think, Mom? Do you think she's nice?"

Nira considered. Serena. What came to mind was a slimmer, younger version of her mother-in-law—fair-haired, serene, a round face, mild-mannered, a fussy mother, soothing, pouring tea, flowered Liberty lawn dresses, heavy legs. "I think she's a bitch," she said.

"Me too," Posey said. "I bet she's a real bitch."

"Why would Daddy like her then?" Heather wondered aloud.

"Maybe she's rich," Posey ventured. "Is she rich, Mom?"

"I don't know," Nira reached over and scooped up some of the baby's chocolate sundae.

"Yeah," Posey said. "I bet she's like a millionaire or something."

"Millionairess," Heather corrected.

"She probably lives in a castle and has horses and stuff like that," Posey embroidered. "And servants to do everything."

"But why would Daddy like that?" Heather said.

"Why shouldn't he?" Posey said. "*I* would . . . Wouldn't you like to live in a castle?"

"No," was Heather's prompt reply. "Would you, Mom?"

"Not really," Nira admitted. "But kids, she might be rich. I don't know, but I don't think on that scale, quite . . . Let's face it. Daddy just fell in love with her."

"Why, though?" Heather persisted. She frowned. "I don't mean to be insulting, Mom, but do you think she's a lot younger than you? Angie's mother says they all trade you in for a younger model because they want fresh unwrinkled skin and stuff."

"Mom doesn't have wrinkles," Posey said staunchly.

"She has four kids," Nira said. "I don't think she can be much younger. . . . He may have just wanted someone nicer in some way."

"In what way?"

"Maybe someone who paid him more attention or something."

"You pay attention to Daddy," Heather said. "Don't you?"

Nira started to cry again.

"Mom, come on, seriously, pull yourself together," Heather said. "We aren't even halfway there."

Nira choked back her tears. "I know, I'm sorry, kids . . . This is really a disgraceful performance. I was supposed to just say Daddy was detained on business."

"I'm glad you told us," Posey said. "I hate it when parents lie."

"Do you feel up to driving?" Heather wanted to know.

"Sure," Nira said.

"I'll sit in front and talk to you," Posey offered. "Jas can sit in back."

"Thanks, Po . . . That would help."

Oddly, the rest of the trip was peaceful, even pleasant. Posey made interesting cheerful conversation, and the effort, the desire to please, comforted Nira as much as the actual words. The baby listened to Heather read stories, dozed heavily, and pointed out the window every time they passed a cow. "Moo," she said.

"Right!" Posey said. "Mom, did you hear? I've been teaching her. She knows eight animal sounds. Jas, what does a horse say?"

That night, after a hasty dinner, they all went to sleep early. Nira felt no desire or ability to think much beyond the moment. When she awoke the next morning, after a sound sleep, she lay in bed peacefully, content. Something was bothering me yesterday, she remembered. What was it?

But once the day got under way—shopping lists, instructions to the mother's helper, Mary, a round-faced, dogged-looking girl—Nira still felt that, between herself and what had happened, a slight emotional gulf existed. It was as though she had been told a good friend had a serious illness and felt guilty at not having gone to visit her. I'm glad he's gone for the whole summer, it'll be easier. She would see what life without him was like. Maybe it was all much exaggerated. Maybe women could manage perfectly well on their own. As long as there's money. That bothered her—that, when Adlai finally called, several days later, she could not, even with virtue shining on her side, become quite as angry and irritable as she would have liked for fear: what if he deserts us? What if we're left with only my salary to manage on?

And, of course, the memory of Jerry, the fact of Jerry made her sense of virtue somewhat more tarnished than she would have liked. Still, she had not deserted the family. She had been discreet—furtive, some might say, but considerate, might say others. Not disrupting the flow of everyday life. The children knew nothing of her own escapade, and she was glad. Oddly, though it might have made it worse, it gave her some small, secret satisfaction. Someone had, for however brief a time, selected her, found her attractive. That was how she liked to look at it. But at other times during the day she thought: rejected by two men. Wasn't that worse?

The Richardsons' house this summer was occupied by two middle-aged gay men, Tim and Blake. Tim had been in design. Blake was an architect. They were extremely, almost egregiously, nice and seemed to enjoy the children. Posey took to having weak gin and tonics with them in the late afternoon. They took both her and Heather to horror movies at the local drive-in, since all four enjoyed them. Nira, in gratitude, had them over for dinner several times. The occasions were pleasant, but her pleasure was marred both by the memory of the dinner with Jerry the summer before and by a fear that she might become one of those women one heard about whose "best friends" were gay men. That was fine, provided there was, at the center of one's life, one firm, heterosexual tie.

How did people manage without sex? She thought of Jill, five years divorced, whose sexual encounters were, at best, spaced about six months apart. In between times, she claimed, she didn't even think of it. Everyone is different. Yeah, I know. Maybe in the winter it would be easier. But the warm, endless summer nights seemed made for dalliance, bodies entwined. If only she were old enough not to need it anymore. When did that happen? Ever? She remembered visiting her great-aunt's old-age home. Two men for every hundred women. Each man had at least four women fawning on him constantly. The moment one of the four died, ten would-be contenders shot into place. Shit.

Despite her hatred of New York in the summer, she was relieved when Murray Farber called, asking if she could come in that Friday. He hated to disturb her vacation but some problems had come up in connection with orders for the fall collection, papers misplaced.

"I may stay over till Sunday," she told Mary. "Do you think you can manage?"

"The baby's no trouble," Mary said. "And the other two are never here anyway." She disapproved of the freedom Nira gave Heather and Posey, who planned endless outings with friends, ties formed when they were barely older than Jasmine.

"Make sure they check in at night and bathe now and then," Nira said. "And their father may call Saturday night. Let them know."

She herself stayed virtuously far away when the girls spoke to Adlai. It was clear that, despite Posey's initial anger, she had been quickly won over by Adlai's promises of an eventual return. "It's just that he needed a vacation," she said. "I don't think it was that woman so much."

Maybe she was right. But what then of his looking so anguished, and those desperate blurtings of agonized love? Maybe, now that he had her, in every sense, every day, the bloom had faded. All that soothing tender care. It gets to be a drag. Nira was so peppy, so outspoken, so full of unexpected remarks. "Stop talking about your wife. I don't want to hear any more about her. She sounds like a wicked, unstable woman. A breakdown, having that affair." "I don't know she had one. She just seemed . . . distant at times." "Of course that was it! And you say she seemed not quite there during sex? How could she, with you such a marvelous lover?" "Am I?" "Yes, yes, wonderful." "Of course, Oswald was . . . and yet you never?" "Never, Adlai darling. I was his wife. I never, never, never even *thought.*" "Of course, darling." "And if we . . . marry, you can rest assured I will be yours forever. Not even a backward glance."

It was pouring rain when Nira got to the office, a heavy tropical rain that seemed to sizzle and steam off the pavement. Going up in the elevator, she felt a pang, suddenly remembering Adlai's remark that day of the baby's party. "You'll be looking for a new. . . ?" What had he meant? A new husband? A new job? A new lover? A new life?

"We're amazed, frankly, at the size of the orders," Murray said. "You were right, Nira, adding that line of suits. They're going over. Maybe a little extra quality can't hurt."

Sol was in the office in the morning, then disappeared. When Nira went to look for him, Murray stopped her in the hall. "He was having a bad day . . . . Can I help you?"

Together they searched for, and found, the necessary papers. It was late afternoon. Nira felt exhausted, but pleasantly so. This could have been any day, any ordinary day six months earlier. Except that, it being Friday, she would have been thinking ahead to the weekend, porno movies of herself and Jerry playing all day in her head while sketching, phoning, writing letters.

"I hate to even suggest this," Murray said, "but could you come in tomorrow? I don't know. I just didn't think we'd get this backed up."

"Sure, I'll come in," Nira said. She stopped and looked up at him.

He smiled. "Listen, it's your husband I should apologize to, but he can spare you for a day, can't he?"

"I don't have a husband," she blurted out grimly.

"You don't?" He looked startled. "I thought you . . . Don't you have three kids?"

"Yeah, but my husband took off. He has a girlfriend and he decided to spend the summer with her."

"No." He looked so genuinely shocked and horrified that Nira wanted to kiss him. He sat down in the chair next to her desk. "How could he do a thing like that?"

"I don't know," Nira said. "I guess he's in love with her or something."

Murray Farber shook his head. "Listen, take it from me, hon. It's never love. It's always sex."

"He called it love," Nira said.

"I don't care *what* he called it. He can call it a pastrami on rye . . . It's always sex."

Nira sighed. "Yeah?"

"Believe me . . . He'll be back. He just has to get it out of his system. You hang in there."

Tears began sliding down Nira's face. Oh God, no. The wailing wall. "I'm trying to," she mumbled.

Murray patted her clumsily on the back. "You poor sweetie," he said. "How could he do a *meshuganah* thing like that?"

"He needed to get it out of his system?" she repeated.

"That's no excuse . . . A beautiful young wife, three little girls. Shame on him! Do you have his number?"

"What?" Through her tears his face looked blurry.

"His phone number."

"He's in Europe," she croaked.

"I don't care. Give me his number. I'm going to call him up. I'm going to give him a good talking to."

For a moment Nira had the illusion that her father had come back to life in another form. "No, really, that's okay," she said. "I'm going to be fine. You see—," she tried to talk, stopped, but he waited patiently. "You see, I've been having an affair myself all year and—"

"You think he found out?"

"No, but . . . I just mean, I'm not a good person. I'm not a virtuous person. I don't deserve any—"

"Listen, Nira, of course you're good. He wasn't paying any attention to you. You needed someone who'd treat you with love, who cared for you a lot, right? Wasn't that it?"

Nira nodded, snuffling. "Yes."

He patted her, half-hugging her. "Look, you're a beautiful woman . . . and I'm not just saying that to make you feel better. Of course you wanted someone."

"But I've lost *him* too," Nira said. "He's divorced and he wants to get married and . . . I love him and I don't know what to do."

Murray was silent a moment. "You know what? You're going to come with me and I'm going to buy you a terrific dinner. You like seafood?"

"Yeah, I love it."

"You're going to have the best seafood dinner you ever ate, and you're going to share a bottle of wine, and you're going to forget all about these *shmendricks*. You got bad taste in men, Nira. Did anyone ever tell you that?"

She laughed. "I do?"

"Sure . . . They both sound like losers. You should have someone who treats you right, who makes you feel loved."

"Jerry did, in the beginning," she said wistfully, getting her bag.

"Who's Jerry? The husband or the other guy?"

"The other guy."

It was a wonderful meal. Nira drank too much wine, and felt sleepy and comforted. "You remind me of my father in a way," she confessed. "I don't mean that you seem old or anything, but he was like you. He always made me feel better."

Murray smiled. "Look, I'm getting false points. If you weren't gorgeous, would I be here?"

"I don't know . . . Would you?"

"You have beautiful eyes. . . . I noticed that right off, right when you came in for that interview. Blue eyes and black hair. I like that combination."

"Are you faithful to your wife?" she asked.

"Sometimes." He smiled.

"How about tonight?" She smiled at him. "Is that going to be one of the times?"

He looked uncomfortable. "I guess I've kind of set this up, haven't I?"

"Maybe . . . What's wrong with that?"

He took her hand. "You're such a nice person. I don't have the solution to any of your problems is all I mean."

"Solutions to problems turn into other problems," Nira said. "How about just for the fun of it? Or doesn't that seem like a good reason? Or is your wife home?"

"She's at our country house . . . I do feel extremely tempted, I must confess."

Nira leaned against him. The wine, his warmth, the long weeks of celibacy caused pangs of lust to charge through her. "You only live once," she reminded him.

"True." He grinned. "Okay, what the hell."

"It'll be an act of charity," she reassured him, finishing her wine. "I'm horribly horny. It's summer, something . . ."

"I know the feeling."

"You have a wife, though."

"Yeah, I have a wife . . . okay, so where should we go? Your place, my place?"

"I'd feel uncomfortable in our apartment," Nira confessed, "though that may sound silly."

"No, I feel the same way about ours . . . Listen, I know. Let's go to The Plaza."

"The Plaza? Isn't that horribly expensive?"

Murray shrugged, waving to the waitress for the check. "You deserve a nice experience, something you'll remember."

That was true; she did. "Okay." She remembered Fay's saying he had a lot of money. Why worry?

The room was gigantic, the bed big enough for ten. "We could have invited all my cousins from the Grand Concourse," Nira said.

"If they're like my cousins, I'm glad you didn't."

Nira took a long, hot bath, luxuriating in the sense of being taken care of. She had grown plumper since Adlai had left. Nights munching on Sara Lee chocolate cake, brooding over Jerry as well, had added at least five extra pounds to her figure. But she felt certain that Murray Farber would not mind. He would consider her well-rounded, Rubenesque, not blubbery and out of shape. She knew, instinctively, he would be the type who didn't mind a little potbelly, ample hips. Thus, emerging naked from the shower, she marched proudly across the room and enjoyed the way his face lit up at the sight of her.

"What have I done to deserve this?" he asked, welcoming her into his arms.

"Tomorrow you'll help an old lady across the street," she whispered, nuzzling against him.

Making love with Murray was pleasant, relaxed, comfortable. None of the piercing shocks of romantic love, the feeling of being torn apart, of sailing to the moon. They nestled together afterward, like a couple married fifty years, pleased at still being able to give each other enjoyment.

"Your husband will come back," he assured her.

"I don't think it was sex so much that drove him away," Nira said. "It was more . . . I don't know."

"He just got a yen for someone," Murray explained. "That happens. You're happily married, you're walking down the street, you meet someone and *whammo.*"

"Did that ever happen to you?"

"Yeah . . . and I survived. And my marriage survived."

"How about your wife?"

He hesitated. "I don't think she knew . . . or maybe she did and just kept it to herself. She's a very . . . She doesn't like scenes."

"Lucky."

"I am. She's great. . . . What I mean is, just sometimes, for no good reason, a man, no matter who he's married to, no matter how good-looking she is, a good mother, a nice person, whatever—"

"You marry an apple, and you want a pear," Nira said drowsily.

"What?"

"That's what my friend Ellie says. Then you get tired of pears and you come home."

He nibbled on her shoulder. "You're a pineapple. Sweet and juicy."

Nira sighed. "I feel good. This was nice, Murray. Thank you."

"Thank *you* . . . Will you sleep okay? Do you feel relaxed?"

"I feel terrific."

You would have thought he had two anorexic daughters in the room with him from the breakfast he ordered. Emerging from a shower, Nira saw a cart loaded with pancakes, bacon, hot muffins.

"I'll be so fat, I'll never get anyone," she said, munching contentedly.

"Men like a little flesh. You have nothing to worry about." He poured more coffee. "So, who's this Jerry? You're really stuck on him, huh?"

She nodded.

"And what's the problem? He's married?"

"No, he's divorced, but he wants—well, he wants someone full-time, someone he can really count on."

"When was he divorced?"

"Just a few months ago, I think."

"Okay, well, listen, there's your problem. You've got to give him time."

"I do?"

"Yeah. See, sweetie, when a guy gets divorced, he's been married, same woman, ten, twenty years, he needs time to fool around a little. He isn't looking for love, marriage right off the bat. He just needs a little foolishness for a year, two years maybe . . . then he'll be ready to settle down."

"Yeah, but—"

"Take my friend Monty. Now his wife died three years ago, four. They were happy, but she died. So now, you should see some of the kids he's gotten stuck with. My wife fixed him up with this lovely woman she's known for years—nothing. He visits us and who does he bring? This walking disaster area. Gorgeous, but an alcoholic at twenty-two! A beautiful girl, but trouble. You didn't have to be in the room with her three *minutes* before you knew: look out . . . But did he listen? Even to me? We've known each other thirty *years!* I took him aside. He said, 'Murray, so she's trouble? I *want* trouble. For twenty years I was happy. I want to do dumb things. Please don't try to stop me.' Do you get what I'm trying to say?"

"Sort of." Nira sighed. "But I think Jerry . . . It's not exactly the same. He's done a lot of dumb things already. He married someone like that . . . I think it's more he's looking for someone very stable, solid, a good mother—he has these two kids."

"Sure," Murray looked understanding. "Everyone wants that."

"I don't know if I am that, though," Nira said. "Apart from my being married."

"Sure you are," he said. "You're solid, you love your kids. . . . The way I see it, you've got to make up your mind what you want. If you could have either of them back, who would you pick?"

God, what a choice! Nira sank back in bed, exhausted by even contemplating it. "I miss Jerry so much I could die at times," she said. "But, for the kids . . . picking him would be selfish. It would be for me. I guess I'd have to say Adlai . . . But why can't I have both?"

He smiled sadly. "It doesn't work that way, sweetie."

"Yeah, I guess not." She stared at him mournfully. "I'll be lucky to get one of them back. Or half, even."

Murray leaned back on the pillow next to her. "So, what should we do? Here I brought you into the city to work."

"We could go in now." Nira looked at her watch. It was nine-twenty.

"I'll tell you what. We have the room till eleven. We might as well use it, right? As long as we have it?"

"Sure," Nira agreed. "It would be rude, just leaving ahead of time. They'd think we didn't like their service or something. They'd be heartbroken . . . We didn't even eat all the muffins."

He leaned over to kiss her breasts. "In twelve hours, I've broken my diet, been unfaithful to my wife, done something my best friend would kill me for . . ."

"Sol? Would he?"

"It's complicated. Let's not tell him, okay?" He slid down to her. "It's even my twenty-fifth wedding anniversary Friday."

Nira kissed him. "Happy anniversary . . . You're supposed to get things made out of silver."

"You're the best present I'll get, Nira. No doubt about it."

So, what did it add up to? And did it matter? They went back to the office. Nira worked hard, felt better, and realized, as Murray had predicted, that none of her problems was any closer to having a solution. But nor were they any further from it.

The summer continued as it had been. The girls active, playing. For them, once the fact of Adlai's absence had been digested, it was a summer like any other. What the baby knew, felt, or thought was anyone's guess. She kept her secrets hidden behind her mask of jovial, babbling geniality. Nira went into the city on Fridays to help out at the business. She and Murray never repeated their escapade, but it made her feel better, not worse, that he knew of her troubles and would ask, from time to time, "So, how's it going, sweetie?" and listened as she told him. Only once did she call Jerry's number in Princeton. His older daughter answered, and Nira hung on, just for a second, then lowered the phone, ashamed, into its cradle. At least it had been his daughter. Which meant nothing. Which didn't mean that upstairs, in his bedroom, he was not entwined with someone, entwined with a Perfect Person who knew the difference between DNA and RNA, and possibly even cared.

Usually she looked forward to Labor Day and the briskness and excitement of fall. Now all that lay ahead seemed to be worries. She would need a substantial raise or would have to look for a new job. And yet she hardly felt up to offering herself. Look, all they care about is your work record. They don't care, won't know about your private life. True. Her conversations with Adlai were usually perfunctory, just hellos before putting the children on. But finally he said that he was flying home at the end of August.

Nira, unable to interpret the tone of his voice, asked only what flight, what day.

"We can talk then," he said.

"Yes."

The children were beside themselves at the thought of his return, so much so that Nira felt guilty. If I had been different, he wouldn't have left. No! If *he* had been different, he wouldn't have left! If something had been different. She dreaded seeing him, despite almost looking forward in advance to the inevitable scene they would have upon his return. He would be abject, would beg her to forgive him for doing such a stupid, irresponsible thing. Should she be haughty and unforgiving? Or kind and melting? "All that counts is that you've come back." In her head she played both roles, savoring now one, now the other; Hedda Gabler or Desdemona?

She remembered his return the summer before—the night she had sat on the porch, watching Jerry's window, unknowing but already wanting him on some subterranean level. The light going off. The woman passing by, too far away to be seen distinctly.

The first three hours of Adlai's arrival were spent with the children. They told him of their summer adventures, greeted him eagerly, enthusiastically, seeming to have forgotten, almost, that he had deserted them. Nira felt a pang at that. Would *she* have been so easily forgiven? By him? By them? Did children have a double standard too?

"You look well," he told her, almost formally.

"Thanks." She hadn't spent hours in the sun, but she felt physically back in control, slimmer.

"Jas is so much larger," he said. "And she's speaking so much more."

"Yes . . . She's had a great summer."

He hesitated. "How was it for you?"

Nira shrugged. "I survived . . . I went into the city a couple of times. They needed me at the job." She looked at him. "How was *your* summer?"

The children were in bed now. She had planned not to force a confrontation, yet her question hung in the air with the force of a loaded revolver.

"We went to the Isle of Wight. Serena's family has a house there."

"It must have been peaceful."

"Yes, well." He smiled. "She has four boys. They weren't there all the time, but . . ."

Nira just stared at him, trying to be, or at least act, cool. "So, what will happen?" she said, unable not to be blunt.

"We want to get married," Adlai said.

Nira felt a shock wave pass through her system. She wondered for one second if he were joking. Or testing her. Did he want her to grovel and beg, plead for him to come back? Or had the time for that passed? In any case, she felt incapable of it. "When?" she stammered.

"As soon as I'm free to." He looked at her questioningly, obviously asking: will you make that difficult?

"And she'll come here to live? With all her children?"

"No, we'd live in England."

"But how about us?" Nira felt her throat go dry, her voice rise to a Mickey-Mouse squeak. "How about the children?"

Adlai looked at her. "I—look, I don't know what to say, Ni. I would take them, but—"

"What do you mean—take them?"

"I mean, I realize it isn't fair to you, having all three, but—"

"I want them!" Nira cried, in agony. "You can't take them!"

"I just thought—"

"How can you move there? What about your job?"

It seemed he had thought of all that, had in fact, been thinking of it all year. He had talked to various publishing houses in London. There was a good offer, equivalent to what he had here, with ties to America so he would have to travel back and forth fairly often. "And of course the children can come over in the summer."

For some reason this struck Nira as the final deviousness, his having set up an alternate job situation, having had talks about it all last winter when she had writhed in what now seemed totally unnecessary guilt. "How are you going to live?" she said. "Two families? Seven kids? You don't have that kind of money."

"Serena's family is quite comfortably fixed."

Nira laughed bitterly at the memory of the castle with horses. "Does that mean piles and piles of money?"

"More or less." He looked uncomfortable. "It's been somewhat of a problem for her, actually."

"In what way?"

"Well, you know, fortune-hunters, that kind of thing . . . Not that Oswald was, at all. They were evidently extraordinarily happy."

"Despite the—wasn't he in a wheelchair?"

"Yes, but . . . they loved each other very much."

Was that an accusation? Or a mere statement?

"She was totally bereft after his death," Adlai went on. "That was why I went to see her last summer actually. Jeremy's stayed in touch with them, and he was a bit worried she might . . . try to do something. She just locked herself up for weeks, didn't see anyone. The first time I went to see her, she hardly spoke, just sat and stared at me. She looked in a really bad way."

Oh, I hate her! Nira thought. I hate widows, I hate suffering rich women. I hate women with four sons. She imagined her in bed. The type with soft, white, silky skin. Never had orgasms, but said it didn't matter. "I just want you to be happy, darling. You can come in my ear, if that'll please you."

She felt nervously certain that at some point in the conversation he would turn to her and bring up Jerry. But evidently his own guilt had clouded any time or ability to focus on her. If he did not exactly grovel and beg for forgiveness, nor did he turn on her with recriminations and counter-accusations, and Nira, with Jerry at the back of her mind, could not bring herself to act shocked or horrified. You have broken our marriage vows! Begone!

"I feel we had a good marriage in so many ways," Adlai said, frowning. "I hate leaving you in the lurch."

"Oh, I'll find somebody," she said blithely. "Maybe I'll find a rich widower."

She had not consciously meant to be nasty, but how else could he take such a remark? He looked ironical. "You may not believe this, but actually Serena's money was more of an impediment than an attraction. It made me hesitate."

"It gave you pause," Nira said, remembering how she and Joel in childhood always guffawed over *it gave him paws,* acting like bears.

"You'll find someone," he assured her. "I know you will."

God, why was everyone so sure she'd find someone? As long as it's not me. "Can I use you for a recommendation?" she said, trying for wryness."

"Sure."

"But actually, I don't think I'll remarry," she said. "I can manage on my own. I'll just have a string of lovers of various races and religions—that might be more fun."

Adlai looked apprehensive. "I think, for the children, it might be best if . . . Well, of course, you have to do what makes you happy."

"Yes," Nira said defiantly. "I do." If only she could import a stoned teenager, preferably black, for the weekend, just to plague him with a few sleepless nights under Serena's flowered coverlet. Maybe Jerry's wife could lend hers, if she still had him.

Upon leaving he said that he would fly back to London, return in a few weeks. Lawyers would meet; arrangements would be made. "There doesn't have to be any ugliness," he said hopefully. "We'll always love each other, through the children, anyway."

We will? Nira searched her heart for such generosity of spirit and found, instead, a void. "You told the kids?"

He nodded. "I think they understood."

A pox on the understanding of children! What did they know of heartbreak and betrayal and crushed hopes, the guileless, forgiving beasts?

Dinner with the four of them, after Adlai's departure, was quiet, the girls eating with unusual speed and neatness.

"He showed us her picture," Posey said.

"What does she look like?" Nira asked.

Just as Posey said, "Pretty," Heather said, "So-so." "She's not a knockout exactly," Heather said dryly.

"I thought she was cute," Posey said. "She's little and she has long brown hair."

"I think Daddy's marrying her for her money," Heather said.

"Me too," said Nira, pleased at this suggestion.

"She isn't *that* rich," Posey said. "Is she? I thought he just said she was comfortable."

"That's a euphemism," Heather said. "I bet she's loaded."

"Yeah, I think she's loaded," Nira said.

"Still," Posey said. "That doesn't mean he's marrying her *for* her money. She could still be nice."

Heather wrinkled her nose. "Four boys . . . ugh."

"Do you think he's going to marry her for her money?" Posey asked Nira.

"Maybe not for," Nira qualified. "I guess he likes her too."

"He said she was . . ." Posey wrinkled her brow. "I can't remember."

"Sensitive, warm, and lovable," quoted Heather.

Nira cringed.

"You're sensitive, warm, and lovable, Mom," Posey said. *"I* think so. You're just not rich, that's all . . . You may have some problems finding someone."

Heather sighed. "You'll have to start going to singles bars . . . Angie's mother says it's murder."

"I am not going to be caught dead in a singles bar," Nira announced, reaching for a second ear of corn. "I'm going to fend for myself."

"How?" Posey asked, curious.

"There are many fish in the sea," Nira announced. "Anyhow, who needs men? We'll manage on our own."

"Angie's mother has a T-shirt," Heather said, "that says: A woman needs a man like a fish needs a bicycle."

That motto had always puzzled Nira. She wished it were true.

"Mom," Posey said. "Would you make sure you marry someone nice, if you do marry someone? Because Daddy was at least nice."

"And someone without kids," Heather put in. "There is nothing more sickening than stepchildren."

"If they're babies I wouldn't mind," Posey said.

"I *would,*" Heather said. "Babies are the worst!"

"I think teenage boys would be the worst . . . Mom, did you know she, whatever her name is—"

"Serena," said Heather.

"—yeah, her . . . she has twins . . . Only Daddy says they're the kind that don't look alike. One of them is color-blind and the other one collects butterflies."

"How come she married someone who was in a wheelchair?" Heather wanted to know.

"Hon, I never met the woman," Nira said. "I haven't the vaguest idea."

"How did they have sex?" Posey wondered. "It must have been uncomfortable."

Heather looked disparaging. "They didn't have to have sex *in* the wheelchair," she said. "Maybe they just did it the regular way."

"I guess she's glad Daddy's not in a wheelchair," Posey reflected. "I mean, she doesn't have to push him around and stuff like that."

"But that's the fun of marriage," Nira said. "Having someone to push around."

They both looked at her, puzzled.

"It was a joke," Nira explained. "Forget it . . . they'll probably live happily ever after." She got up to clear. "Watermelon, everyone?"

In front of the children Nira put up a front of jocularity, as much for her own sake as theirs. But that night she woke up at three in the morning, shaking, her body covered in sweat. She sat on the porch, feeling chilled and numb despite her warm socks and the heavy robe she put on over her nightgown.

She thought of the first few months after she had gotten out of the mental hospital. Before she had gone in, she had been frantic and depressed but in what struck her later as a hopefully crazy way— eager to grab at any suggestion anyone offered, picking up books to see if there was some cure for depression she hadn't heard of or tried, some drug, untested perhaps but miraculous. But when she came out, it was different, a feeling of total emptiness; she felt no use for, or belief in, anything. It was as though the pieces of her life were strewn around her like a jigsaw puzzle, yet she had no idea how to begin putting them back together again.

As a psychiatrist's daughter, she had grown up believing in Freud the way ministers' daughters believed in God. His kindly, tormented face hung, framed, in the hallway of her parents' apartment. She passed it every day on the way through her father's waiting room. He was like a super-version of her father, someone whose insights kept the world going. Without psychiatry—she and her brother had gone since childhood to a variety of handpicked experts—the world would spin crazily off its axis. Poor Freud. Maybe that confusion and sadness she had seen in his expression even as a child came from the realization that, after all, he had just discovered another art form, not a science, just a way for a few more idealistic or money-mad doctors to earn a living and support their families.

Before being in the hospital, she had always given lip service to the cruelty and corruption of the world, but she had never seen it or felt it, or even, at bottom, believed in it. But it had turned out to be true! Her experience had been no different from that of an earnest, sheltered young man going off to war, no different from a million peoples' experiences with the harshness of reality. The madness of the world, its irrationality, sadism, power struggles, could be read on the pages of any day's newspaper. But it had never been anything real, just statistics. I wish I didn't know that, Nira had thought. It had been nicer not knowing.

Sitting on the porch, she thought: that was when we got divorced. She recalled it all: the shouted accusations at Adlai for not getting her out of the hospital, the bitterness at his leaving her alone there while living at home in such a self-enclosed, contented way with the children, the afternoon when he had taken her on a visit away from the hospital and then refused to leave her alone with the children for ten minutes for fear she might harm them in some way. Maybe her hysteria had driven him to Serena or had created the need for something like it. What a wonderfully symbolic name for her to have! My wife is hysteria; my mistress is serenity. But for her it had been the betrayal of trust, a quality she had always, without thinking about it, thought underlay her marriage, and had discovered that it did not.

And the irony—that the one desperate night they had made love two months before she escaped, an act having no connection with love or lust, simply a failed desire to feel something, anything—that night had led to Jasmine's conception, their least-wanted child and, for no reason that made any sense, the one with the sunniest, most carefree disposition.

Now she was really, truly alone, but she had—maybe this was lucky!—gone through it before, without being able to explain to anyone why she felt as she did. With such a fine dress rehearsal, surely the performance would go smoothly. "Depressions are time limited," some doctor had informed her before her breakdown. "One day you'll be walking down the street and for no reason—just because the sky is blue!—you'll feel happy." Like all clichés, it had been partly true. Connections—to work, to family, to friends—hooked themselves up seemingly without effort. One day they were there! And this realization brought an almost first-lovelike dazzle with it. Reclaiming the world, being reclaimed by it, was intoxicating. It could work without rules, without beliefs; it could work even if Freud had been wrong. Nira had felt like a skier with an amputated leg who finds, for some reason, that he skiis better, more effortlessly than he did before his operation.

Would anyone want her again? Jerry she had chased away by wanting too much, Adlai by wanting too little. Intricate lessons. She wasn't sure she had found any solutions. The questions seemed simply to have multiplied, like cancer cells. It will come back, she told herself, trying to smother the sparks of panic that flew up within her. Even without Jerry, without Adlai. It will come back. Wait. Be patient. "Do not fear, all will be well." Her father's catch-all phrase. The warmth of the porch began lulling her into drowsiness. Without knowing when, she fell asleep on the small cot in the corner, the old knitted afghan, which her grandmother had made, drawn up over her. When she woke in the morning, she found Posey curled up, asleep, beside her. "I had a bad dream," Posey said, stretching, her head touching Nira's on the pillow. "But I can't remember what it was."

Spring-Fall 1981

Meredith was squatting beside the dollhouse, peering in. "Do the lights still work?" she asked.

Penny shook her head. "I should get new ones . . . Maybe we can stop in the store later."

"Great." Meredith looked pensive. "It's funny, I don't really regret not having had kids . . . but I would like to have had a dollhouse."

"Get one for yourself," Penny suggested.

"Wouldn't that seem strange?" Meredith said, adding quickly, "Not that it matters, I guess."

"Most of the people in the dollhouse stores are adults, collecting for themselves. The things are so delicate, you couldn't give them to kids. Plates costing twenty dollars each! Chess sets."

Meredith stood up and stretched. She had stayed over the night before and was going to go to the stable with Penny, though she hated riding. It was such lovely weather, she told Penny, she would just sit under a tree and read. "Do you ever regret that?" she said suddenly. "Not having had kids?"

Penny hesitated. "Sometimes."

"I've never even gotten pregnant."

"Never?"

"Oh wait, there was that one time, before Rick and I were married. I remember I spent about a week, toying with the thought of having it." She smiled. "She—or he—would be in high school now."

"So, do you wish—"

Meredith frowned. "It's so hard to imagine. I've had one kind of life, with a certain amount of freedom in relation to my work, men, and I've grown to like that. It suits me . . . with a child everything would've been different. It's just now, realizing that if I don't in five years, say, that's it . . . I guess that's middle age, realizing there are some things you'll *never* do. You won't have another chance." She looked at Penny. "Do you know what I mean?"

"For me it wasn't the freedom so much," Penny said. "It's more the solitude. I really like being alone, having time to myself . . . and Cal is so demanding when he's here . . . wants so much of me. I knew it would be like having two children. He'd love the *idea* of a baby, but the reality would be him off in L.A. and me here."

"It's funny," Meredith said. "I wouldn't mind that. In fact, I'd prefer it. I'd *rather* raise a kid on my own. Maybe because my parents argued so much about everything. I feel if it was mine, I could raise it however I liked."

"No, I'd want . . ." Penny stopped.

"What?"

"Well, I like the idea of sharing it, somehow, even the not agreeing about everything, having another point of view. The way Jerry says he feels he and his wife have helped each other. I like that."

Meredith smiled. "How is he, by the way? You haven't mentioned him lately."

Penny hesitated. "Okay."

"What's wrong? You're not in love with him, are you?" She sounded alarmed; probably, Penny knew, because she had always talked about Jerry in such a lighthearted, concealing way.

"Yeah, afraid so."

"Pen."

"I know! . . . I wanted to be gay and devil-may-care. Maybe in my next incarnation."

Meredith was gazing at her with an intent, but sympathetic expression. "What is it you love about him?"

Penny knew she was asking, not just as a person who was fascinated by people's feelings, but as a friend. And she wanted to talk about it, not having done it with anyone, as though not talking might make the feelings themselves vanish. "The way he loves his kids. That's so touching to me. Maybe it's that he's more or less had to raise them himself, his first wife being so irresponsible and, well, I gather he married the second one thinking she was so good with her own kids, but by the time they married she'd had it with all that and was on to the career thing. He's always worrying about them, if they go into this career will it work out, if they marry this one, will they be happy? He's like a Jewish mother!" She smiled fondly. "I guess it reminds me of my father."

"What else?" Meredith asked.

"I'm not doing this in order of. You just want to know—?"

"Right, any order."

"He remembers things," Penny said. "I mean, like he knows all about you, all about your affairs, and your mother and her heart problems, and your wanting to give up smoking. And he thinks to

ask, 'How's Meredith?' He seems to *care* about all the trivia of my
life."

Meredith laughed. "I'm the trivia of your life?"

Penny smiled. "You know what I mean, all the little things. Men
don't always. Cal is so jealous of any relationship I have with anyone
but him, even with you. And that's flattering, but it's slightly oppres-
sive too. It means there's so much I can't share."

"And how is the sex part of it?"

"Wonderful," Penny admitted quickly, "but it's not, well, not a
thing of, you know, suddenly feeling things I never felt before, etc.,
etc. He's—I don't know how to describe it. He's just caring in a cer-
tain way I love. He makes me feel cherished." She blushed, as though
having admitted something much more intimate. "I love the way he
calls me 'dear.' It's such a subdued kind of endearment . . . as though
we were married."

"Uh-oh," Meredith said.

"Don't panic . . . I said 'as though.' Is there a law against
fantasies?"

"There's no law against it," Meredith said, "but fantasies have a
sneaky way of attaching themselves to reality."

"Never!" Penny said. "You can set your mind at rest. . . . No, it's
funny, I was thinking—all the men I've ever liked, loved, so few really,
but they've all had that quality of sweetness, like Ferdinand the Bull,
preferring to sit under the cork tree and smell the flowers. Jerry says
he's not really like that, that he's competitive and wants to do well;
but still, it isn't in that ruthless, mindless way some men have."

"And what are the bad things?" Meredith said, "or is he per-
fect?"

"Am I going to have to pay sixty dollars for this?" Penny asked.

"My rates have gone up . . . Seventy-five, except for starving
artists and confused friends."

"Double for us, huh? . . . Well, it's not a trait so much. It's
more—and he's not *always* like this—but there's a way he has of being
preoccupied, exhausted seeming. I feel so awful complaining about it
because it's connected to something I like in him so much, that he
takes all his responsibilities so seriously: his work, his marriage, *his*
kids, *her* kids . . . but sometimes I feel like I'm at the end of a long line,
and he just doesn't have the time or energy for me. I want to come
first with him, I guess is what it boils down to, and I don't, at least
not always, not in any solid way. . . . Just to give an example, once I
was at his apartment and the phone rang. It was one of his step-
daughters, calling from college with some kind of problem, and he

was so nice . . . to *her!* He stayed on the phone for half an hour, listening and giving advice. I felt so furious, so jealous! It was like he forgot I was there! I finally wrote on a piece of paper, 'I have to go now,' and he took it, looked at it, kept on talking and just smiled at me as I left, like I was the cleaning lady or something!" Penny sighed. "Oh shit." She looked at Meredith. "You know, you'd be a good psychiatrist."

"How so?"

"Well, you've let me burble on with all these hideous things, but you haven't made me feel ashamed or as though I'm an awful person."

"Why should you be ashamed?" Meredith asked gently.

"Oh, because, well, even leaving the adultery part aside. Okay, I know Cal does it and you think I have no cause to feel guilty. So let's leave that aside. But here I am luring—or trying to, in some way— someone away from his wife! And even with him, I feel sometimes like I'm some little dog clinging to his pants leg, yapping, 'Pay attention to me, pay attention to me!' "

"That's *all* you're doing?"

"I don't know *what* the hell I'm doing," Penny said, "and that's the truth."

They went outside. It was almost spring, warm, sunny, the air still a little crisp. "On days like this, I can almost see why you live out here in the boonies," Meredith said.

They got into the car. Penny drove mechanically, preoccupied. Neither of them spoke. Once she glanced over at Meredith, but she, too, seemed lost in thought. At the stable, she asked, "Will you stay in the car?"

"I'll sit over there, under that tree . . . is anything wrong? You have a funny expression."

"Well . . . I think I'm pregnant, actually."

Meredith did a double take. "What?"

Penny laughed. "We'll talk about it when I get back, okay?"

She had known for two weeks, had bought one of those do-it-yourself pregnancy kits and passed the test with flying colors three times. Three seemed a magical number. You couldn't fool a test three times running. For some reason there seemed a symbolic significance in whom she would choose to tell first. Partly, she would have liked to tell no one and even debated that—or at least debated waiting until she was several months along, past the stage when an abortion would be convenient. But she knew she was too dependent on other people's opinions to do that, wanted Meredith's reaction, Helen's . . . and, of course Cal's, Jerry's. *I'm going to do it anyway*, she told them all in her head, to forestall imagined protests. *I don't care what any of you say.* She had already had such long, exhausting arguments in her head with all of them, that it was often with surprise that she remembered she still had not told anyone.

Penny came back from riding feeling relaxed, but exhausted. She had been sleeping poorly since she had found out, would wake up at four or five at night, and instantly these imaginary arguments would begin playing in her head. By the time they had played themselves out, it would be almost time to get up and go to work.

Meredith was sitting under the tree, immersed in the journal she had brought, her soft auburn hair loose in a pony tail down her back. Approaching her, Penny tried to imagine the teenage daughter or son Meredith might have had, but it was impossible.

"Do you think it was mental telepathy?" Meredith asked, as they got into the car. "My mentioning it today?"

"I don't know. We've known each other so long. I think people do tune into each other's thoughts somehow, but I don't believe in it in any firm way."

Meredith smiled. "You have the dollhouse already . . . You'd better have a girl."

"You're assuming I'm going to have it?"

"Yeah . . . Aren't you?"

"Yes."

There was a pause.

"Told Cal yet?"

Penny shook her head.

"How come?"

"Various reasons . . . It might not be his. That's not the main one, though," she added hastily.

"What's the main one?"

"I don't know if it's any of his business," Penny said, surprised at the curtness of her voice.

"Even if it is his? Or do you know for sure it's not?"

"I don't know for sure."

"Do you care?"

Penny glanced at her. "Do you think I should?"

"Pen, what's all this *should?* There is no *should.*"

"I guess it would be easier if it were Cal's."

"I assume your author friend is the only other—"

"Right."

"Doesn't he have a whole passel of them already?"

"Four . . . Is that a whole passel?"

"Definitely . . . Look, I think it's wonderful, Pen, really. I feel excited, vicariously."

"You don't think it's selfish?"

"In what way?"

"Well, I'd have to keep on working, right from Day One. . . . Even if it is Cal's, even if he decides to stay married to me, he won't be around all that much."

Meredith looked horrified. "What do you mean, even if he decides to stay married to you?"

"Well, he doesn't have to."

"I don't get it . . . What grounds would he have for upping and leaving now?"

"Adultery?"

"You've *got* to be kidding."

"Cal is funny."

"Well, screw him, then."

Penny stared out the window. "Yeah."

Meredith stared at her. "I'm sorry. That was a little . . . I just truly can't see Cal getting up on some high horse and screaming about your so-called infidelity after all these years of—"

"Oh, he wouldn't do it that way." They were at the house. Penny opened the door and climbed out. "He'd more pout . . . He'd be wounded to the core, that kind of thing."

"Oh Christ, men!"

"Sure, okay, men . . . But what's the alternative?"

"True . . . But, well, say he did pull out? I don't think he *will*, but what then? Would you get rid of it?"

"No!"

"Good. I was getting a little worried."

"I don't want to be frivolous though."

"Pen, one could accuse you of many things, but—"

"I mean, it's a real *person*. I don't earn much. I'm not one of these instinctive, earth-motherish types."

"That's all bullshit."

"Would you be this sure of yourself if it were you?"

Meredith smiled. "Probably not . . . But you'll be great, I know it. Look, I'll move out here and we can raise it together."

"What about your practice?"

"I'll start a practice out here."

"Would you really?"

"I don't know . . . I've only had two minutes to think about it. But why not? Then, if it works out, I'll have one too."

Penny sighed. "It sounds too much like one of those feminist movies we both can't stand."

"Yeah . . . Well, anyway, are you going to tell him? Or Jerry? Or will you just put it off until it becomes visible to the naked eye, as it were?"

"What would *you* do?"

"Well, I'd tell everyone the second I found out. But you know me. To me nothing has happened until I've polled all my friends and gotten their opinion."

"I'm afraid my sister will be furious."

"So? How about Jerry?"

Penny thought. "He's . . . I really hate to get him involved in any way. He's so conscientious, somehow. He'd feel all involved and worried and responsible."

"You could marry him, if Cal—"

"Yes, I've thought of that actually." That was all she said, and Meredith knew better than to press.

They didn't talk about it much more that weekend, but Penny felt relieved at having it out in the open. She knew now that she'd done it, that she had told Meredith first, simply because Meredith was so relaxed and uncondemning about everything. She had been, for that reason, the opposite of a test case. She had always been that way, even before she'd become a psychiatrist, but certainly now, after years of hearing people's psyches laid bare, nothing seemed to faze her. Helen, despite her rebellious nature, was more conventional, particularly where children were concerned. Where Meredith's main concern was how the baby would fit into Penny's life, Helen would worry about the baby; would *it* be getting a fair deal? Penny didn't know which view she herself ascribed to most. It did seem frivolous to have a baby just to satisfy a yen, just because, as Meredith had said, time was passing, and soon it would be too late. Oughtn't one to have some sense that one would be a good mother as well? You'll be good, she argued with herself. Look at all those teenage kids getting knocked up. You're responsible, hard working.

She hated herself for being so desperately eager for Cal's good opinion. In the abstract she totally agreed with Meredith. For him to protest in any way ought to be unthinkable. Or, why tell him that it might not be his? Babies looked like each other more than like any particular person. Those issues all seemed so heavy and weighty—who is the father? Who is my "real" father?

Cal was coming to stay for a month in May, before he did another summer-stock stint in the Poconos. Two months away. Maybe, then. She would be in her fourth month, but probably wouldn't show too much. She recalled how Helen, who was small-boned and slim, had hardly showed till the end, with any of hers.

Sometimes, in her middle-of-the-night worryings, Penny would imagine sending everyone a postcard informing them of the news: "Penelope Howard wishes to announce her pregnancy and forthcoming motherhood." And everyone could send letters as in one of those epistolary novels. "I was most overjoyed to receive the news of your . . ." "My sincerest wishes for a most relaxed and successful confinement . . ." It puzzled Penny that Helen, who seemed to have been born with a desire to flout convention, had, at bottom, done what most women of her generation had done: married young, had children, put off a career till they were mostly grown. And she, who disliked standing out in a crowd or being controversial, had a marriage which made no sense by anyone's standards, including her own, had put off motherhood for no good reason—certainly not because her "career" was so involving and demanding it left her no interest in anything else—and now, at a time which had no special convenience, was pregnant with a baby whose father might be unavailable, even angry.

She thought of how Meredith had said she didn't feel anything had happened till she had told all her friends. Penny had always been the opposite. She liked to decide everything in private. The thought of turning to others bothered her, maybe because she knew she would then care about everyone's opinion and try to please everyone. Whereas Meredith, no matter what all her friends advised, went right ahead and did whatever she felt like, anyway.

But first she wanted to tell Jerry.

She wanted the baby to be his. Didn't it have to be? Statistically it seemed so much more likely—she'd only seen Cal half a dozen times in the past few months. It wasn't just what she had told Meredith, that she thought Jerry would be a good father, that having a child with Cal would be equivalent in many ways to being a single parent. It was that she felt sure that, once Jerry knew, he would want to leave his wife. Sure, people stayed in marriages like the one he had forever, marriages of duty and obligation, where all the magic and excitement that had been there at first had vanished. But that was only because they had no options. They were resigned, and tried, for any number of reasons, to make the best of it. But he had *her!* And everything else was so much simpler than in most such cases. No problem with past children—his and hers were grown. No need for alimony—his wife was more than self-supporting. He'd said once she earned twice what he did. Maybe she'd pay *him* alimony!

Penny had a few qualms when she thought about Nira, about what her chances would be to get someone else if Jerry left. But maybe—or was this too wonderfully convenient?—maybe she had someone already. Maybe all those trips to Paris had been just an excuse. Or, if not an excuse, maybe on one of these trips she'd met some dapper, charming Frenchman and found him irresistible. Why not? That thought consoled Penny. She didn't like the idea of starting a new life founded on someone else's misery.

And she would make Jerry happy, she knew that. He would have someone to talk to. *She* would have someone to talk to! All the repressed resentment she had felt toward Cal for being so manically absorbed in his own career, and so little interested in hers, burbled to the surface. He always made fun of her colleagues, called them stuffy academics. Maybe they were. But now she wouldn't have to bother even putting up a pretense about all his idiot, strung-out actor friends. She would never go to L.A. again! Never! Not even if she lived to be eighty-nine, like her grandmother.

She wasn't old. If she married Jerry now, at thirty-six, they could be married forty years or more. Nira would become a vague, hazy memory, someone who had been there when his life was in too great a state of confusion for him to have the energy to look elsewhere.

They hadn't talked directly about marriage much but once, when she had mentioned the idea of Nira's having a lover, he'd looked almost pleased, as though it would be a relief to him also. He wouldn't have to feel guilty then was what that smile had said to her. Not that he had to anyway, in Penny's opinion. It sounded like he'd been an exemplary husband, really caring and involved. Maybe if he hadn't met her, he could have gone on that way for the rest of his life. But he found her "irresistible." That was what he had said once. "You know my irresistible weakness for you." Something like that. That was almost as good as her other favorite compliment. He had once been describing some woman he knew as "the pal type." "Like me?" Penny had inquired. "No, I think of you more as the temptress type," he'd said. Not even ironically! She had looked at herself ten times a day in the mirror for weeks after that, trying to spy in her familiar features some trace of a temptress, an irresistible temptress.

They had just made love. Sleepy, feeling wonderful, Penny snuggled against him. It was the first time they had made love since she had known she was pregnant. She thought of how often Jerry had said he regretted not having a son, much as he loved his daughters. Lying there, eyes closed, she pictured him with a smaller version of himself, playing outside her parents' house. She knew he would be good as the father of a son, devoted, caring. He wouldn't get into that competitive thing so many fathers did. Penny opened her eyes. She looked at Jerry.

He turned to her. "How're things with Cal?" he said.

She was surprised. A few times, at the beginning, they had indulged in a mild orgy of complaining about their spouses, but since then he hardly ever referred to Cal, or she to Nira. "He's fine," she said awkwardly. "He . . . might be coming to visit in a few months."

"Good," he said. "That should be nice for you."

Penny stared at him. Was he being ironical? "How're things with you and Nira?" she said, trying to sound arch, mocking him.

"Very, very good," he said. "We had a really wonderful talk over the weekend."

Penny felt as though he had sliced her up into five separate, bloody pieces. She lay stiffly, frozen. "What was your talk about?" she managed finally.

"Well, you know how busy she's been this year, traveling to Paris so often? And I *have* resented it in a way, no matter what I said. It was hard. Well, she said she's decided not to use the funding they raised in Paris, that they would simply look further here. She said she realized it just wasn't worth it, at this point in her life, to sacrifice all we'd built up together, and that success didn't seem that much to her."

"So, what *is* she going to do—stay home and raise geraniums?"

He continued, oblivious. "What was interesting was she began telling me how she felt her father, though he was so supportive of her in a way, had crippled her somehow, making her so dependent on him, and that in some way she felt the same way about me, as though becoming a success in the world meant proving to him, even though he's dead, *and* to me that she was worthwhile . . . I'd never realized that was what it was all about, the intensity with which she threw herself into her work."

"That sounds like the kind of conversation you have on a first date," Penny said coldly. "You mean, you've been married ten years and never discussed any of that?"

From his expression it was clear something of her mood had filtered through to him. "Nira and I've hardly seen each other this year," he said. "One reason I'm here is that—"

"Oh great," Penny said, so hurt she turned away, wanting to cry or hit him. "I'm the second team, then? Cheaper than going to a massage parlor?"

"Penny, I—"

"Men are such fools!" she said violently, sitting up. "Here she obviously senses you're straying, so she gives you this idiotic spiel and you fall for the whole thing! It's despicable! I don't even *believe* it!"

"She has no idea about us," he said curtly.

"How about the time you said my name in your sleep?"

"She thought I said Jenny . . . we had a dog named Jenny once."

"Bullshit!" Penny could hardly sit still, she felt so furious. "She's just a desperate, middle-aged woman whom no one wants and—"

"She's beautiful," Jerry said. "She gets five propositions a week. She could leave me in one second with someone earning twice what I do."

Penny was horrified. How could he coolly have kept a trump card like that up his sleeve for so long? "You never said she was beautiful," she said accusingly.

"What did you assume, that I'd marry a monster?"

"I thought looks didn't matter to you."

He laughed. "What made you think that?"

Part of what had made her think that was that she didn't think of herself as beautiful, yet he seemed to think she was. But she said, "That woman we met on the street once, the one you had that thing with . . . she didn't seem like such a knockout."

"I have catholic tastes . . . Isn't Cal handsome?"

"He has to be," Penny snapped. "That's his profession." *I am acting very badly,* she thought with a combination of remorse and satisfaction. "Look, *I* don't care," she rushed on. "It's *your* marriage. If that's the kind of marriage you want, wonderful! In which nothing is honest, in which you both lie about everything. If you want to be married to someone who never reads a single book—"

"I never said that," he stammered.

"You *did!*" Penny yelled. "You said she *never* reads. You said she was a functioning illiterate."

Jerry laughed. "Penny, I *never* said that. You know I didn't."

"You said she never reads," Penny retreated.

"What I meant," he said carefully, "is that she doesn't read scientific things. That's totally understandable. It's not a field that's accessible to outsiders. It—"

"You said she never reads period," Penny shouted. "You said that!"

"So she's not an intellectual. That doesn't make her stupid. She knows more about design than either of us will ever know."

"Design! Big deal." Penny stared at him contemptuously. "So, she's the world's authority on mashed potatoes? Look, why not just admit that you want to be married to someone whose profession you can regard with contempt, just so you can go around thumping yourself on the chest, saying, 'I'm the intellectual, I'm the intellectual'? "

"I wasn't aware I did that with such tremendous frequency."

"You could *never* be married to someone like me," Penny said. "You say how wonderful it is that I can understand your books, but it makes you nervous. I might be critical. You'd rather have someone who sews ruffles on skirts!"

"I can't be married to you because I'm married," he said. "And I was under the impression you were too."

"That's *not* the reason." She turned away and stared out the window. "Oh, who cares! We'd be miserable. It would be awful. Look at this argument."

"I don't happen to agree with you. Obviously, if you had tantrums like this, we'd have some major blowouts. But I think there might be some wonderful things too."

"There wouldn't be," Penny insisted. "It would *all* be awful! You'd take up with some idiot person three seconds after we were married, and say all the awful things about me you used to say about Nira."

Jerry was looking at her, obviously trying to be patient. "I don't want to choose between you, that's all," he said quietly.

"I'm not asking you to. You're just here for a free fuck, right? So? You had it. Leave! Get dressed and leave."

He didn't move. "I thought we were here to make love, not war."

"You had the love part . . . That was Act One. This is Act Two."

Jerry laughed. "I don't like Act Two . . . Why don't we stick with Act One?"

"Because that's what you *always* do," Penny screamed. "You do Act One nine million times. I don't *want* that! I wanted us to love each other forever. Twenty years is a one-night stand for me."

"Twenty years of this would finish me off in no time," he said. "Twenty *minutes* is plenty, in fact."

"I—," Penny began, but he interrupted her.

"Shut up for one second," he said. "You've done enough yelling for one afternoon. I'm going to tell you something about my marriage."

Penny put her hands over her ears. "I don't want to hear anything about your marriage."

He grabbed her hands away and pushed her violently back against the pillow. "Well, you're going to . . . whether you want to or not."

Penny was amazed, frightened. He had never spoken to her in that tone of voice. She watched in silence as he got dressed and went over to sit down in the chair facing the bed. "Don't interrupt me," he said.

She didn't reply. But feeling overly vulnerable being naked, she draped the sheet around herself and watched him.

"When I married Nira, she was just beginning to find herself, whatever the right expression is, starting up in her career after having put it aside for raising kids. She wasn't bitter about the lost years, but she was eager to get started again. And she did, slowly; she kept at it. And did well. Not super well, but well. She was satisfied, happy with it. . . . Then six years ago one of our daughters was killed."

"One of yours or one of hers?"

"One of hers. Posey." Jerry was talking more slowly, as though it was painful for him. "She was a wonderful child, very perky, impulsive, beautiful, full of life. I guess I felt a special attachment to her because my girls don't have that. Their lives have been so difficult. Posey bubbled; she was so natural, so sweet . . ."

"How did it happen?"

"She was visiting her father in England one summer. They were on a boat. She jumped off to swim and got caught in the current. Everyone else was down below, resting. She shouldn't have done it without asking, but she was like that—impulsive." He stopped. "It was . . . You don't have children, you can't imagine what it's like. Nothing in the world is like losing a child, nothing. Nira collapsed. She'd put so much of herself into the children, and Posey was special to her too. Not that it would have been different if it was one of the others, but—"

"How do you mean, collapsed?"

"Just . . . Well, she'd had a breakdown earlier, after her father died. This wasn't like that. She wasn't hospitalized. But she quit her job. She stayed home; she slept; she roamed around. She'd call me at work, distraught, weeping. I was terrified. My first wife had gone through something like that after we were divorced and I couldn't reach her. With her, it was as though her illness was a way of not wanting to be reached. But Nira *wanted* to be. She let me help her. She said I saved her life. I don't think it's true. You don't, in the end, save anyone's life. They have to do it themselves. But it's the thing in my life I feel most proud of, having been there for her, getting her through it. It's why I tried to choke down my resentment when she rushed into work again. I understood it on a rational level, the desire to forget, immerse herself. I've done that."

He was sitting there, staring out the window. Penny felt divided in two, part of her cold and detached—who cares if your whole family died in a concentration camp!—the other part moved and involved, as though she were hearing the story from someone else, under different circumstances. "And what is the moral of the story?" she asked gently.

His voice was much quieter. He looked directly at her. "The moral of the story is that we love each other, that there's a tremendously strong bond between us, that marriage isn't—for me—a game that you play a few rounds of and then quit."

"And what am I?" Penny asked, unable to keep the bitterness and hurt out of her voice. "An intermission in the main drama? A pleasant interlude? I want to be part of your *life,* Jerry! Not just—"

"You *are* part of my life."

"But—"

"But, I can't sacrifice everything for you. I love you in a lot of ways. I want you to be happy. But I can't divide myself up emotionally. I'm one person." He looked at her, frowning. "I wish you would see me as I really am."

"How are you, really?"

"I'm not rushing out after other women. Your jealousy is flattering, but unfounded. I did all that. That's the past. That's not what I am now. When you're younger, sex is just a physical drive. But at my age it's psychological."

"I guess for me it's always been psychological," Penny said.

"Well, for women it is, I think." Smiling, he put up his hand as she started to interrupt. "No feminist speeches!"

"Calm down, I was *agreeing* with you."

"I thought I caught a gleam in your eye."

"No gleam," she said sadly.

"Darling, it's this—my life is a struggle to balance a lot of complicated things. I'm trying to be fair. It's not just you and Nira. My work, so many things! That's why I hesitated when you wanted to get involved. I knew it would be like this. I knew you'd want so much, and I knew I couldn't give it to you."

"Am I that awful?" Penny said, the image of the demanding woman rising up before her.

"No, just human . . . Look, I *want* to give it to you. That's why it's a struggle. But if I do, my marriage would collapse. Nira's sensitive, intuitive. She picks up on things. . . . Once, one afternoon after we'd been together, I came home and she'd fixed this lovely dinner. I felt rotten. That's such an ugly feeling! You don't have that. Cal's away all the time. You wouldn't like it either, believe me."

Penny let the sheet drop and lay back, naked, staring at the ceiling. "What will happen, then?" she asked, as much to the ceiling as to him. "With us, I mean . . . *Will* we love each other forever?"

Jerry got up and came over to the bed. He knelt beside her. "Is that what you want?"

"Yes." She put her arms around him. "I want to visit you in your old-age home when you're ninety and bribe the nurses to let me take you out for a ride in your wheelchair, and then I want to jump into your lap and push us downhill."

"Will there be brakes on the wheelchair?" he said, taking off his clothes and getting into bed with her.

"I don't know," Penny said, kissing him. "Are there? I'll be whispering obscene, affectionate things into your ear, and you'll be saying, 'Who are you? I think I've seen you someplace before.' "

He was inside her. "I'll remember you, darling . . . Don't worry."

Later, after he left, she realized she had forgotten to tell him she was pregnant.

For a week or so after their encounter, Penny almost forgot about the baby. All she could think of was Nira, his wife. At night she lay in bed composing anonymous letters to her. "I am bearing your husband's child." The tone of the letters varied, sometimes openly sadistic, sometimes coolly enigmatic. But always at the end she pictured Nira opening the letter, beautiful Nira who still got propositioned in her forties—or was that a lie she had made up for his sake?—and dissolving into tears. Or, instead of tears, an outburst of rage, ordering Jerry from the house, his marriage, his life shattered forever.

One night, unable to sleep, she got up and actually wrote out such a letter. She worked on it for hours, as though it were a manuscript that had been submitted to her, changing a word here, a phrase there. Finally, when it was perfect, she typed it up and then sat, staring at it. Carefully, Penny took the letter, crumpled it up and threw it into the wastebasket. *You are not the kind of person who does this kind of thing,* she told herself severely. *Go back to bed.*

Once she called their apartment and a woman, whom she assumed to be Nira, answered. For a second Penny lost her wits and was about to hang up. Then she thought: *that has been done. I must spare myself one cliché of being in this situation.* "Is Jerry there?" she said after Nira had said hello twice.

"Oh . . . no, I'm afraid he isn't right now. Who is this?"

"This is . . . Penny Howard." Thank God she had remembered her own name at the last minute! "His editor. I was calling about some changes that have to be made in his manuscript." To her infinite relief, the English language began seeming native to her by the end of the sentence.

"I'll have him call you back as soon as he gets in," Nira said. "Does he have your number?"

Penny hesitated. "I think so."

"Why don't you give it to me just in case?"

Penny hung up, feeling sick. You're throwing up because you're pregnant, she told herself, hanging over the toilet bowl. It's called morning sickness.

But in the next two months, though she spoke to Jerry once a week on the phone and met him for lunch once, she never mentioned being pregnant. The lunch was unbearably awkward. He came out to Princeton. His manner to her was cordial, almost elaborately sympathetic and interested, as though they were married, in the worst sense of the word. Did you have a nice day, dear? Wives become mothers, girlfriends become wives, a friend had once said, that being supposedly, the tragedy of women's relationships to men, or vice versa. His attentiveness seemed forced, so at odds with the way, early on in their relationship, his face had lighted up when she walked into a room, when everything she said seemed to delight or amuse him.

Toward the end of the lunch, a young woman came in, carrying a baby. She set it in its infant seat on the table and proceeded to eat a hamburger. Penny looked at the baby. Plump, dressed in a blue terry-cloth stretch suit, he was crooning softly, chewing on some rubber teething beads. Jerry looked at the baby too. This is the moment, Penny thought. The baby seemed to have been brought in as a prop. But she said nothing.

As he was paying, she thought: if you invite him back to the house, I'm never speaking to you again.

"I guess I better get back," he said. "I have a lot of work to do."

The lie pained her as much as the fact of his not wanting to come to the house. "Me too," she said.

They looked out at the rain. "What I think," he said carefully, as though he had rehearsed it, "is that we can have the closeness and the intimacy without necessarily—"

"Oh sure," Penny agreed over-hastily. Like not having your cake and not eating it.

In fact, she did have work to do, but, unable to face being alone with her thoughts, she went to the closest movie which, as luck would have it, turned out to be about a married woman having an affair. In one scene the woman fell down on the ground and lay there in the grass without moving. Jumping to her feet, Penny started to walk out of the theatre. Then she sat down again in an aisle seat. Tears were streaming down her face; she could hardly see the screen. You have to see the rest of the movie, she told herself. You cannot leave the theatre. I can't sit through it, it's unbearable. It's a movie. Look, see, it's a screen. They're French. It's just a movie.

That day was the worst. Later, she remembered it as a turning point and was left only with a reluctance to ever see a movie made by that particular director again.

Inertia made not telling Cal and Helen easy. After the first few phone conversations with them, in which she knew and didn't tell, it seemed easier not to refer to it. Often she hung up and thought: oh yes, she still doesn't know. But during the conversation, the baby would have not even entered her head. Only sometimes, seemingly by perverse chance, Cal or Helen would bring up stories of friends' pregnancies or babies, and she would listen, nervously, trying to respond as she might have six months earlier.

. "He's adorable," Cal said of Karen's baby, who had been born the week before. "A real head of hair—bright red, just like Dan's."

"So he's the father?" Penny said and instantly thought: why say that, dope?

"Sure." Cal said. "They seem really happy. I guess I was wrong."

"So, she was pregnant when they got married?"

"Yeah, sure, maybe they wouldn't have done it otherwise, gotten married, I mean . . . But she says she's never been happier. She looks great. I mean, you know Karen. She's always seemed so off-the-wall, so scatterbrained. But she's taking this really seriously."

There was a pause.

"That's nice," Penny said finally. She found herself doodling a giant baby on the pad in front of her.

"I know you never liked her," Cal said, misinterpreting her silence."

"No, it's not that." Penny hesitated. She penciled in a few curlicues of hair on top of the baby's head. "Did she care whether it was a boy or girl?"

"I don't think so . . . He's cute. I'll bring a photo of him when I come. I took a whole bunch at the hospital."

"Okay, good."

It was he who broke the silence again by saying, "I'm really looking forward to it. We haven't had a long stretch together in such a long time."

"I know." After a second she added quietly, "I'm looking forward to it too."

Hanging up, she stared at the drawing of the baby: its giant head, its round, lopsided grin, its few androgynous blades of hair. She wondered how Cal would react to their having a boy. He had always said he had no interest in having a son, that fathers and sons got along terribly. His only paternal vision had been of himself and a baby girl, doting, cuddly, sweet. "Look at my father," he would say. "He was a rotten father with me, but he was terrific with Dina." "Was he terrific, or did he just baby her and spoil her? That's just as bad," Penny used to say. "No, he did that a bit, but when she contradicted him or stood up for herself, he thought it was cute and pugnacious. When I did, he threw a fit." "You wouldn't be the same way," Penny had said. "Maybe. But I've practically never met a man who liked his father," Cal said. "And I've met dozens of women who adored theirs."

Maybe he had convinced her, or maybe it was because she had only seen her own father as a father of girls, but Penny had felt won over to his side and when she found out, upon having an amniocentesis test, that the baby would be a boy, she felt uneasy. If Cal were looking for a chance to pull out, maybe this would be just another weapon. Also, the reality of knowing the baby's sex made the whole thing more real. Now that she was actually pregnant, she realized that many of the myths she had entertained about pregnancy were, at least as far as she was concerned, untrue. It had always seemed to her that pregnant women walking along the street, or in supermarkets, at parties, had a serene, peaceful, almost smug air. She was sure that whatever they did, no matter how trivial the action, it was imbued somehow with an aura of destiny and calm, a sense of purpose. All those petty doubts and uncertainties about the future, the past would, so Penny had thought, be temporarily suspended.

But it was not so. Or maybe she was odd, abnormal in that way. Most of the time, even after she began to feel the baby move and had to let out the waistlines of her dresses, she forgot she was pregnant for about eighty percent of the day. At work, it would leave her mind totally. She would be just as obsessed with trivial concerns that she knew would remove themselves a week later, would get just as flustered, as alarmed when things went wrong. Most of the time, even when she did think of the baby, it was mainly as another worry. Would it wreck her life? Would she be a terrible mother? Would Cal leave? How would she manage? That's natural, she would try to argue with herself. If this were a regular baby, if you had a husband who would be around, if you knew, for certain, who the father was, then you *would* be like those women you used to see. I don't know, would I?

"How did you feel when you were pregnant?" she asked Helen one night. She had a perfect lead-in because Helen had just been talking about her older daughter's having imagined she might need an abortion, then finding out she wasn't pregnant after all.

"No special way," Helen said. "Gosh, I can hardly remember. It's odd. You just forget."

"Were you radiant and glowing, all of that?"

"You saw me . . . Was I? I didn't *feel* it, that's for sure."

It was true that, except during Helen's first pregnancy, there had always been so many babies underfoot that the possibility or time to be or act composed and radiant had hardly presented itself. "You never got very fat," Penny remembered.

"Yes, I did," Helen said. "With Stuart I gained thirty pounds. I was a cow."

"I guess I didn't see you then," Penny said. "Did it take a long time to lose?"

"Not much . . . I just stopped eating for a couple of weeks. Living with George always gave me enough to worry about; that was one of its dubious virtues . . . Oh listen, thanks for sending the address of that Japanese guy. Bernie said they had him to dinner, and he and Shirley really hit it off."

"In what way?" Penny asked.

"Who knows . . . But they evidently took a long walk in the garden, and he told her all about his three wives and how he admires unconventional women and how devastated he was that she was married and if she ever considered divorce, she should send him a card."

"She told Bernie all of that?"

"Sure! She wants him to think other men still go for her. . . . So, how's life back East? Is Cal there yet?"

"In a month," Penny paused. "Hel?"

"Still here."

"Remember what we were talking about at the beginning?"

"Josie and her boyfriend?"

"Well, that she thought she might need an abortion, but she didn't?"

"Yeah?"

"Well, I have sort of a vaguely similar problem . . . in relation to my life."

Helen laughed. "How vague? When did you have it?"

"Have what?"

"The abortion."

"I didn't have an abortion."

"You didn't?"

"No, I never even considered it."

"Pen, could we backtrack a little? It's just—I'm not sure what we're talking about actually. *I* thought we were talking about your having or not having an abortion."

"We are, sort of . . . But I didn't. I decided to have it is what I'm trying to say."

"You're pregnant?" Helen sounded astounded, almost disbelieving.

"Right."

"Jesus, talk about indirect openers!"

Penny hesitated. "I guess I was afraid you'd be mad."

"At what? Why?"

"I don't know."

Penny could almost hear Helen try to pull herself together. "I think it's marvelous, Pen . . . I mean, I don't think it was something you *had* to do. I know lots of women who are happy as clams without them. But I always thought you'd be a terrific mother."

"Did you?" Penny said, obsequiously grateful. "Why?"

"Well, you're so organized, so efficient . . . not like me."

"Yeah, but I . . . And maybe that's bad. I'm afraid I'll be obsessive and rigid, and hover a lot."

"So?"

"You don't think it matters?"

"You know what I think? I really don't think *any* of it matters much. I have friends who've been warm and relaxed and marvelous, and others who've hung them by their toes in the dark woods and fed them on gingersnap crumbs . . . and at eighteen the kids are all exactly the same. But *exactly.*"

Penny just sighed.

"Does that mean you haven't told Cal yet, that sigh?"

"Among other things."

"Other things?"

"I don't know if it's his, for one."

"I thought you were always crooning on about having such a tediously virtuous life, the joys of celibacy and all that. It always sounded insane to me, but you were so convincingly vehement. So how—"

"Well, remember that writer I met for dinner?"

"The monk's brother? Oh Lord . . . Didn't he have dozens of children and a horde of ex-wives or something?"

"Kind of . . . But that's not the problem."

"What is then?"

"Well," she paused. "I'm afraid Cal might mind."

"Of course he'll mind!"

"He will?" Penny had been hoping for a "Don't be silly; he'll be beside himself with joy."

"I assume you're referring to the 'who is the father' bit, not the fact itself."

"Both, though it's true more . . . But, do you think he has a *right* to mind? I mean, here for years he—"

"Sweetie! Welcome to the world of the double standard."

"But Cal isn't like that, I don't *think.* . . . He always *said* if I wanted to have affairs, that was fine with him. He used to encourage me."

"Fiddle-faddle. Just because he knew you wouldn't . . . That's one of the oldest tricks going."

"You may be right."

"No *maybe* about it. I'm right . . . which makes your dilemma as simple as pie. Just don't tell him."

"You don't think that's dishonest?"

"Of course! Look, find me one instance, only *one*, where honesty was ever of the tiniest help in relations between the sexes."

"I like being honest, though," Penny said, giggling.

"Sure you do. So do we all. But Pen, it's a luxury. If you want to get kicks out of being honest, go ahead, lose your husband, go on welfare, struggle, and agonize. I thought you wanted down-to-earth, commonsense advice."

"I do."

"Babies all look alike anyway. He'll never notice."

"It's true. They both have blue eyes."

"Sure . . . Anyway, it'll look like you. The first one always does."

For a day or two after the talk with Helen, Penny felt totally relaxed. Helen was right. She *was* always right. Why raise or create moral issues when it benefited no one? Maybe her motives weren't lofty or noble at all. And look at all the adopted babies. They were just as loved and cared for. Maybe she could tell Cal years later, just as Jonah or Benjamin (those were her favorite names so far) was graduating college. "I've always been surprised at how good he is at science Pen, considering neither of us. . . ." "Well, actually, dear, there's something I've always meant to tell you."

In April, two weeks before Cal was due to arrive, Penny went into the city to see her doctor. She was at the beginning of her fifth month. She had called Jerry earlier in the week and said she would drop his galleys off after her appointment. She had just said she had "a doctor's appointment" late in the afternoon.

"You could stay for dinner," he suggested.

"Oh . . . okay." She had always wanted, though been apprehensive, to meet Nira. Under the present circumstances, she was slightly more so.

"Nira's away," he added, sensing her thoughts. "But both my daughters will be around. I'd like you to meet them."

The doctor pronounced her in good shape. "I guess you might invest in a few maternity dresses," he said, glancing at her barely expanded waistline. "It can be uncomfortable in the summer."

Penny knew she didn't show at all yet. And the Design Research dress she was wearing had a vague waistline. Going up in the elevator to Jerry's apartment, she was relieved at that, but still more self-conscious about her appearance than usual.

"You look lovely!" he exclaimed, almost in surprise as he answered the door. "What a beautiful dress."

"Thank you." But her heart sank a little. She felt suddenly uncomfortable and wished she had said she didn't have time to stay for dinner. She handed him the galleys.

As it turned out, they ate alone. His stepdaughter, the one she had met the first time she had visited, confessed to having had a turkey sandwich and a chocolate milkshake with a friend after gymnastics class. "Can you save some for me?" she said, peering as Jerry put the fish in the oven. "I might have a little bit, later." To Penny she asked, "Do you like fish?"

"Yes, most kinds."

"The only kind *I* don't like is squid." She wrinkled her nose. "Mommy says it's cheap, but so what if it tastes horrible?"

"Some people like the taste, darling," Jerry said.

But she had wandered out of the room, her clogs clomping as before. Hearing him call someone other than herself darling sent a pang through her.

"Do you ever worry about her being so beautiful?" Penny asked. "I mean, that it might be a problem?"

"A little. . . . People used to ask Nira a lot about the possibility of her modeling. But we both felt it would spoil her one way or another. She seems pretty oblivious of it so far, or contemptuous, even . . . But then boys haven't entered the picture yet. Will you have some wine?"

Penny nodded.

"Could you open it? It's in the refrigerator."

It had been a month since they had had lunch. She was trying, since that was what he obviously wanted, to think of the sexual part of their relationship as something comfortably in the past, years past, and was bothered by the fact that, watching him cook even, she remembered their being in bed, how he had felt, how he had touched her.

"Couldn't you find it?"

"What?"

"The wine."

Penny frowned. "I'm sorry . . . What was I supposed to do? I wasn't listening."

He smiled. "It must have been a hard week. I just wondered if you could open the wine. It's on the first shelf there."

She tried, but couldn't. The cork crumbled. For some reason, though it was totally trivial, Penny felt upset. "I just can't do it," she said, handing the bottle to him, her voice shaking. "I don't know what's wrong."

Her voice sounded so distraught he looked at her in surprise. "That's okay, Penny." He touched her arm. "The doctor didn't . . . You're okay?"

"It's something I feel . . . Could we talk about it later?"

"Of course."

During dinner he did most of the talking. Penny ate mechanically, hoping she looked as though she were following the conversation. Toward the end of the meal, the front door slammed and a teenage girl entered the room. She was a tall, healthy-looking young woman with thick brown hair in a braid that hung jauntily down her back. Not beautiful, but she radiated an air of affable, good-natured directness. "Hi, Jer," she called from the hall.

"Heather, come in and meet Penelope Howard. She's the editor for my book."

Heather swung into the room and waved at Penny. "Hi . . . It's a great book, isn't it?"

Penny nodded. She was surprised that his daughter had read it. "We're really excited about it. The advance orders are terrific."

Heather hugged Jerry from the back. "See, I told you!" she said. "I want him to write a best-seller and send us all around the world on his royalties."

"Not too likely," Jerry said. He looked at her affectionately. "Want some dinner, sweetie? There's a lot left over."

She shook her head. "I've got to run . . . Joe and I are going to the movies. Is that okay? Will you be here for Jas?"

"Sure . . . Have fun," he called, but she had vanished down the hall, braid swinging.

"I didn't know any of your daughters had read it," Penny said.

"Well, Heather's the only one in the family who has any kind of science background. Ironical in a way, since she's my stepdaughter. She's very bright. She's going to get an MD, PhD at Cornell, starting in the fall . . . Jane's read it too, but more for literary content." He smiled. "She doesn't think I'll be the next Henry James." He stood up. "You don't seem too hungry."

Penny looked up at him. "No, I'm sorry. It was good. I just—" She stopped.

"Do you want to go into my study?" he said. "It might be more private, talking there."

"Okay." She followed him, feeling as though she were a daughter having to explain why she had failed a crucial exam or been expelled from school.

The study was cool and darker, despite the one lighted lamp on his desk. Penny lay down on her back on the couch, and closed her eyes for a minute.

"If you'd rather not talk about it, that's okay," Jerry said gently.

"It's nothing bad! It's something good. I'm going to have a baby, that's all." Penny said angrily.

There was a pause.

"Do you want me to congratulate you?"

"I don't want you to do anything!" She glared at him.

"I think it's wonderful, Penny," he said finally.

"In what way?"

"Well, you said you'd always thought of having a child . . . I would think your husband must be very happy."

"He doesn't know about it."

"Aren't you going to tell him?"

"Maybe . . . eventually." She felt such rage, it was hard for her to talk.

"I would think . . . well, this might make a big difference in your marriage."

"What kind of difference?"

"Well, it could . . . There seem to be a lot of things you don't talk about. Maybe—"

"Do *you* talk about everything with Nira?" she threw out. "Do you tell her about us? About our sleeping together?" Her voice rose.

He smiled. "Could you lower your voice?"

"Why? I thought she was out."

"We're not alone in the house."

She shrugged.

"If you didn't want it, couldn't you have had an abortion?" he asked. His manner toward her was wary, tentative, as though she were a heap of explosives that might burst into flame at any moment.

"Of course I could have!"

"Then, I'm not sure I understand—"

Penny bit her lip. "I don't know what's going to happen," she wailed. "I don't know who the father is. I don't know if Cal will leave me. I don't know anything!"

Jerry walked over and sat down next to her. "You think it's mine?"

"I don't know."

He was silent. "Don't you believe in birth control?" he asked wryly.

Penny glared at him. "Of course I believe in it! I have an IUD. Nothing's foolproof, you know."

He looked at her. "Well . . . I'm sorry."

"Don't be. Be glad!"

"I would, if you seemed less upset. . . . Are you afraid about managing financially, is that it?"

Suddenly Penny felt the anger drain out of her. She felt exhausted. "No, nothing that—" She reached out and touched him. "I'm sorry, Jerry. It's not your fault."

"If I can help in some way—"

"No, I'm fine. It's the heat, something." She started.

"What is it?"

"He moved . . . I've just begun feeling him this past month." She smiled suddenly, pleased and excited.

Jerry put his hand on her stomach. The baby fluttered again and was quiet.

"I think a lot of men envy women being able to give birth," he said.

"Sure, as an abstraction . . . but the reality of it?"

"Nira feels having kids was the best thing she ever did."

"So? I'm not Nira!" She flared up again. "I'm not some great earth-motherish person who wants to breast-feed in public and all that."

"She wasn't either. She thought it would be a disaster. She thought she'd be an awful mother. And she's been wonderful."

"I thought you said she was lousy, that your daughters hated her."

He looked horrified. "I didn't say that. I said Stacey and she . . . But Stacey's a difficult girl. *I* find her difficult."

Penny gazed off out the window. "I don't want to talk about how wonderful Nira is," she said grumpily.

"Okay."

"If she's so wonderful, why were you unfaithful to her?"

He laughed. "Maybe *I'm* not so wonderful. . . . Come on, give me a break, okay? My marriage is like anyone else's. I never said it was perfect. When we met it was a little . . . shaky."

"And now everything's all lovey-dovey, and you're billing and cooing from morn till midnight?"

"Not exactly."

He sat watching her, not angrily, but there was a tension and awkwardness between them. Penny felt awful. Suddenly she wanted him to act warm and loving and concerned, and say she was beautiful and witty and better than his wife in every way. She wanted him to make love to her, to show that he still found her desirable, even with the baby inside her.

"You have a strange expression," he said finally.

She stared at him, dreamily, from a distance. "I wish we could make love."

Jerry sighed. "Penny."

"Let's lock the door and do it here, on the couch."

"There is no lock."

"Would you want to, if there were?"

"I think it would be a terrible mistake from every point of view."

"Why?" She laughed. "I can't get pregnant."

"Look . . . It's what I said in the beginning, and I certainly wasn't thinking of this. But all I've done is complicate your life. I haven't helped you."

"If it's your baby, you've given me something to obsess about for the next twenty years." She smiled. "You *have* helped me, Jerry; that's not true."

"Have I?" He looked uncertain and vulnerable. "How?"

"Just making me feel, I don't know, that you cared for me in a way, not just the sex. It was important."

He took her hand and held it, stroking her fingers. "I'm glad . . . you helped me too."

They stared at each other. He kissed her lightly, obviously willing himself not to let it become passionate.

"I knew you looked different when you came in," he said softly. "Glowing somehow."

"Oh dear," Penny sighed. "Should I tell Cal? What do you think? Helen thinks it would be a mistake. She doesn't think it's necessary."

"I agree."

"You don't think being truthful—"

He shook his head.

"I guess." Penny sat up. "Can you get the galleys back by next week?"

"Sure . . . When is your baby due?"

"Labor Day, fittingly enough." She smiled. "I'll send you a card from the hospital."

"We'll see each other before that." He hesitated. "If there's anything I can—"

"I feel fine now . . . It's funny. Maybe that's why people go to psychiatrists, just to pour everything out."

He walked her to the door and hugged her. She went down in the elevator feeling good again, as though they *had* made love. He was right and Helen was right. She would definitely not tell Cal. To do it would only be a form of cruelty. Cruelty masquerading as truthfulness. That was the worst kind, pretending to do things for lofty reasons when underneath one's motives were only petty and self-serving. I'll have a skeleton in the closet, she thought, and in her present mood that seemed amusing. Everyone had always accused her of being too precise and straightforward. It would be good to go against type for a change.

The month that Cal stayed, May, was one of the nicest months they had ever had together. Penny couldn't tell if it was because of her own feeling from being pregnant—a kind of tenderness she felt for him—or just that he was here, on her own turf, separated from the world he usually lived in where she always felt so unwanted and alien. During the day, she left for work while he was asleep. He stayed up late at night reading and slept till nearly noon. When she returned, at five or six, he would be lying in a hammock in the backyard, usually writing; he was working on a screenplay. Once, she found him asleep. She stood over the hammock, gazing down at his sleeping face. She knew she would never find any man's face as beautiful as Cal's. Was it that they had met as children and that she would always see, no matter how old he was, that trace of the child in him? He still had those irregular, delicate features, thick eyebrows, but with time his face had gotten thinner, the cheekbones more prominent, like some medieval saint carved out of stone. It would be nice to have a son that looked like that. People used to say, in high school, that they looked like brother and sister, so maybe it was true— the baby would look like some version of the two of them, so intertwined that no one could tell.

Often he had gone shopping during the day and even started fixing supper. He claimed that years as a bachelor—that was how he referred to his years in L.A.—had made him an expert on certain kinds of dishes. He had an Indian cookbook that he'd brought and, if in the mood, he prepared elaborate vegetable curries, finding stores in Princeton she had never known existed. They would eat outside— unless the mosquitos became too fierce—sitting there while the light faded.

"Maybe in five years you'll have a mid-life crisis," she said one night, "and switch to some completely different field . . . and we could live like this all the time."

Cal smiled. "Would you like that? You used to say it would drive you crazy to have me around all the time."

"You seem different . . . You *are* when you're here."

"How?"

"Not so crazed and frantic."

"Maybe I'm just on good behavior since it's only for a month."

"Is that it?" She smiled.

"A little . . . I like being crazed and frantic. Here, I feel I'm being

such a disgustingly good husband, doing all the shopping, the cook-
ing—"

Penny laughed. "You *have* been good. I'm going to put a bronze
statue of you in the town square."

"Listen to this, Pen! I even vacuumed today. How do you like
that?"

"Wonderful . . . What's it all for?"

He put his head to one side. "To win my way back into your
good graces."

"You're not *out* of my good graces."

"Sure I am."

"In what way?"

"Well, you haven't mentioned that you're pregnant, for one."

Penny gazed at him, glad the wine made their whole conversa-
tion seem a little distant. "Am I pregnant?"

"Unless your body is going through some peculiar transforma-
tion."

"I didn't think I showed." She flushed, glad of the protective
darkness around them.

"Maybe not to a passing stranger . . . I guess I know your body
pretty well by now."

"Evidently. . . . It's a boy, Cal."

"How do you know?"

"I had one of those tests done . . . . amniocentesis. You know, to
make sure it wouldn't be born with any strange complications."

"In addition to being crazed and frantic?"

Penny kept gazing at him, feeling almost hypnotized and float-
ing. His eyes were between blue and green, not plain blue like Jerry's.
"I feel happy about it," she said softly. "At first I wasn't. I thought it
was a terrible mistake. But now I'm glad."

"Me too."

"You always said you wanted a girl."

"It doesn't matter." He stood up and embraced her. "I'm really
happy about it, Pen."

She accepted his embrace. "I was afraid you might be angry . . .
or even leave for good."

"Why would I do that?"

"I don't know."

They made love as they had almost every night, but this time it
seemed different to Penny, knowing that he knew. Afterward he put
his head on her belly and listened. "I could feel him before," he
whispered. "It's strange, isn't it, all three of us making love together?"

"Yeah . . ."

"Maybe we should have lots of kids . . . six, like your sister. Three girls and three boys."

"Sure, and I'll raise them all by myself, in a shoe."

"I'll quit acting . . . We'll open a general store. You'll get fat and jolly and wear an apron and sell home-baked pies, and I'll sit on a stool and chew tobacco and tell yarns of my wild youth in Hollywood."

"Help!"

"What's wrong with it?" he pursued. "I think it's a wonderful idea."

She couldn't tell where he was poised between irony and genuine enthusiasm. "How about your monthly allotment of adoring starlets?"

"I'll import a few, COD . . . Or I can switch to nubile coeds."

"And me, what will *I* do?"

His voice was strangely soft, almost ethereal in the darkness. "Whatever makes you happy."

"That's complicated," she found herself saying, not sure what they were talking about.

"It always is."

The month that he was there, Penny finally felt as she imagined pregnant women might feel: full, glowing, sexual, healthy. She gave way to reveries of herself with a child at her breast, considered baking bread, envisioned herself and Cal at their hypothetical general store. And then, into the fantasy, the hypothetical nubile coeds would intrude, peering in at the door, asking for Cal. This is a fantasy, Penny rebuked them. Get out. But they insisted on being there, as no doubt they would insist on being there in real life. And their presence, she knew, would be a thousand times harder to handle than girls she would never know or meet three thousand miles away.

They didn't discuss their marriage anymore, lived the rest of the month just as though they were any couple on vacation anywhere. Only once, when they were lying together on a blanket on the grass, Cal said, into the air more than to her, "What we have is real."

"Yes."

"And we don't have it with anyone else."

"No." She propped herself up and looked at him. "And so?"

Cal took her hand. "And so we should value it and cherish it."

Penny hesitated. "I do, Cal . . . I always have."

"I always have too . . . despite everything." He looked away, up at the sky again. "Karen was saying that the reason she knew she

wanted to marry Dan was that, when she found out she was preg-
nant, she didn't want to have an abortion. She'd had around three.
She knew if it was his child, she wanted to have it . . . I feel like that. I
wouldn't want anyone but you to have my child."

Penny was silent.

"Do you think that's sexist?"

"A bit, yeah."

He smiled. "But you do appreciate the sentiment?"

She bent over and kissed him. "I do . . . If I hadn't married you, I
wouldn't have married anyone," she said. The thought had just come
to her, and she knew it was true.

"Me too . . . I never wanted to be married. We were too young to
know what we were doing. I'm glad."

She laughed. *"He* better not get married that young, though,"
she said, pointing to her belly.

"We'll disown him," Cal said. "Oh listen, it'll be different for
him. By then, no one'll be getting married."

"Sure they will." She unbuttoned his denim shirt and kissed his
collarbone. "You have nice bones," she observed.

"Thanks . . . You sound like you're evaluating an ancient work
of art you just dug up."

"I am." She slid her hands under him. "Definitely a find, defi-
nitely worth preserving."

It was he, being beneath her, who could look up while they made
love and see the sky and trees overhead. But Penny, smelling the grass
around them, thought it was the best way to celebrate their twentieth
wedding anniversary, which both of them had forgotten until that
moment.

Jerry's book was due out the same week as her baby. The sym-
bolism of this irritated Penny, especially when his book was early and
her baby was late. She had always disliked comparisons between
artistic creativity and giving birth; they seemed both dishonest and
inaccurate. But in the August heat, her belly swelling in front of her,
almost anything seemed to annoy her. She felt that her month of
feeling ripe and sexual and blooming had given way to a feeling of
being overripe and fetid, like a piece of fruit that no one has picked,
which hangs, turning brown, only to finally plop to the ground.

Meredith was coming out for the weekend. Cal had come,
briefly, the weekend she was due and then had to fly back to be on
location in Hawaii. He was playing the transvestite friend of a crazed
killer in a low-budget horror movie. Penny was glad Meredith was

coming. She had no special panic about giving birth, but she wanted someone there while it happened, just in case. And Meredith claimed to have actually delivered hundreds of babies in med school, even having toyed with the idea of becoming an obstetrician. "Not that I remember a damn thing about it," she said reassuringly. "But it'll come back to me, if need be. It's like riding a bicycle."

Everyone in the office, perhaps due to their sex, regarded her with a mixture of consideration and anxiety. She was moved into the only air-conditioned office, offered numerous glasses of water each day. To her amazement, even casually obscene jokes, which previously might have been made in her presence, were now, with sidelong glances, censored, as though her imminent motherhood made her especially delicate and refined. One might, given the cause of motherhood, have expected it to be the other way around, she thought.

In the middle of Friday afternoon the phone rang.

"Is this Penelope Howard?"

"Yes?"

"This is Nira Goldschmitt, Jerry Gardener's wife? I'm just calling because Jerry got your note about the book being ready, but he's out of town for a few days, and I'll be in Princeton this afternoon. I'm at the train station now, actually. I wondered if I could stop by and pick it up."

"Sure," Penny said, her throat suddenly going dry. "That's . . . fine. Um, when do you think—"

"Would five be too late? I know some people like to leave early for the weekend."

"No, that'll be terrific." In fact, she had intended to leave with Meredith at five-thirty.

By four, almost everyone had left the office. Penny felt too exhausted mentally and physically to do anything, to even be anxious about finally meeting Jerry's wife. She lay down on a couch in the corner of her office and fell asleep.

Some time later she was awakened by a knock on the door and leapt up, groggy from a deep sleep. "Just a sec," she called out, and went to open the door.

"Hi." It was Nira. Penny recognized her from the photo. "I'm sorry to be so late."

Penny felt half asleep. Traces of some strange dream were still in her mind. She and Helen had been pressing currants and trying to decide what to cook with them. She turned on the overhead light. "I'm glad you were late," she said. "It gave me a chance to rest."

"When is your baby due?" Nira asked.

"Any second." Penny laughed. "I have a friend, a doctor, who's coming to stay with me this weekend. My husband's away."

Nira shook her head. "They always are, aren't they? Mine was always away with all three."

Penny remembered that this did not mean Jerry. She looked at Nira more carefully, trying to keep in mind Nira's connection with Jerry without totally losing her composure. She looked, as one might expect, older than in the photo—slender, with soft, pale skin. Her hair was still dark, short, and fluffy but streaked with gray. Beautiful blue eyes. Penny had expected someone ultra-elegant, perhaps because of the connection with fashion. But Nira was dressed just in slacks and a shirt, nothing very high style or unusual.

"The books are in a box," she said. "Over in the corner there. Can you manage them? I don't trust myself to lift them."

"Oh sure." Nira took one off the top and inspected it. "It looks impressive. I'm really looking forward to reading it."

"You haven't already?" Penny decided to pretend total lack of knowledge of anything about her, for fear of making some misstep.

Nira smiled. "I could never follow the other one, the history-of-science one. I'm just awful at science! I failed biology . . . It's disgraceful, really. But this sounds more like just a regular novel."

"It's a fascinating combination," Penny said. Sitting at her desk, she felt more professional and detached. "If someone had described it to me, I wouldn't have thought it would work, but it does."

"Do you think someone like me could understand it?" Nira said, leafing through it. "It's not too technical?"

"Just a few parts. . . . No, we're hoping for a more general audience than we have for most of our books. You'd be a good test case."

Nira looked at her thoughtfully. "My older daughter's read it. . . . She admires Jerry so much. She thinks it's extraordinary. It's so funny, how things work out—"

"How?" Penny said, her heart thumping.

"Well, when I met Jerry he was thinking of switching to teaching and perhaps having time to write, but it seemed such a remote possibility. Teaching jobs were so hard to get. And he doesn't have a doctorate in the history of science, just in biochemistry . . . But it all happened. Everything fell into place." Her voice was soft, bemused.

"You're not a scientist?" Penny asked nervously, remembering a moment too late Nira's previous remark about failing biology. But she didn't seem to notice.

"No, I design clothes." Nira looked at her, her hands over the title of the book. "This has been an important year for me. I've set up my own business with a friend. But I've gone crazy, flying back and forth to Paris every month. It's nice having the freedom of making all the decisions yourself. I've always worked for other people. It's scary in a way, though. . . . Will you keep working after your baby's born?"

Penny nodded. "I have to, financially . . . But even if I didn't, I think I'm the kind of person who needs something—"

"Oh, yes," Nira interrupted. "Everyone does."

"Do you think so? So many women seem to take a few years off. I feel somewhat guilty."

"Don't," she urged. "It's such a mistake. I did that . . . and then, when you want to get back in, it's so hard. You start from scratch and that can be so demoralizing, working for people much younger than you."

"So, if you had it to do over," Penny asked, "you'd—"

"Work straight through," Nira said, leaning forward. "Definitely . . . I mean, now it doesn't seem to matter so much, but those first few years were murder. And with Jerry trying to switch fields too. . . . Is your husband in publishing?"

"No . . . He's an actor."

"Oh . . . What kind?"

"Well, he started out wanting to do plays, but now it's mostly TV and movies."

"Would I have heard of him? Is he famous?"

"Well, not famous, no . . . He was in something recently on TV. That series about the Roman uprising. He played the general, the one who kills himself."

Nira's face lit up. "I saw that! He was wonderful. Goodness, that was your husband? He's gorgeous."

Penny smiled. "He is."

"I love that kind of looks in men, that blond, crisp, steely thing. Well, Jerry has it a bit. You've met him? Of course, you must have— to have worked together."

Penny swallowed. "Yes, we—"

"How was he to work with?" Nira asked. "I always wondered. He can be so . . . rigorous. I mean, insisting on having his own way."

"Yes," Penny said. "He *was* like that at first, but in the end he accepted a lot of the suggestions I offered."

"Good," Nira said. She smiled. "I'm glad they gave him a woman editor. That's good for him . . . Well, perhaps he'll do more books for you?"

"Maybe," Penny said faintly. For no reason that she could fathom, images of herself in bed with Jerry started invading her thoughts. She felt as though Nira could see all of them. There was a knock on the door. "Come in," Penny called, grateful at the interruption.

It was Meredith. In her confusion Penny had completely forgotten. "Oh hi . . . Meredith, this is Nira Goldschmitt. She's the wife of one of our authors whose book just came out today." Her eyes signaled to Meredith silently. "This is my friend, Meredith West."

"You're the doctor?"

"Yes. But it's been *years* since I've delivered a baby. I'm just hoping Pen will have a nice long labor. First babies usually are."

"*I* thought that," Nira said, looking from one of them to the other. "And my first was born in around two hours! It really scared me. I had the next two induced, just to be on the safe side." She stood up. "Well, thanks so much . . . I'll carry the box."

"Are you going back to New York?" Meredith asked.

"Yes . . . I think there's a train at six-thirty."

"I could drive you . . . I came by car."

"Would you? That would really help."

The three of them went downstairs together, Nira first. Meredith didn't even look at Penny, to her immense relief. Nira got in front, next to Meredith, and Penny took the backseat.

"Jerry's going to be so excited," Nira said, more to Meredith. "I think this book means more to him than the other one. I hope it does well."

"Has he published other things?" Meredith asked.

"A history-of-science textbook . . . But this is more like a novel."

"Yes, Penny's described it . . . I always feel *I* ought to write a novel. I'm a psychiatrist and I get so much material every day. I'd have to change it, of course."

"You could use a pseudonym," Nira suggested.

"I have a friend who did."

Meredith glanced in the mirror at Penny. "Are you okay, Pen? You look a little funny."

"I'm just exhausted," Penny said quickly.

"You should take the next week off," Nira suggested. "If you're so close. And with the heat."

"She's one of these puritanical types," Meredith said. "All work, no play."

There was a pause.

"What are you hoping for?" Nira asked, turning around. "A boy or a girl?"

"Well, I would have liked a girl, but it's going to be a boy. I had an amniocentesis test."

"I have three girls," Nira said. She stopped. Her face looked so stricken, Penny was taken aback. "No, I have two, actually . . . I used to have three. One of my daughters died, Posey."

Penny stared at her. Nira's face had gone white.

"I'm so sorry," Penny said.

Nira had turned around again. "They say you get over things like that," she said quietly. "But you don't really, not ever. I think about her every day."

They drove the rest of the way in silence. Nira gathered up the box of books. "Thanks so much," she said to Meredith and, turning to Penny, added, "Good luck with your baby."

She was soon out of sight. Penny, stretched out on the backseat, let out a low moan. Meredith turned around. "What's wrong?"

"This is the worst day of my life," Penny said.

Meredith laughed. "Never fear. There'll be worse ones . . . What was it, the thing about the child?"

"Everything," Penny said. "It was everything. I feel so sick and terrible. I feel like an evil, irresponsible person who ought to be stoned to death."

"Could you be a little more—"

"She's nice!" Penny wailed. "She's a nice person!"

"So? What did you expect? The bride of Frankenstein?"

"I don't know . . . I guess I expected some cold, imperious Joan Crawford type who would make biting, witty remarks and blow smoke rings."

"You've been seeing too many old movies."

"She *was* nice, wasn't she? Didn't you think she was?"

"Yeah, well . . . Actually, she reminded me quite a bit of you."

"Me?" Penny's eyes flew open. "How?"

"Just a certain . . . tentativeness, not being that sure of herself. I didn't mean it as an insult."

"Then why does he need *me?*" Penny asked. "Tell me."

"First of all, most people are drawn to a certain basic type. That's natural. And you're a different person. I'm not saying you're identical twins."

Penny turned over as best she could, her arm hanging down. "I don't want this baby," she said. "I don't want to be pregnant."

Meredith just looked at her.

"I won't have it . . . I don't want to have it. I'm going to have an abortion."

"You're more likely to go into labor if you keep writhing around like that."

Penny sat up. "I don't want to have it!" she shouted. "Aren't you listening to me?"

"Pen, I'm listening. Just calm down, will you? This is a mood. It will pass."

"It's *not* a mood! I *hate* babies! I don't *want* a baby . . . Look what she said. They die! *I* might die; *Cal* might die; *it* might die."

"Look, the statistical likelihood is that we'll all be blown to smithereens by some crazed little Dr. Strangelove type . . . if that will set your mind at rest."

"Mer, will *you* take the baby? Will you raise it for me? You said you would. Please."

Meredith sighed. "I don't want a baby."

"So, why tell *me* to have one?"

"Look, it isn't like you asked me ahead of time. I just think now is hardly the moment to—"

"Mer, I never told you this, but I actually *hate* babies. I mean, I have a real aversion to them. Like some people do with dogs. They scare me . . . And they *know* I don't like them. They back out of the room when I come near. They sense it."

"With your own it's different."

"It's going to be like *Rosemary's Baby,*" Penny said. "It'll be born with horns and tiny red eyes. Conceived in sin . . ."

Meredith sighed. "Stay away from the movies for a while, okay?"

"She was a nice person!" Penny screamed.

"Okay! So she was a nice person? . . . Did he tell you she was a monster?"

"No."

"You don't even know it's his kid, do you?"

"No."

"And one thing I can tell you absolutely—she hasn't a suspicion in hell about you. Not one."

"That's supposed to make me feel better?"

"Yes . . . You'd be happy if she knew and was secretly miserable and jealous? Pen, listen to me. You're exhausted. She's right. You're not going in to work next week. You're coming back to the house with me and have a nice, relaxing supper and a little iced tea, and you're going straight to bed . . . and you'll have a beautiful baby, and you're not an evil person."

Penny began to cry. Meredith drove back to the house.

The baby, Jonah, was born Sunday night. Meredith drove Penny to the hospital. He was born in four hours, and the doctor gave Penny gas because it was a breech birth. He was beautiful and had all the requisite fingers and toes. Penny came home on Wednesday and was back at work the following Monday. During the day, she left Jonah with a Mrs. Tucker who lived down the road. Mrs. Tucker had three pre-school children and "took in" babies, four of them. Life changed and did not change. Jonah was a good baby and slept through the night at five weeks. Meredith offered to raise him after all, and Penny said no; she had changed her mind. The baby did not seem to know or sense that she hated babies. He smiled when she came near, grew fat, and his physical perfection was marred only by a heat rash on his forehead and legs.

When the baby had his first month birthday, Penny took him in his carriage for a walk. If serenity had eluded her, the hysteria of that day in the office had also passed. Life seemed no more comprehensible than before, but nor did it seem horrifying or impossible. She was going to buy a wedding present for Helen, who had called the night before from Hawaii.

"Did you bring George?" Penny asked, upon hearing Helen and Bernie were on their honeymoon.

"He's chained up outside the door, baying," Helen said. "No, we managed to elude him, somehow. He sent a huge bouquet of flowers before we left, though."

"He sent me a five-hundred-dollar gift certificate for FAO Schwarz," Penny said. "Should I keep it?"

"Of course! That'll keep you in Steiff bears until Jonah's in high school."

"I wish you could see him," Penny said.

"He looks gorgeous. I got the photos."

"Cal adores him . . . Isn't it funny?"

"No, not at all."

"He wants us to have five more, like you and—"

"I'm having my marriage to George annulled," Helen said. "I'm having it legally declared a figment of my imagination."

"Is that possible after six kids?"

"It is . . . There's a new Figment-of-Imagination law which has been passed just in the state of California."

Penny hesitated. "Are you happy?"

"Frighteningly."

"And Shirley is really going to marry that Japanese historian?"

"So she says. She's moved in with him. His sister is threatening hara-kiri every day, but I think that appeals to Shirley's sense of drama. Anyway, she's off our back. . . . So listen, Bernie is waving at me from our heart-shaped bathtub. We have to do all the requisite insane things so we'll have a honeymoon to describe to our grandchildren."

"Have fun."

"You too, sweetie. Kiss the baby for me."

Thinking of the conversation, Penny smiled as she walked along in the early October sunlight. October was her favorite month. She was smiling as she almost bumped into Jerry and his daughter who were coming from the other direction.

"Penny!" He took her arm.

"Hi, Jerry."

"Penny, I don't think you met my daughter Jane . . . Jane, this is Penelope Howard who edited my book."

"Hello." His daughter was almost as tall as he was and very thin, with long, blond hair hanging limply to her shoulders. She had sad, penetrating eyes.

Jerry was looking into the carriage. "He's beautiful," he said.

The baby was lying on his stomach, his face to one side, the side that had the heat rash. "Well, he's—" Penny started. "He is wonderful . . . and he's beautiful on the other side."

"Is he yours?" Jane asked in a very soft voice, looking in also.

Penny nodded. "Jonah."

"What?"

"That's his name."

Jane stared down at the baby. "Babies always make me nervous."

"It's different with your own," Penny and Jerry said in unison, and laughed.

"Where are you going?" Jerry asked.

"I need to get my sister a wedding present."

"We're looking for one too," Jerry said. "Heather's getting married next month."

"Who's she?"

"My stepsister," Jane said.

"You met her that night," Jerry said. "The night you came for dinner."

The memory of that night passed swiftly through Penny's mind, lying in his dark study, acting impossible. And then, on the tail of it came the day she had met Nira and screamed, "She's a nice person!" and wanted to die from shame. "Yes, I remember now," she said.

They all three walked along together.

"Who's she marrying?" Penny asked.

"A fellow student . . . Jon something."

"Daddy never can remember his name," Jane said, affectionately exasperated.

"Oedipal, no doubt," Jerry said.

"I thought she was your stepdaughter," Penny said.

"It doesn't matter."

Jane looked at him. Then she said to Penny, "He was married before. Heather's my stepmother's daughter."

"Yes, I know." Suddenly she turned to Jerry. "I met Nira—that day she came for the books . . . She's nice. She *is* beautiful."

He smiled. "Yes, she is."

"I wish my mother would get married," Jane said to no one in particular.

"Why?" Jerry asked. "She's happy as she is."

"No, she's not," Jane said. "She's *not* happy."

Jerry looked flustered. "She's as happy as she would be married."

"She did love this one person," Jane said intensely to Penny. "Only he was black. And he was thirty years older than her. So she didn't marry him . . . She's very conventional in some ways." She looked contemptuous. "I wouldn't care what color someone was, would you?"

"No," Penny said. "But—"

"When she's old, she won't have anyone to look after her," Jane said accusingly. "I'm afraid she'll end up like those shopping bag ladies on Broadway."

"Darling," Jerry said.

"You just don't care about her!"

"I do . . . I can't be married to two people at the same time, that's all."

Jane stared at him. Then she laughed. "I guess that's true," she said. "And she wouldn't want you back, anyway. That's what she says." She looked at Penny. "Are *you* married?"

Penny nodded. "My husband lives in California, though. . . . He's a movie actor."

Jane made a face. "Is he very conceited?"

"No."

"I once had an actor for a boyfriend, and he stared at himself all *day* in the mirror. Once we went to a party, and someone said I looked pretty and they didn't say anything to him . . . and he wouldn't talk to me all the next day."

"Was he that shaggy one with the glasses?" Jerry asked.

"No! Daddy, what's wrong with you? You keep getting people mixed up! That was Jack."

"It's age," Jerry said, smiling at Penny.

"You're only fifty, not eighty-five!"

They went into a small gift shop. The woman who ran it said the carriage would have to be left outside. "I'd take the baby in with you," she said. "We had a baby-snatcher last week. Maybe you read about it in the paper."

"No, I didn't," Penny said.

"It was just a teenager playing a prank, but the poor mother! She almost died."

Penny took the sleeping baby with her into the store. She walked around slowly, looking at things. Helen had most things already, but she wanted to get her something. She saw a large ceramic platter with small green fish painted on it. "I think I'd like that," she said to Jerry who was standing beside her. Jane was on the upper level of the store.

"Maybe we should get one of those too," he said. "It's lovely."

"It's one of a kind, sir," the woman who ran the store said. "But we have another very like it by the same artist."

Jerry liked the other platter and bought it, though to Penny it didn't seem as nice.

"I've been meaning to get you a baby present," he said. "But I can't think what. I want it to be something special."

Penny just looked at him. She wondered if they would ever go to bed together again.

"What would you like?" he asked.

"I don't know," Penny said.

They stared at each other for a long moment.

"Daddy, there's something great up here," Jane called. "Look!" She held up a multi-colored straw basket.

"I got something already, sweetie," Jerry called. He and Penny watched as his daughter climbed down the stairs.

Summer 1971 - Fall 1972

Make few changes in time of stress.

That was one of the cardinal rules in all those infuriatingly cheerful self-help books that Nira bought during her divorce. Implying that there were dozens of changes you *could* make! Murray gave her a raise, thus sparing her the indignities of further job-hunting. Their housekeeper stayed on, her kindness and efficiency now larded with off-the-cuff remarks about Adlai. "A man who leaves his family, three little girls," she murmured darkly. "He must have no conscience. I had an uncle like that once. He ended up in jail, embezzlement." But it was Serena who belonged in jail, under the embezzlement-of-husbands law which had, alas, not been enacted yet. As for Adlai, he was scarcely around long enough to scream at, flying back and forth from London to New York, caught in the mayhem and excitement of creating a new home.

Friends were kind but apologetic.

"I'd introduce you to someone if I knew anyone," Ellie said.

"Steal someone's husband" was Fay's advice. "It's the only way. Forget sisterhood for a while."

"I don't want anyone!" Nira shrieked. "Men are schmucks. Who needs them?"

"Yeah, well, that's a stage," Fay said.

It was worse than a stage. It wasn't even true. She did need someone, desperately, in a way so ugly and needful, it made her ashamed to even look men in the face at parties. She slunk in corners, eating too many canapés, waiting for the party to be over so that she could go home and, in darkness, pretend it was someone other than herself luring her into the oblivion of physical pleasure, then sleep.

Murray Farber and his wife had her to dinner and introduced her to his friend Monty, the widower who was looking for trouble. Either he had passed on to another stage or she looked troublesome, but he seemed quite taken with her and, on her front door, swept her up into a passionate embrace, chomping on her front lip with an avidity that might have scared her, had she not recognized how many nights of restless loneliness went into it. Though she felt no responsive feeling, there was a sense of sympathy. "I guess I'm not ready to get involved with anyone yet," she begged off but felt obliged, through guilt, to ask him in and then listen to the story of his marriage—how happy they had been; how wonderful his deceased wife was.

"Was it really like that?" Nira couldn't help asking. It was three in the morning—too late for politeness. "Or does it just seem that way now that she's gone?"

"Both," he admitted. "I guess it was that we knew each other right through, everything. You don't have that with so many people."

"No," Nira agreed.

"I'm ready to marry a lamppost," he said, sighing. "Know any good ones?"

"Oh, me too," Nira said.

"I thought you said you weren't ready—"

"I'm not. I just meant . . ." Oh, what did she mean? She didn't know herself, anymore. By four it seemed easier to go to bed with him than to pitch him out. He made love swiftly and silently, like someone jumping over a fence. It was neither wonderful nor terrible. It had no future, which was perhaps its one advantage.

The girls saved her, Nira thought, as fall wore on. All those family responsibilities, which previously had seemed a drag, especially after she began work, now seemed doubly welcome. Having someone to come home to, to cook for, to care about, to love. And the baby's clutching, avid neediness splashed over her. With Adlai gone, she was more clinging, and Nira wanted to be clung to, wanted to be "everything" to someone, if only for the moment. The girls, sensing her loneliness, tried stratagems themselves. Heather brought home her math teacher for dinner.

Timothy Easterman looked in his early thirties, a careful, precise man who gasped with horror when he spilled a glass of wine on the tablecloth. He had never been married. "I love children," he said dolefully. "But of course teaching gives one that vicarious satisfaction."

"Yes," Nira said. Or did she mean no? Or didn't it matter?

"Heather is a very talented student," he assured her. "You must be proud . . ."

"Yes," Nira assured him. "I am."

"I was very sorry to hear of your husband's untimely demise."

"What?"

He blushed. "Heather told me . . . I gather the death was very sudden. Sometimes it's best that way."

Later she was to learn that Heather had decided "death" sounded more romantic than "divorce." "I figured if you really liked each other, you could explain later."

"Hon, I think the truth is usually easier all around."

"You said the opposite last week," she reprimanded her. "You said the truth serves no purpose whatsoever, quote, unquote." Teenage condescension had begun creeping into Heather's normally precise diction.

How could she remember a week ago? It was another life. After Mr. Easterman had left, Nira opened her mail and found, once again, a letter from her former mother-in-law, Lily (Amaryllis) Goldschmitt. It gave her a pang, just to see the smooth, even, violet script on the familiar parchment stationery. They had written to each other once a month for sixteen years. In anger at Adlai, Nira had stopped answering her letters, but they continued, never reproving, only worried. This one read:

> Dearest Nira,
>
> I understand what you must be feeling. I hope that, in time, our friendship can continue as it was, unattached to the dreadful consequences of my son's behavior. Please understand that I don't wish to force myself on you, at a time when you must have so many duties and responsibilities. I'm writing simply to let you know that I'll be in New York next month, stopping over en route to Bermuda to visit an old school friend. If you would like to have lunch, I would be so happy. I'll call you from the hotel. My warmest love to the children.
>
> Lily

They had been friends, it was true. And what was the etiquette on relations with former mothers-in-law? None of it was her fault, Nira told herself, but it didn't quite work. It wasn't so much that Lily had given birth to Adlai as that her new daughter-in-law was English, and Nira felt certain that that must, in some way, be enjoyable to her, in addition to the pleasure of having Adlai so near by. But when Lily called that October, Nira said yes, of course she would come to the Carlyle for lunch; of course she wanted to see her.

Adlai's parents had been English versions of her own, socialists who lived in opulent comfort on a small estate in Devon, ready, when the revolution came, to give it all up but wanting to savor it for all it was worth until that was necessary. Of their three sons, Adlai was the only one who was, strictly speaking, legitimate. Conventional to the teeth, the Goldschmitts had felt "free love" was their socialist duty, and lived in a supremely bourgeois version of living in sin amidst ironstone crockery and flowered chintz armchairs. Lily had once confided to Nira that she missed those days, the long years of feeling smugly different, the glow from fending off curious questions from neighbors. "But Thurston never could quite accept it," she said. "He always felt it wasn't fair to me." Nira's own parents' version had consisted of sneaking out at night to buy *The Daily Worker* from an eight-room Madison Avenue apartment. The inconsistencies of it were as familiar to her as milk.

"I'm so glad you came, Nira," Lily said, welcoming her into the suite. She had said she thought it would be more comfortable and relaxed if they had lunch in her room. "I have a lovely view," she had added, as though an extra lure might be necessary.

In the almost twenty years that she had known her, Lily had changed so subtly that it often seemed to Nira she had not changed at all. Her hair had been that same soft white at forty-five as at sixty-five—hereditary, she had once explained, on both sides—her figure already rounded beyond fashionability, her blue eyes alternately keen or misty, depending on mood, her bifocals poised charmingly on the tip of her daintily uptilted nose which, luckily, Heather had inherited. Her only vanity was her legs, which were still, into her sixties, slim as a girl's. She wore high-heeeled sandals with ankle straps, and sat, legs crossed, like someone ready to be picked up at a bar. She still smoked half a pack of cigarettes a day, puffing quickly and intently, and snuffing each one out with an impatient, decisive gesture.

Nira had sometimes wondered about Lily's sex life, though Adlai had claimed it was nonexistent. "Everyone thinks that about his mother," Nira had said, but he insisted, and she finally, having no counter-evidence, gave way. Thurston Goldschmitt had died on Adlai's twenty-first birthday, two winters before Nira had come to England. There had been a few years when Adlai had muttered darkly about the carpenter-handyman who tended the grounds, evidently fearing some autumnal rerun of Lady Chatterley. The carpenter was bearded, stocky, and rubicund, given to quoting Shelley and Keats. He had, according to Lily, "An absolute genius for plants and flowers. He just touches them and they bloom." Whether this metaphor was sexual or merely horticultural, they never discovered. Lily continued, as serene and unperturbed in her widowhood as she had been as an unwed mother of two and member of the local garden club.

"Are you finding it very difficult?" Lily inquired now as they waited for room service. "I was a disaster after Thurston's death so I can imagine."

"Were you?" Nira was surprised. "You always seemed so—calm and self-possessed."

"I did?" Lily blushed. "Goodness, how wonderful. . . . That was what I was aiming for, of course, but I always thought anyone from a hundred yards could see what a sham it was. If it hadn't been for Peter—"

"Was he the gardener you had? The man with the beard?"

Lily beamed. "I still have him," she said. "I mean, he still . . . works for me."

"It wasn't sexual, then?" Nira probed. She felt divorce had given her the right to be rude. "We always wondered. Adlai worried—"

Lily's cool laugh splashed over this rumor, congealing it at once. "Goodness no. Peter? He was gay. I thought Adlai knew that. And in any case, it wasn't that kind of thing."

"What *did* you do about sex?" Nira asked. "I know this sounds rude, but—"

"Not at all, darling," Lily looked pensive. "I guess basically nothing, really . . . I mean, I had the odd run-in with this one or that. But somehow . . . I'm not a terribly sexual person, I don't think. I know that's ghastly to say nowadays. I mean, I miss terribly being held and kissed and cared for, but the act itself seems to me, well, dispensable somehow."

Nira sighed.

"You'll find a lover," Lily assured her. "At first it's hard. I was angry at Thurston for dying, so I can imagine how—"

"It's that I didn't know," Nira said intensely. "It was so sudden. I didn't suspect anything. And yet he seems so happy . . . Does he to you?"

"Oh, I don't *care* about whether he's 'happy' or not!" Lily shot back. "That's no excuse at all. She's a dreadful woman, simply unspeakable . . . You should have *seen* her with her husband. Making such a fuss over him, practically *feeding* him at dinner parties. It was sickening . . . I knew from the day Adlai went to visit her, he was a dead duck. I just hate women like that, you know, the kind that fawn on men. It's perverse."

"I don't know," Nira said. "Maybe one has to, a bit."

"A bit! Of course a bit . . . and she's done the same thing with her boys. Spoiled sick. The twins have criminal records, did you know that? Oh, they're dreadful boys. The kind that probably tore the wings off birds when they were young. And I'm sure Serena sat there, smiling, as though they were painting the Sistine chapel."

All of this was balm to Nira. She wondered how much it was exaggerated for her benefit. "Actually, we're managing all right," she said. "It's better than I thought."

"Even the baby?"

"Especially her . . . She's so beautiful, I wish you could see her."

"Would you let me?"

Her tone was so gentle, Nira was touched. "Of course. Any time."

"I was afraid to ask." Lily lit another cigarette. "Nira, this may seem presumptuous. I assume financial matters have been . . . settled?"

"Pretty much."

"You'll be able to manage?"

"I think so . . . I'm working now, and that helps."

"Yes, I know . . . Well, really, what I wanted to say was, if it would ever make life easier for you, I'd be glad to take them for a year. I have so much room, as you know. For me it would just be a joy."

"I don't think I could right now," Nira tried to explain. "It's hard with them in some ways, but without them it would be worse. They're like a lifeline."

Lily stamped out her cigarette. "Yes, I know what you mean . . . but you'll bear it in mind, darling, if ever . . ."

They had chicken salad and white wine. Nira remembered the last time she had been in a hotel—with Murray, that boiling summer day, the gigantic breakfast, his nurturing, parental sweetness, how he had rolled back his eyes after they made love the second time and said, "I think I've died and gone to heaven."

"What you ought to do," Lily said, sipping her wine as she puffed her cigarette in small, quick sips, "is come to England and visit. Stay with me . . . I think you'll like English men, Nira. There's more to them, from what I've seen. Americans seem so straightforward and blunt, lunging at you, somehow. English men are more like women. You can talk to them; they prevaricate; they have interesting weaknesses. You used to say you liked challenges."

Nira smiled. "Maybe I better get over that . . . just find some bouncy, ardent person who thinks I'm wonderful and loves the girls."

"*Are* you in love with anyone?"

Nira turned red. How had she known or guessed? "Well, maybe. I hope not, but perhaps . . . It's someone from the past," she said vaguely, not quite ready to confess to mutual marital infidelities.

"Someone unavailable?" Lily said, her eyes bright and concerned.

"In a way . . . I—" She stopped.

"We don't have to talk about it, if you don't want," Lily said. She poured Nira more wine. "To love," she said.

"Okay," Nira said. "Why not? To love."

But the encounter with her mother-in-law unsettled her. She wished, somehow, she could hate her, could snap off the past with a quick nip, like biting a thread. Instead, the past seeped into the present, eroding it, sustaining it at the same time. Thanksgiving came. Madame Jacobe invited them as usual, but Nira refused. She didn't feel up to the friendly concern which she knew would pour over her and the girls. Instead, with a grim determination, she roasted a large turkey, mashed sweet potatoes, set the table for the four of them with cloth napkins and the bird napkin rings she and Adlai had bought on a trip to Mexico many years earlier. The baby tried to eat her napkin ring and seemed displeased at the bitter hardness of it. Posey plied her with marshmallows instead.

"They're sweet," she said. "They're good, see? Even if they're burned."

"Mom, how come they're burned?" Heather asked.

"I left them in too long," Nira said, her mood as dark and unlifting as the rain which beat down. She had carved the turkey with reckless abandon, shearing off legs and wings, dismembering it as though it were her former husband. The girls overate doggedly and then collapsed in front of the TV, too stuffed to even want to go out to a movie.

Nira cleared up and then felt a stab of panic at the long weekend ahead. Someone had invited her to a party Saturday, but apart from that there were four frighteningly empty days. Maybe I'll go see Jerry. She was not sure where that thought came from. Since the lunch with Lily, she had begun thinking of him more often again. It was a habit which, at this point in her life, she lacked the energy to curtail. She remembered the Thanksgiving a year ago, the drive to her parents' country house, making love in the chilly room on the corduroy spread, showing him her artwork.

"Girls, I have to go out," Nira said, entering the bedroom where the TV was nestled into a white wall-system. Jasmine was sitting on Posey, who was lying belly down, her legs in the air. Heather sat propped against a large velvet pillow, her newly acquired glasses on her nose.

"It's pouring rain," Heather said, not moving her eyes from the screen.

"It's a sick friend," Nira invented. "She needs someone to talk to. If she's in really bad shape, I may have to stay over. Can you manage Jas?"

"What are our options?" Heather inquired coolly.

"You can call Thelma tomorrow if you get desperate. She said she was free."

"I know!" Posey said. "We can take Jas to the Museum of Natural History." She turned around to look at the baby, who was thoughtfully stroking Posey's ears. "Would you like that, Jas? Museum?"

"Mu," the baby said.

"Last time she got scared," Heather said. "Don't you remember? She thought the animals were real."

"That was when she was a baby," Posey said. "Don't worry Mom . . . We'll be fine."

"Is there a number where we can reach you?" Heather asked.

"No," Nira said quickly.

"How come? Doesn't she have a phone?"

"I'll call you," Nira said.

"How come she doesn't have a phone?" Heather persisted.

"Maybe she lives in the country," Posey suggested.

"So? People in the country have phones," Heather said.

"Not always," said Posey. "Sometimes they're poor, and they can't afford it. Is that it, Mom? Is she poor?"

"Very poor," Nira said, escaping before the conversation could get further out of hand.

"That doesn't make sense," Heather was saying. "Susie's poor and she has a phone."

"But she doesn't live in the country," Posey said.

Outside the rain fell heavily and darkly. It was early evening but could have been midnight. Nira hated driving in the dark or in rain, but a sense of necessity had overcome her. She felt like a fighter pilot about to embark on a suicidal mission to save France. What if he's there with someone? What if he's in San Francisco visiting his brother? So, I'll drive back. She knew his address; once, months earlier, she'd called the biology department at Princeton, pretending to be the county courthouse checking on his address for jury duty. What if he's moved?

Nira had driven to Princeton once, a few years earlier, to visit a friend; she remembered the route. She decided to drive slowly, listening to music on the radio to soothe her nerves. But the radio music was all odd—Russian operas with endless basso profundo arias, a psychiatrist analyzing *Don Giovanni* with phrases like "I would like to take this opportunity to go out on a proverbial limb." Finally, she snapped it off and allowed her thoughts to wander aimlessly: "Mother Abandons Children on Thanksgiving Weekend, found dead on New Jersey turnpike. Children found" . . . Oh hush. They're old enough; they'll be fine. But guilt made her pull over at nine o'clock and call from a roadside phone.

"How are things?" she asked.

"Fine," Posey said. "How come you're calling, Mom? I thought you said she didn't have a phone."

"I'm not there yet."

"Jas fell asleep. She didn't have her bath."

"That's okay."

"I ate all the marshmallows."

"I thought I threw them out."

"They were right on top of the garbage. They're just burned, but they're really good."

"Po, burned stuff isn't good for you."

"Yes it is . . . Cavemen ate burned meat."

Touching base proved to be a good idea. The remaining hour passed swiftly, as though she were asleep but still alert enough to focus on driving. In fact, she did feel sleepy, having awakened, as she often did these days, at six, lying in bed with no idle thoughts to soothe her back to sleep. She drove slowly down Prospect Street, looking for the right number. There was a light on in the living room. It was just past ten. Okay, so what if he's there with her? What are you going to say? I'm from the country courthouse. I want to see if he's available for jury duty. Quit worrying. I'll rely on the inspiration of the moment.

Nira rang the door bell. Her heart was pounding with sickening fear as steps came down the hall. The door opened; it was his older daughter, Jane. She was dressed in a long flannel nightgown and had bare feet. Nira was in a yellow slicker, with a broad-brimmed hat to match. Rain dripped from the hat as from a roof. "Hi," she croaked.

"Hi," Jane said. "Daddy's not here."

"That's okay," Nira said. "Can I come in?" She was relieved at having been recognized.

"Sure." Jane stepped aside. "Are you Nira?"

Nira sneezed. "Yes," she said.

"We're watching TV. Do you want to come in? There's a fire-place."

The room was cosy and old-American seeming, with a hook rug and a fire which had burned down but was still warm and glowing. Stacey was curled up under a knitted afghan. Nira felt like Alice through the Looking Glass. The same scene as in her own house, but with two light-haired girls instead of two dark ones, and different furniture.

"Daddy's at a party," Jane explained. "He might be back late. He said we could stay up till ten-thirty. We took our baths already."

The younger girl was in pajamas with feet. Her eyelids were dropping, as though she had stayed up this late more to prove that she could than because the TV program was that fascinating. Nira hung her coat in the hall closet. She checked for women's coats but saw none. Would he return with someone from the party?

"Do you want to watch with us?" Jane offered. "It's this movie about a man who gets lost on a desert island."

"Yeah, I've seen it," Nira said. But she sat down beside them and watched, not really following the plot. Her own eyes began feeling heavy. Without realizing it, she dozed off briefly. When she opened her eyes, she saw that Stacey had fallen asleep, one arm hanging over the edge of the couch, mouth slightly open. The TV had been turned off. Jane, cross-legged, was reading *The Bell Jar.*

"I'm going to get a snack before I go to sleep," Jane said, looking up. "Do you want one too?"

"Sure," Nira said, following her into the kitchen. "What should we do about Stacey, though?"

"Oh, Daddy'll carry her to bed . . . That's why she does it. She just wants him to carry her to bed. She's really neurotic. Daddy says it's because of Mommy. Like she walks in her sleep! But she walks into Daddy's room and falls asleep on the floor. Stuff like that. She just wants to get attention."

The kitchen was big and comfortable. Nira sat down at the table as Jane got out some apples and oatmeal cookies. "Did you ever read *The Bell Jar?*" Jane asked.

Nira nodded.

"Did you like it?"

"Yeah, quite a lot . . . I like her poetry better, though."

"I haven't read much of that. Daddy thinks I shouldn't read it till I'm older. I don't see why. I can understand." She hesitated. "It's sort of depressing, though."

"She had a lot of problems," Nira said. "She ended up killing herself."

"I know." The girl's blue eyes focused intently on her. "I sometimes get feelings like that," she said.

"Like what?"

"Just, you know, like the girl in the book."

"Well, I guess everyone does," Nira said, feeling close to her. "I did at that age too."

"Did you have those feelings about boys?"

Nira nodded.

"And then what happened?" Jane asked.

Nira frowned. "I guess I . . . I met someone and got married."

"I don't want to get married," Jane said darkly. "Ever, to anyone."

"Well, lots of people don't," Nira offered.

"Daddy says I'll change my mind, but he's wrong. I'm *never* going to. I don't want children, so why should I get married?"

"Sometimes people do it just to . . . have a friend," Nira said lamely. "Someone to talk to."

"You don't have to get married for that! You can just have friends."

"True."

The girl stood at the door, still hesitant. "Do you think you could do me a favor?"

"Sure."

"Could you come upstairs with me and stay in my room till I get into bed?"

Jane's room was small, with two wooden, framed beds side by side and a small desk near the window. "We could have our own rooms," she explained, "but she doesn't like to sleep alone."

Nira waited while she brushed her teeth and climbed into bed.

"Keep the hall light on," Jane called.

"Sleep tight," Nira called again, going down the stairs.

"You too!" came the reply.

It was past midnight. Nira felt too exhausted to even think or worry any more about Jerry, when he would return, whom he might be with. She curled up on the other end of the couch, sharing the afghan with Stacey, and fell sound asleep.

When Jerry touched her and she opened her eyes to see his face looking down at her, for one confused second Nira thought they were back in his apartment, that she had fallen asleep after making love, that he had touched her because he wanted her again. And then the room swam into view and, with it, remembrance.

"When did you get here?" he asked. His manner was more friendly than abrupt.

"A few hours ago . . . Jane went to sleep, but Stacey—" Nira looked and saw Stacey wasn't there.

"I carried her upstairs," Jerry said.

Nira looked around, into the front hall. Was there someone with him? "I just came," she said, not knowing what explanation or apology to offer. "I wanted to see you."

He was gazing at her with an intent, thoughtful expression. "I'm glad you came," he said.

Nira didn't reply.

"I've been in the city several times," he said. "I thought of calling you, but . . ." He let the sentence go unfinished. "I'm going to have something to drink," he said. "Do you want anything?"

Nira shook her head but followed him into the kitchen where he drank a glass of orange juice. "How is your teaching working out?" she asked.

"It's really been good." He looked excited. "The students are first-rate. I'm teaching it with someone, did I mention that? That makes it easier, of course. . . . How have things been with you?"

"Okay." Her heart started thumping again. She didn't want to tell him about Adlai or the divorce. "Pretty much the same."

There was a long pause.

"I don't think I'm up to driving back tonight," Nira said, "Could I—could I stay over?"

"Of course." He looked puzzled at the question.

They moved out of the kitchen. Nira felt as though she had fallen from a cliff. Her whole body seemed to ache. She could hardly move. She hated him for having such terrible power over her. The longing that swept through her hardly seemed sexual; more like some primeval pain. Jerry touched her arm, guiding her. "Let's go upstairs," he said.

She followed him silently, like a dog, padding up the carpeted stairs in her bare feet. Her damp sneakers were on the living room floor near the fire.

Jerry's bedroom was dominated by a large four-poster bed. Otherwise, like his bedroom in New York, it was messy, with piles of books and newspapers everywhere. He saw her glance and smiled.

"They have traditional tastes," Nira said, sitting on the edge of the bed, "the couple you rented from."

"Yes . . . He's a history professor. They're in France this year."

She was glad when he disappeared into the bathroom; she wanted to undress without his seeing. She slipped under the cover furtively, like a virginal bride, pulling the patchwork quilt up to her neck. The sheets felt cold. When Jerry came out of the bathroom, she was in bed, her clothes tossed hurriedly on the floor in a heap. She watched as he undressed, hanging his clothes on a bentwood rocker in a corner of the room. He was erect as he walked toward her. Nira moved over. Jerry snapped off the small bed-light. She was unspeakably grateful for the sudden enveloping blackness of the room.

In the dark, their bodies said everything for which she could never have found the words. His mouth never left hers, he seemed impelled by an almost angry passion, and she struggled against it and with him, not sure if they were engaged in combat with each other or mutual seekers after the same prize. "Jerry, I love you," Nira whispered. "I can't help it. I'm sorry . . . I tried—"

Afterward he pulled her close, his arms locked around her. They fell asleep that way, their legs still entwined, his cock half inside her, their skin seeming welded together. Nira slept as she had not in months, deeply and soundlessly, with no dreams, as though at the bottom of the sea.

In the morning, when Nira awoke, sun streamed in the window. She was alone in bed. She showered and dressed, and went downstairs before she could think about the night before or anything else. At the table in the kitchen his daughters, still in their nightgowns, were having breakfast.

"You slept over," his younger daughter said, slightly accusingly.

"Yes," Nira said. She poured herself a bowl of cereal.

"Daddy's on the phone," Jane explained. "He made some coffee, though."

"It's that woman who dropped her necklace down the drain," Stacey told her.

"She doesn't know her," Jane said.

"Her name's Francoise," Stacey said. "She just dropped it down the drain! Then she started to cry. She said it was her grandmother's."

"She was a dope," Jane said.

"She's a teacher," said Stacey. "How can she be a dope?"

Jerry came into the room. He was dressed in jeans and a heavy dark-green sweater. "Did you have some coffee?" he asked Nira.

"I thought you might be in San Francisco," Nira said. "Visiting your brother."

"We couldn't go because Mommy's in the hospital," Stacey said.

Nira looked at Jerry questioningly.

"Are we going to visit her today?" Jane asked. "You said we could."

"We'll visit her in the afternoon," Jerry said stiffly.

Stacey looked at Nira. "I remember you," she said. "You came to the wedding with us. You're the one with the baby."

"Right." Nira smiled. "Only she's big now. She's a year and a half." She took some recent photos out of her purse. "See."

The two girls and Jerry looked at the color photos Nira spread out on the kitchen table.

"She's cute," Stacey said enthusiastically. "She looks really different. . . . Is it the same baby?"

"Of course it's the same baby," Jane said. "Is she walking yet?"

Nira nodded.

"We didn't walk till we were two. Mom thought we were retarded."

"Darling, that's—"

"I didn't say we *were* retarded," said Jane. "I said Mom thought so."

"So?" Stacey said. "She's crazy . . . What does she know?"

Nira felt her stomach tighten.

"She's not crazy," Jerry said finally.

Jane sighed. "Yeah, she's just confused, right? Daddy thinks it's because she was on drugs."

Jerry said, "Nira and I are going for a walk, kids. We'll be back a little later."

"I'm going to make Mommy a Thanksgiving Day card," Stacey said. "I don't care if she is crazy."

"She might rip it up like last time," Jane warned.

"I think that's a nice idea," Jerry said. He turned to Nira. "Do you have time?"

"I have time."

He drove her to a large meadow outside town, and they walked into the field. The day was bright and sunny. Nira felt, despite everything, insanely, wildly happy. She had done a reckless, foolish thing, driving out to see him, and it had worked. He had made love to her;

he was glad to see her. He smiled, taking her hand as they walked. "I'm glad to see you looking so well," he said, "so happy."

Nira, smiled, not wanting to add it was illusory, due to being with him. "I am happy," she said. After a second she asked, "Are you?"

Jerry didn't reply for a moment. "Well, this thing with Claire has—"

"How long has she been in the hospital?"

"Two months, about. . . . It was visiting her parents. That's always a disaster. Her father especially. . . . Then they call me up frantically, as though *I* were responsible for her. They actually wanted me to fly to Paris to get her. They'd put her in a hospital there, drugged up with Thorazine, with doctors who didn't know a word of English, and went off to their summerhouse in the south of France."

"So, you went?"

"I went. I got her discharged. She seemed happy to see me. She was fine on the plane coming home, very quiet but okay, nothing irrational. I brought her back here . . . and after a couple of days, she started getting the way she used to be, strange remarks, taunting the kids, threatening to cut their hair off in the middle of the night."

"And now?"

He shrugged. "I don't know . . . Am I going to be doing this for the next thirty years? We're divorced, supposedly."

"She doesn't have anyone but you."

"I know."

You're not in a hospital, Nira told herself. You were, but now you're here, in a sunny field with your lover, holding his hand. "What happened with Paige?" she said.

He glanced down at her. "It didn't work out," he said.

Nira laughed. "It was because of me."

"In a way, yes," he agreed.

She hadn't meant it that way. "No, I just meant I stuck pins in a voodoo doll of her. I wished she would give you VD and hate your kids, and they would hate her."

Jerry laughed. "Simple solutions, huh? None of that was necessary. It was all much more prosaic."

"And the woman who dropped her necklace down the drain?" Nira said, more sharply than she'd intended.

"How did you know about that?" He looked flustered.

"Your children."

"She's French," he said briefly.

"And?"

"And what?"

"And did you have sex with her? Often?" Her voice was shrill.

"A couple of times . . . So?" he said curtly. "I'm not asking you how many times you've had sex with your husband in the last six months."

Nira stared at him. "We haven't . . . if that sets your mind at rest."

He looked wary. "What do you mean?"

She told him. When she was done, he said, "Why didn't you tell me last night? You said everything was the same."

"I didn't want you to fuck me as a charity case," Nira said, stomping ahead of him in the long grass.

"That's not my specialty."

"What is—rescuing crazy married women from their boorish husbands?"

"Your husband never struck me as especially boorish."

"You're supposed to say *I* never struck you as especially crazy."

"Ni, why are you trying to pick a fight? I felt we were so happy."

She stood stock-still. "Because I can't go through this again!" she cried, turning to him. "I love you. I can't start up and stop and start up and stop. I'd rather you shot me. It's too painful. I think about you every second! I hate it! It's demeaning and awful . . . I wanted you to die, Jerry. I couldn't—"

He held her close. "Listen, things are different now."

"Are they?"

"Yes . . . We'll start again, differently."

"I'm the same person, though," she said quietly.

"I'm the same person too."

They went back to the house. The children were in the living room. Stacey was working on an altair design from a book. She held it up and showed it to them. "It's beautiful, sweetie," Jerry said.

It was. Nira was struck, as she had been by the girl's drawing the day of the wedding, at her astounding use of color.

"Will Mommy like it?" Stacey asked.

"Of course she will," Jerry said. "She'll love it."

"*I* wrote her a poem," Jane said.

They went upstairs, leaving the children to complete what they were doing, and made love again in the four-poster bed. This time the room was light; they could see each other. It was more like swimming in a tropical sea than being tossed by icy breakers, not knowing if they would crash over your head. Afterward they lay quietly together, not speaking.

"I should go back," Nira said finally.

"We should get going too," Jerry said. "Visiting hours are only till six on Sunday . . . God, I dread it. I wish—"

"Go," Nira said. "You have to go."

"Sometimes she doesn't even speak!" he said. "You don't know what it's like, Ni."

"I do," she cried. "Of course I know!"

"Were *you* like that?" he said, bewildered. "Really?"

She would have given anything to lie, but she said, "Yes, I was like that."

He stared ahead. "I just don't know," he said.

"She'll get better," Nira promised him.

"And then she'll get worse again."

"Maybe . . . You don't know that."

As she was leaving, he said he would be in the city the following week. They arranged to meet. It was a Saturday. "Maybe you can come to our apartment," Nira said. "You've never seen it."

The first time he came into the city, they just met for lunch near her job. It was strange to Nira, seeing him waiting in the lobby. For that whole year, he had been something separate from her job, her family. It would take some getting used to, to integrate him even mentally. Murray Farber came down in the elevator with her. She introduced them.

At lunch Jerry said, "Is he the one that was always giving you so much trouble?"

"No, that's Sol . . . Murray's a sweetie. He was so wonderful to me over the summer, after Adlai left." She told him about The Plaza.

"That's being wonderful?" Jerry said. "Taking advantage of a distraught employee, fucking her? *That's* being a sweetie."

"He did it to be nice. It *was* nice. He made me feel good, taken care of. Both of you had run off, with barely a nod. I was feeling like a worm . . . I'd never been to The Plaza. We had room service, blueberry muffins for breakfast . . ." She beamed at the memory.

Jerry continued looking irritated. "So what is this—something you do often, like women buy a new hat to cheer themselves up? Just fuck whoever passes by because they'll buy you blueberry muffins?"

Nira laughed nervously. "Yeah, I'm a cheap date . . . I've even been known to put out for a poached egg, given the right circumstances."

"Who else has been offering you poached eggs?"

She wished so much she had dozens of threatening, dashing conquests to offer. "Murray introduced me to a friend of his, a mournful widower."

He raised his eyebrows. "And he gave you a long, sad story about how miserable he was with his wife?"

"No! The opposite! How happy . . . only she died."

"And you went to bed with him because you felt sorry for him, right?"

Nira scooped up more chicken salad. "I have a tender heart . . . Look, Jerry, Christ, you did it with thirty people! I have a meager what, three, four."

"It's different for men."

Nira just stared at him. "Goodness, my corset is really pinching me . . . Is this 1890? Different for men! God, I can't believe anyone would have the effrontery to even *think* something like that, much less voice it. Shame on you!"

"I didn't mean—," he started, taken aback.

"You're off screwing women who drop their necklaces down the drain, gooey-eyed graduate students—"

"Who said anything about gooey-eyed graduate students?"

"Come on . . . You mean to say you've been there six months, and you haven't made it with at least one forlorn, bedraggled specimen who's spent eight hundred years doing her dissertation? Or do you limit yourself to assistant professors?"

He smiled. "You're very intuitive."

"Intuitive, shit! Of course I'm intuitive. I have all that feminine—"

"She wasn't bedraggled and it wasn't eight hundred years."

"What did *she* drop down the drain?"

"She wouldn't have noticed if she had . . . Anyway, she never came home with me."

"Please don't tell me you did it on the floor of your office. Wait till I finish my chicken salad."

"She had her own apartment."

"Whew . . . So here *you* are, nipping off with all these mindless blobs, and *I'm* begrudged one measly blueberry muffin."

"You deserve at least one," he said, smiling.

Fay was not as delighted as Nira would have liked at Jerry's reappearance in her life. "Two fucked-up kids, a mad wife who'll need alimony forever . . . That's the best you could do?"

"They're not fucked-up."

"One walks in her sleep, the other writes poems about suicide at twelve?"

"Who am I to cast the first stone?" Nira wondered aloud. "My own record isn't that terrific."

"Your kids are terrific."

"Yeah, but . . ."

"You're sure he doesn't have any schizophrenic cousins that come with the package?"

"There *is* no package," Nira said. "We're dating, okay?"

"Dating!"

"Well, what else does one call it?"

"Your guess is as good as mine."

The first time Jerry came to the house, the girls eyed him suspiciously. It was, in truth, Nira's first date. It was two weeks before Christmas.

"You're the one who came to dinner," Heather informed him. "You have two daughters. One of them fell asleep, and the other was reading *Anne of Green Gables.*"

"You have a good memory," Jerry said.

"I don't remember you," Posey admitted.

The baby, who had recently taken to babbling eagerly to every passerby, was dumbstruck, and she huddled in a corner of the room, watching him suspiciously.

"Hi," Jerry called over to her.

"Don't try to win her over," Heather advised him. "That never works." She saw him eyeing the photos on the mantelpiece. "We're a matriarchy," she informed him. "That's a society of women. They used to have them in the old days. Our father is in England. He's going to marry someone named Serena Bassington."

"I know," Jerry said.

"How do you know?" Posey asked, surprised.

"I told him," Nira called. She was in the kitchen, fixing him a drink.

"Do you know her?" Posey asked.

"No," Jerry said.

"Her husband used to be in a wheelchair," Posey said, "but then he died . . . But they still had four children. Boys!"

"We're going to fly over for the wedding," Heather said. "It's on Christmas. Mom made us velvet dresses. Do you want to see them?"

Jerry nodded. They ran off to get the dresses. Nira moved into the living room and sat down beside him. The baby ran over and buried her face in Nira's lap. "I didn't know you sewed," he said.

"I sew, I reap . . . I have many hidden talents and virtues," she admitted. "Jas . . . this is Jerry."

Jasmine opened one huge, black-lashed blue eye. "Man," she identified him.

"You probably don't remember," Nira said, "but he took your photo when you were a baby. You were just three months old."

"Fo?" Jasmine said, sitting up and pointing to the mantelpiece. "Right."

Heather and Posey returned in their floor-length, burgundy velvet dresses. "Our hair will be different," Heather said, "but you get the idea."

"Jasmine isn't going," Posey said. "She's too young."

"She doesn't know he's getting married," Heather said. "She doesn't know much."

Jasmine scrambled up and quickly returned with a silver-framed photo of Adlai and Nira getting married. "Marry," she said.

"Yeah, but that was the old days," Heather said, taking the photo from her. "That's all over with. . . . Mom, how come you didn't wear a long dress?"

"I was a rebel," Nira said.

"What were you rebelling against?"

"God knows . . . It was thousands of years ago."

"Did *you* have a long dress when you got married?" Posey asked Jerry, then turned red. "I mean, your wife."

"Sure," Heather said, sipping from Nira's sherry glass. "He wore a long, white dress with a train and a lace veil."

"I said her!" Posey said.

Jerry frowned. "I don't remember exactly," he said. "I think it was quite long."

"It had pink spots," Nira reminded him, "standing for all her past boyfriends."

He laughed. "How in the world did you know that?"

"My female intuition."

"Hey, that's a great idea," Heather said. "I want to do that."

"Were they big spots or little ones?" Posey wanted to know.

That winter, Jerry came in twice a week. Princeton, he said, had promised him that a full-time, tenured position would be available in two years. He would teach one course a semester till then, and continue running his lab at Rockefeller.

"It sounds hectic," Nira commented.

"If it comes through, it'll be a chance of a lifetime," he said. "I can't afford to give up my job at Rockefeller."

"Because the Princeton thing might fall through?"

"Because I need to eat . . . and feed two daughters *and* a collapsing ex-wife."

"I thought her family had money."

"It's tied up in all kinds of crazy trust funds. The bottom line is that she's safe, but till then—"

When he came in, he usually had to return the same day. They took lunch hours, making love in the apartment of a friend of his who worked all day. Weekends, Nira sometimes drove the girls to Princeton or just visited him alone. But it seemed unsatisfactory. There was something truncated, unsettled about it all—the hasty, though still wonderful sex, his up-in-the-air plans for the future, his ex-wife.

By spring Claire got out of the hospital and moved in with a woman friend in a big, old house near Princeton. The woman was a college friend who happened to be a psychiatric nurse.

"Sounds perfect," Nira said.

"Claire is funny," Jerry said. "She desperately wants to be taken care of, but as soon as she feels she's becoming too dependent on someone, she flares up and attacks them. She feels they're preying on her. Mary can handle it, I think, but still. . . . Anyway, she seems better for now, and the girls see her every weekend."

One Saturday evening Jerry took Nira to Jane's school play. They were doing *The Importance of Being Earnest.* Jane played Miss Prism. Nira had gone over her lines with her. She varied from good to bad in a way that seemed unpredictable. Sometimes she would cry with exasperation at forgetting a line. *"I* can't act at all," Nira would try and reassure her. Or, "It's just a school production." "But Mommy and Daddy will be in the audience," Jane wailed.

"Is Claire going to come?" Nira asked Jerry. She was curious—she had so many images of her in her mind.

"She has a big record of not showing when people expect her to," he said. "A kind of negative power, I guess . . . I wouldn't count on it."

"Won't Jane be disappointed?"

"Of course, that's the point."

"I don't think that's the point," Nira argued with him. "Maybe it makes her nervous. Maybe she feels like she's being on trial in some way. Maybe—"

"I don't care," he cut her off. "I've spent too many goddamn years speculating about all that. Either she'll come or she won't come. Okay?"

Jerry found a parking space in front of the school building. They got out. Stacey was going with a school friend. Just as they were standing there, Nira heard a voice calling her name. "Nira, Nira!" It was a cool, high voice, coming from somewhere off to the side of the building. It was too dark to see. Suddenly a woman materialized in front of them. She was pushing a bicycle. "Hi," she said. "I'm Claire."

"Oh hi," Nira said nervously. Somehow she had expected that Claire would be smaller—smaller than she was at any rate—petite, delicate. Instead she was a tall, thin woman with waist-length hair that blew in the wind. She was wearing a corduroy jacket, desert boots, and a funny, Scottish knitted cap.

"I don't know where to park my bicycle!" she said, laughing. "Do you think it's safe, without a lock?" She talked easily, as though they were old friends.

"I would think," Nira said. "Here in the country—"

"I know," Claire said. "I think it's terrific for the kids, the fresh air. It's wonderful. I—I don't know. I don't know what I think for myself. It's so quiet at night. Have you noticed that?"

"I live in the city," Nira said. Although Jerry was standing right beside her, Claire had not so much as glanced at him once, had not even seemed to see him.

"So, you live in the city? I thought you lived out here."

"No, I . . . I work in the city too."

"Yeah, I work in the city," Claire said. "I used to. I have . . . but now I'm trying to just . . . I haven't been well."

"It's peaceful out here," Nira said.

"Do you live here?" Claire said. "I thought you said you lived in the city?"

"I come out, sometimes," Nira said. "I drive out."

"Do you know how to drive?" Claire sighed. "I keep meaning to learn. Except I like bicycles. And you're not polluting the environment, you know? They're safer . . . except you can get killed by drunken drivers. That happened to my friend. He was just driving down a country road on his bike, and he was killed."

"I'm sorry," Nira said. God, Jerry, talk, do something. We'll be out here all night!

"And his wife," Claire said. "They'd been married ten years, fifteen years . . . you can imagine."

"I think we better find our seats," Jerry said finally. He had been standing there as though cast in bronze.

For the first time Claire looked at him. "Oh, are you going too?" she said contemptuously.

"Yes, I'm going too," Jerry said, taking Nira's arm.

"I'm so glad I met you," Claire said to Nira again. "Enjoy the play! Have fun!"

"Aren't you going?" Nira asked, aware of Jerry's arm pressuring her to move.

"Oh yes . . . But I have to park my bike." She pointed to it. "I think it'll be safe. It's a used bike."

They said nothing until they were in their seats.

"I didn't think she saw you at first," Nira said.

Jerry said nothing.

"She's—"

"Let's not talk about it, okay?"

"No, I want to talk about it," Nira said. "She's an important person in your life."

"Ni, please . . . We'll talk about it some other time. I want to enjoy the play."

If he had just sounded angry, she would not have given in, but he sounded anxious. "I just wanted to say that I thought she was quite beautiful in a strange kind of way," Nira said. "She has lovely hair."

Jerry put his arm around her, squeezing her shoulder tightly.

They didn't see Claire after the show. They went backstage to see Jane, who was radiant and happy. "Did Mom come?" she said. "I didn't see her."

"We saw her outside before the performance," Nira said.

"You were wonderful, sweetie," Jerry said, though he later confessed to Nira that he hadn't been able to concentrate on the play at all and had scarcely heard a word.

First wives. Nira wondered how Adlai had described her to Serena, what image of her Serena had formed, how accurate it was. It was almost spring now, and the oddity of her relationship with Jerry was beginning to bother her. Where were they headed? And what did she want? It was he who brought up the summer.

"I thought we might share a house together."

"All of us? The kids too?"

"Sure . . . only I'd pay you rent and we'll split everything down the middle."

Nira laughed.

"No, listen, it's important. I don't want you to just pitch me out if we have a fight. If I pay my half, I'll have some rights."

"Are we going to have fights?"

"Sure we are . . . You've never lived with me."

"What horrors lie in store? Could you give me a preview?"

He took the question seriously. "I'll be trying to finish up my book. I get very preoccupied and irritable. I don't answer questions. I don't even hear them."

"And I'm to trot around on tiptoe like Tolstoy's wife, whispering to the children, 'The master is at work'?"

"It may have overtones of that."

"Wonderful. It sounds like a dream summer."

"It's reality, okay?"

"What are the compensations? Will we have long rapturous hours making love in the afternoons?"

"With five kids in the house?"

"There is a wonderful invention called a lock, which can be installed on bedroom doors . . . Listen, if you're too busy, I can always go back to The Plaza."

"Sex is not going to be our major problem."

"Let's be grateful for small blessings."

Jerry was taking six weeks off, Nira four. She left him with the children and headed back to the city. The month started pleasantly. Alliances formed among the girls and re-formed. Posey and Stacey became friends and disappeared, as Posey and Heather had in summers past. Heather occasionally accompanied them, but this summer she had a new group of friends her own age with whom she went to parties and listened to rock music. Nira encouraged Jane, who was the same age, to join them, but she refused. She took long walks by herself or sat near Nira on the beach, gathering shells, reading, engaging her in long existential talks about the meaning of life. The baby, now two, preferred Nira's company and played happily in the sand, reluctant to move far away.

Jerry worked in the mornings and sometimes in the afternoon. He came out of his study with a glazed look and once or twice walked past Nira without seeing her. Jasmine fell in love with Jerry. She followed him around, studying him gravely. Once, Nira opened the study door and found her sitting in the corner, leafing through some picture books, babbling quietly to herself, pointing to figures on each page.

"But you said you couldn't work with any noise or distraction," Nira reminded him, stabbed with jealousy.

"She's soothing," he said. "It's like white noise."

When mealtimes came, Jasmine walked over to where Jerry was typing. She stood silently, watching him, and would stand thus for five or ten minutes, watching with fascination as he typed. Finally she would place one fat, satiny hand on his. "Come," she would say with quiet definiteness, and Jerry would come.

She's two, Nira would argue with herself. You can't be jealous of a two-year-old. But in fact, she was; not just of the intimacy the two of them shared in the study, but of the hours he spent reading to her while she cuddled against him, stroking his hair, regarding him dreamily while he said, "This is an oboe, Jasmine."

To please him, she memorized lists of musical instruments, wild flowers, national holidays, tools. "She knows what an awl is," Posey said, impressed.

"So?" said Jane. "Big deal."

Nira felt a bond of common resentment. "I don't know what an awl is," she admitted.

"I think it's something you do something with," Posey said.

"I'll give you my awl," Nira sang, covering her jealousy with attempts at wit, which no one seemed to notice.

But there was sex, and that was good. With it all, the entanglements and tensions of daily life seemed bearable, possible, muted. The bedroom was cool, even in the afternoon. This won't last, Nira warned herself. Savor it while it does. Jerry disagreed. "Why shouldn't it last?" he wanted to know.

"Ecstasy has a six-month time limit," she quoted. "Romantic love has a two-year time limit."

"Isn't that a little cynical?" he said.

"Do you think it is?" she said happily. "How long do *you* think it can last?"

"Forever," he said.

"Forever? Even when we're sixty or seventy? We'll still want to do it with each other?"

"Sure."

That he could even entertain that illusion filled her with such joy, she felt like shouting, or turning headlong cartwheels around the room. The only bad moment came one afternoon when Stacey began beating on the bedroom door yelling, "Daddy! Daddy!" and, finding no answer, finally, "What are you *doing* in there?"

"We're fucking!" Nira yelled.

Jerry instantly lost his erection. "How could you say a thing like that?" he said, horrified.

"Well, it's the truth . . . I don't want lurking daughters with seething oedipal longings cringing outside the door."

"She wasn't cringing. She needed me for something."

"Sure . . . She knew what we were doing."

"I think four-letter words are undignified."

"Pardon me . . . I'll consult my book of euphemisms at once."

But the two facts—their daughters getting along, the sex being so satisfying—gave an idyllic feeling to the summer. Nira dreaded its ending.

"Do you think you'll move into the city in the fall?" she asked as Labor Day approached.

"I don't think so," Jerry said. "The kids are settled out there; the schools are good. I'd rather commute myself."

"But what about us?"

He just looked at her. "What do you mean?"

"I mean, what's going to happen, Jerry?"

"We'll keep on seeing each other, of course."

Nira felt a cold dread sweep over her, and she sat down. "I thought—I thought we would get married," she said.

Jerry looked uncomfortable. "Do you still believe in marriage?" he asked, as though out of curiosity.

"Well, it's not a matter of believing. I don't believe in anything, but . . ."

"It's just a piece of paper."

"So's the Constitution. So's the Bill of Rights."

"I thought you prided yourself on being so unconventional."

"Jerry, I have three kids! Living in sin is for teenagers or swinging singles." She couldn't look at him. "I thought we were getting along so well."

"We are, but . . ."

She came closer. They were in his study. It was just before dinner. "So, what do you want, the right to go charging off with dopey people who drop things down drains? Is that what you can't bear to give up?"

"That has nothing to do with it," he said curtly.

"So what does it have to do with?"

"I'm just not ready," he stammered.

"Why not?"

"Look, I had a crazy, rotten marriage. It's just ended. I—"

"Just ended! You've been divorced three years! We've known each other for two . . . When *are* you going to be ready, for Christ's sake?"

"I don't know."

"Everyone has crazy, rotten marriages," Nira said. "What does that have to do with anything?"

"They don't . . . You're trying to blur everything. Look, Ni, you're asking me to take on a family of five kids. Just the financial aspect of that alone . . . Say you suddenly wanted to have more babies?"

"More babies!" She was incredulous. "Jerry, listen, *you're* more likely to have more babies than me. I should have had an abortion with Jas. She was a horrible, horrible mistake."

Jerry looked around nervously. "Don't talk so loudly," he said. "She may be right outside the door."

"I don't care. I don't care *who's* right outside the door! How can you *say* more babies? What do you know of me that you can say that?"

He looked flustered. "Sometimes it just happens. Claire got pregnant on our honeymoon."

"Will you cut it out about Claire!" Nira yelled. "I am not Claire, okay? And it never 'just happens.' It has never in the whole history of the *world* just happened. And believe me, if by one chance in a million I ever got pregnant again, I would find a doctor to scrape it out faster than you say *boo.*"

He had a more nervous and horrified expression. "You say that now, but women—"

"You know nothing about women!" Nira said. "Don't *tell* me about women. I'm not telling *you* about men."

"Okay." He was silent. After a moment he said, "The money issue seems irrelevant and minor to you. To me it's crucial. Supporting five children—"

"Who's asking you to support five children? How about my income?"

"You earn nine thousand dollars a year—that's not an income. And maybe you'll quit and want to stay at home and weave or something."

Nira thought she was going to kill him. "Listen, you, there's one thing I can tell you. I am going to be earning more money than you in ten years."

Jerry laughed. "You are?"

"Of course I am . . . You are totally barking up the wrong whatever. I am a creative, ambitious person, and in ten years I'm going to have my own firm and be traveling around the world. . . . Weaving! Jesus, are you condescending! Do I claim *you're* going to stay at home and weave?"

"Women," he began, but Nira screamed.

"Stop! If you say 'women' one more time, you're leaving this house. Out! I mean it."

"Stop pressuring me," he yelled. "I can't take it."

"Then go! Get the hell out of this house and take your daughters and your damn manuscript. I mean it. I want you out of this house by . . . ten tonight."

"We are not going anywhere," Jerry said coldly. "I've paid the rent till Labor Day, and that's that."

"Okay," Nira said. "Okay, but I'll tell you one thing. I am not cooking your meals or shopping or saying a word to you *ever again* . . . and I don't want you saying one *word* to my children. And stay away from my baby!"

"What if she wants to be with me?"

"I don't care . . . You're seducing a two-year-old child. That's evil and cruel."

"Ni—"

"If you say one word to any of us, I'm going to pitch that fucking manuscript into the sea!"

She stormed out of the room. Oh, she wanted to kill him! She remembered how he said Claire used to attack him physically, saying *she* wanted to kill him. Maybe they should get together. Maybe she should call Claire. Phrases from their argument kept shooting through her mind. "Stop pressuring me." "Weaving!" Damn him.

For a week they did not speak. Posey and Stacey seemed unaware that anything had happened. Heather clearly noticed, but was off with her own friends and not willing to devote a lot of time to what was going on. But Jane, quiet, gentle, perceptive Jane, watched Nira with a sad, understanding expression. Nira felt she knew everything, and her silence was wonderful and helpful. Only once, when they sat together on the beach, Jane said tentatively, "Daddy sometimes gets in a funny mood when he's working on something." Nira just nodded, not trusting herself to speak. But it was the baby who created the greatest problem, being beyond or not up to the point of reason. Jerry tried to avoid her, but she continued to follow him around. Once Nira entered the living room and caught them in flagrante. Jerry was reading her *Madeline* while she sat on the floor, playing with his toes. "In an old house in Paris that was covered with vines . . ."

Nira marched over to him, snatched the book out of his hands, scooped up the baby, and marched out of the room. Jasmine began to howl, but Nira would not let her out of the kitchen and bribed her shamelessly with seedless grapes, ice cream, and chocolate kisses, even though it was an hour before dinner.

She was ashamed, ashamed of herself, humiliated by the fight.

How could he stay on in the house with someone who hated him, who wanted to kill him? Was he a sadist who enjoyed watching someone in pain? Or did he hope that one day she would slither into a groveling heap at his feet out of "feminine" weakness? At night she slept alone in the large bed, hardly sleeping. Sometimes, in the middle of the night, she turned on the light and read; then, during the day, she fell into heavy naps on the beach. One week more till Labor Day. A week, looked at rationally, was not a long time. But she could not *be* rational—about time, about him, about anything. She swam far out in the ocean, hoping to be sucked under by some magical subterranean current, but always found herself back on shore, tanning to a deep, tropical brown, empty and despairing inside.

One night, at two, she got up and went to the kitchen for a snack. Jerry was sitting at the kitchen table, eating a piece of apple pie. Nira had tried to avoid looking at him in the week since they had had the fight. Now she looked. He seemed thinner to her. He had scarcely been at the beach all summer and was pale. When he was tense, he stopped eating, whereas she overate. Jack Sprat and his wife. She saw herself as rotund, dark, menacingly healthy, whereas he looked pathetically thin and needy, aesthetic. All week she had slept in one of Heather's old, rumpled T-shirts which bore, in large black letters, the inappropriate message: Heck, why not? Other than a pair of bikini underpants, that was all she was wearing. Jerry, in light-blue, tailored pajamas that looked ironed, looked up as she came in.

Nira went to the refrigerator and took out an orange. She held it in her hand, not wanting to eat in front of him or even peel it. She stood there in silence for several minutes. Then, without thinking about it or planning it, she went over and put her hand on Jerry's neck. He reached up and held her hand. Without speaking, she slid into his lap and kissed him lightly, softly on the mouth, tasting him like some favorite food she had had to give up on an especially rigorous diet. Kissing him, she heard the wheels going around in his head, felt the moment when he decided to forgive her. He pulled the T-shirt over her head. She felt at a disadvantage somehow, almost naked in his lap, her breasts oddly white against her dark tan. And part of her was still angry at him! Even as he nuzzled her and kissed her ravenously, and eased off her bikini underpants. Okay, so they had good sex? Where had that gotten them? What would that resolve? What was the use of it? When they were in bed, he entered her with no preliminary caresses, knowing, with a cavalierness she found insufferable, that she was ready. Nira pummeled his back, biting him, whimpering aloud as much in pleasure as in humiliation that she had broken down so easily, after her long week of resolve and carefully hoarded anger.

"I hate sex," she said when they were lying side by side afterward.

Jerry laughed.

"I want to be married," she said. "I want fanfare and ceremony. I want you to wear a ring. I'm too nervous to be a noncomformist."

"Do you want me to wear it through my nose or will my finger suffice?"

"I want both. I want you to be branded, 'Married,' on your forehead, like a bull."

He reached for her hand and stroked it, finger by finger. "You're really going to earn more money than me?"

"I swear . . . People will come up to you at parties and call you Mr. Goldschmitt. You'll feel horribly threatened, and rush off and do foolish things with giggling schizophrenic girls in sandals."

Jerry gasped in mock horror. "God no, anything but that."

"I just want us to love each other forever," Nira said. "I don't want to go *through* this again. If you die, that's one thing. But not another divorce."

"You think I want another divorce?" Jerry's voice became quiet. "Ni, that's what we were arguing about. . . . *I* can't go through this again either. I mean it. It would finish me."

"I will not take to weaving and I will not have more babies," Nira said, kissing him. "I can promise you that."

"Then I will love and cherish you forever," he said. "Will you do the same to me?"

"I will."

It sounded good. She would make him happy. She would not have another breakdown. She would slide, effortlessly, from abandoned, neurotic first wife, to cheerful, resilient second.

"Five daughters," Jerry murmured, his head on her breast.

"You can preside. It'll be like Jane Austen. They'll cluster around you. You can give sage, paternal advice at the end of a long oaken table."

"That sounds lovely, I must admit."

"It will be," Nira promised. "Truly."

The wedding was the week of October 20th, the same week as Posey's birthday, in fact the same day. "Do you mind?" Nira said. "Does that bother you?"

"No," Posey said. "That makes it special. Then you'll always think of me on your anniversary."

The girls decided to wear the same velvet dresses they had worn to Adlai's wedding. Nira offered to make some for Jane and Stacey. Jane accepted, but Stacey refused. "I want to wear a white dress," she said.

"White is for brides," Jane said. *"You're* not getting married."

"I don't care."

She had a long white dress that Claire's parents had bought her, encrusted with handmade lace, a beauty. The others, including Jasmine, were in dark red velvet, overdressed for the balmy day which was scarcely touched by fall yet. Nira wore a long velvet skirt and a white lace blouse. She wanted to look Victorian and lush; her tan was still glowing.

The day of the wedding Jasmine spent most of the morning in front of the mirror, admiring herself. "I look pretty," she said to anyone who came by.

"You're not supposed to say that about yourself," Posey said. "You're supposed to wait till someone says it to you." She squirted her with some perfume. The air was heavy with conflicting floral scents. Jerry said it smelled like a Portuguese whorehouse.

The girls spent so much time getting ready, one would have thought it was they who were getting married. Heather was furious she'd woken up with a swollen pink eye. "What'll I do?" she wailed. "I'll look like a monster in the photos . . . Mom, can't you put it off another week?"

"Of course she can't," Posey said, regarding her with satisfaction. "Just keep your eyes closed in the photos."

"Then I'll look weird . . . It looks like I'm an albino, like I have red eyes."

"Can't win 'em all," Posey said cheerfully.

They were to be married at noon. At eleven, Claire called. "I want to come to the wedding," she said.

Nira sat down. "I—I don't know," she said.

"I'd invite Jerry to my wedding if I were getting married," she said. "Why shouldn't I be there?"

"There isn't that much room," Nira said weakly.

"Let me speak to Jerry."

Nira went into the bathroom where Jerry was shaving. "It's Claire."

She stayed in the bathroom while he talked. She put on eye makeup, stroking each eyelash with care. When she came out, he was sitting on the bed, gazing off into space.

"Is she coming?" Nira asked.

Jerry just looked at her. He patted the bed, motioning for her to sit beside him. She had her fancy blouse on and a slip, but that was all. "It's going to be different with us," she assured him.

"I know," he said wearily.

"In a weird way, I wish she could have come," Nira said. "It's a nice idea, but—"

The door opened. It was Jasmine. "Look at me," she commanded them. Two feet high, she looked like a Spanish infanta, with her vividly pink cheeks and sultry eyes.

"You look beautiful," Jerry said.

"So do you," Jasmine said to him.

"Hey, how about me?" Nira said, striking a sexy pose. "I'm the bride."

They both turned to her. Jerry smiled. Jasmine hugged her around the knees, stroking the lace of Nira's slip. Outside the house the Unitarian minister drove up in his blue Chevrolet. It was time to start.